Y0-BLU-006
8-20-11
148

PC LEARNING LABS TEACHES MICROSOFT OFFICE

PLEASE NOTE—USE OF THE DISK AND THE PROGRAMS INCLUDED ON THE DISK PACKAGED WITH THIS BOOK AND THE PROGRAM LISTINGS INCLUDED IN THIS BOOK IS SUBJECT TO AN END-USER LICENSE AGREEMENT (THE "AGREEMENT") FOUND AT THE BACK OF THE BOOK. PLEASE READ THE AGREEMENT CAREFULLY BEFORE MAKING YOUR PURCHASE DECISION. PURCHASE OF THE BOOK AND USE OF THE DISKS, PROGRAMS, AND PROGRAM LISTINGS WILL CONSTITUTE ACCEPTANCE OF THE AGREEMENT.

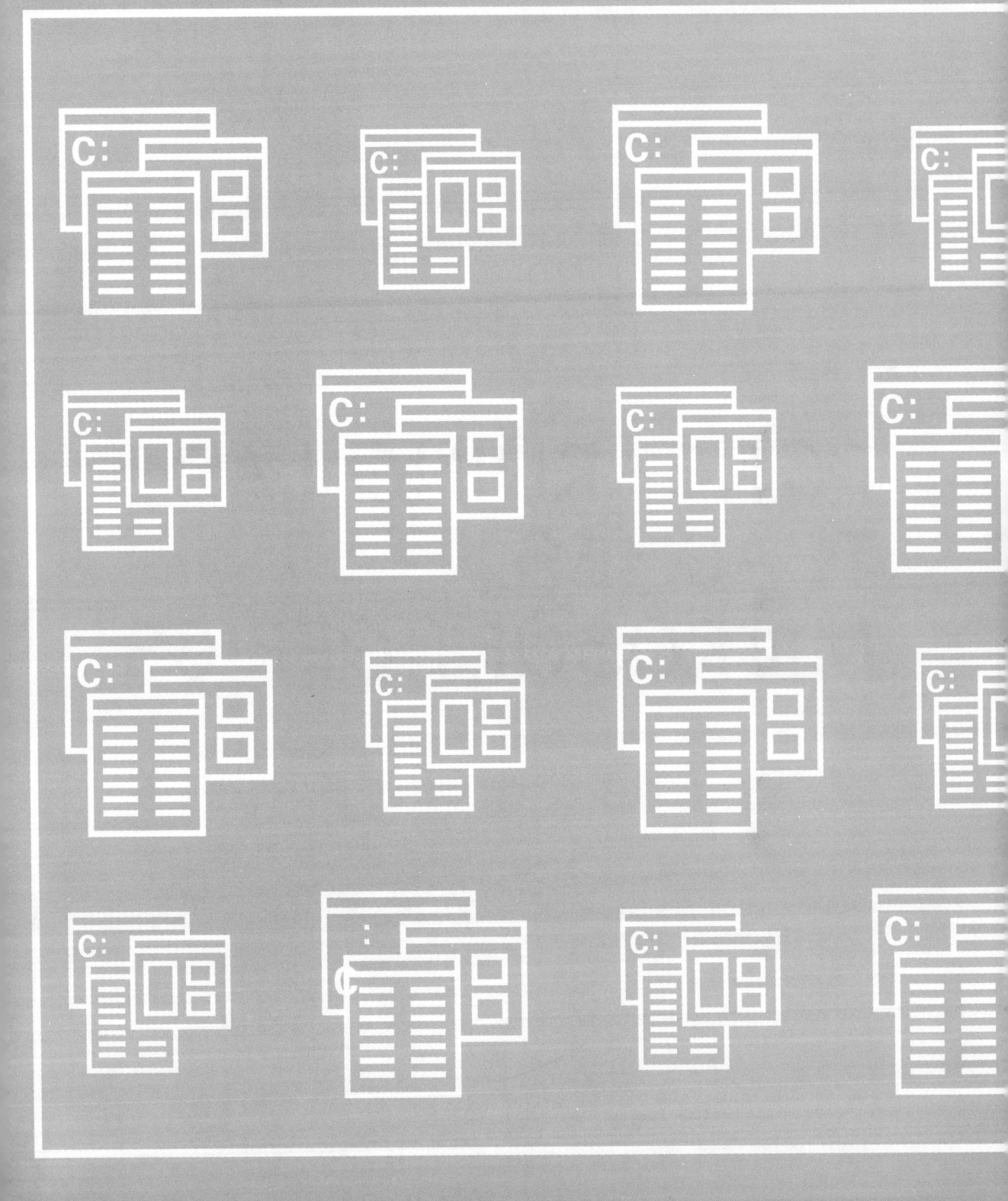

PC LEARNING LABS TEACHES MICROSOFT OFFICE

By Robert N. Kulik and Richard Scott for

Logical Operations®

Ziff-Davis Press
Emeryville, California

Writers	Robert N. Kulik and Richard Scott
Curriculum Development	Logical Operations
Editor	Janice Jue
Technical Reviewer	LO/Kathy Blasi
Project Coordinator	Cort Day
Proofreader	Carol Burbo
Production Coordinator, Logical Operations	Marie Boyers
Cover Illustration	Dave Feasey
Cover Design	Carrie English
Book Design	Laura Lamar/MAX, San Francisco
Screen Graphics Editor	P. Diamond
Technical Illustration	Dave Feasey
Word Processing	Howard Blechman
Page Layout	M.D. Barrera
Indexer	Carol Burbo

Ziff-Davis Press books are produced on a Macintosh computer system with the following applications: FrameMaker®, Microsoft® Word, QuarkXPress®, Adobe Illustrator®, Adobe Photoshop®, Adobe Streamline™, MacLink® *Plus*, Aldus® FreeHand™, Collage Plus™.

If you have comments or questions or would like to receive a free catalog, call or write:
Ziff-Davis Press
5903 Christie Avenue
Emeryville, CA 94608
1-800-688-0448

Copyright © 1994 by Ziff-Davis Press. All rights reserved.
PART OF A CONTINUING SERIES

Ziff-Davis Press, ZD Press, PC Learning Labs, and PC Learning Labs Teaches are trademarks of Ziff Communications Company.

All other product names and services identified throughout this book are trademarks or registered trademarks of their respective companies. They are used throughout this book in editorial fashion only and for the benefit of such companies. No such uses, or the use of any trade name, is intended to convey endorsement or other affiliation with the book.

No part of this publication may be reproduced in any form, or stored in a database or retrieval system, or transmitted or distributed in any form by any means, electronic, mechanical photocopying, recording, or otherwise, without the prior written permission of Ziff-Davis Press, except as permitted by the Copyright Act of 1976 and the End-User License Agreement at the back of this book, and except that program listings may be entered, stored, and executed in a computer system.

EXCEPT FOR THE LIMITED WARRANTY COVERING THE PHYSICAL DISK PACKAGED WITH THIS BOOK AS PROVIDED IN THE END-USER LICENSE AGREEMENT AT THE BACK OF THIS BOOK, THE INFORMATION AND MATERIAL CONTAINED IN THIS BOOK ARE PROVIDED "AS IS," WITHOUT WARRANTY OF ANY KIND, EXPRESS OR IMPLIED, INCLUDING WITHOUT LIMITATION ANY WARRANTY CONCERNING THE ACCURACY, ADEQUACY, OR COMPLETENESS OF SUCH INFORMATION OR MATERIAL OR THE RESULTS TO BE OBTAINED FROM USING SUCH INFORMATION OR MATERIAL. NEITHER ZIFF-DAVIS PRESS NOR THE AUTHOR SHALL BE RESPONSIBLE FOR ANY CLAIMS ATTRIBUTABLE TO ERRORS, OMISSIONS, OR OTHER INACCURACIES IN THE INFORMATION OR MATERIAL CONTAINED IN THIS BOOK, AND IN NO EVENT SHALL ZIFF-DAVIS PRESS OR THE AUTHOR BE LIABLE FOR DIRECT, INDIRECT, SPECIAL, INCIDENTAL, OR CONSEQUENTIAL DAMAGES ARISING OUT OF THE USE OF SUCH INFORMATION OR MATERIAL.

ISBN 1-56276-272-9

Manufactured in the United States of America
⊕ This book is printed on paper that contains 50% total recycled fiber of which 20% is de-inked postconsumer fiber.
10 9 8 7 6 5 4 3 2 1

CONTENTS AT A GLANCE

Introduction xv

Chapter 1: First Things First 1

Chapter 2: A Quick Tour of Microsoft Office Manager 6

Chapter 3: Getting Help from the Office Manager 22

Chapter 4: Copying and Pasting Data between Applications 40

Chapter 5: Linking Data to Office Applications 54

Chapter 6: Embedding Data in Office Applications 84

Chapter 7: Examining Office in Greater Detail 104

Chapter 8: Using One Application to Access Others 128

Chapter 9: Additional Office Techniques 146

Chapter 10: Working with Microsoft Mail 166

Appendix A: Installing Microsoft Office 4.2 188

Appendix B: Sharing Information on a Network 194

Index 199

Table of Contents

Introduction xv

Chapter 1: First Things First 1
    Conventions Used in This Book 2
    Creating Your Work Directory 3
    Before You Proceed Further 4

Chapter 2: A Quick Tour of Microsoft Office Manager 6
    Issuing Office Commands 8
        The Office Toolbar 8
        The Office Menu 9
        The Office Shortcut Menu 9
    Starting Office Automatically 10
    Starting Office Applications 13
        Practice Your Skills 14
    Switching between Running Office Applications 14
        Practice Your Skills 15
    A Note on Office's Memory Requirements 17
    Exiting Office Applications 18
        Practice Your Skills 18
    Exiting Office 19
        Practice Your Skills 19

Starting Office Manually 19
    Practice Your Skills 19

Summary 19

A Note on How to Proceed 21

Chapter 3: Getting Help from the Office Manager 22

The Office Help System 24
    General Help 25
    Practice Your Skills 31
    Exiting Help 32
    Practice Your Skills 32
    Dialog-box Help 32
    Practice Your Skills 34
    Getting Help on Individual Applications 34

Using Office Cue Cards for Step-by-step Help 34
    Practice Your Skills 36

Summary 37

Chapter 4: Copying and Pasting Data between Applications 40

Cut, Copy, and Paste 42
    The Windows Clipboard 43

Using the Cut and Paste Commands 43
    Moving Word Text to a PowerPoint Slide 44
    Practice Your Skills 46
    Modifying the Moved Text 46
    Practice Your Skills 47

Using the Copy and Paste Commands 47
    Copying Excel Data to a PowerPoint Slide 48
    Practice Your Skills 49
    Modifying the Copied Data 50
    Copying Data to Multiple Applications 51
    Practice Your Skills 52

Summary 53

Chapter 5: Linking Data to Office Applications 54

Object Linking and Embedding (OLE) 56

Linking Data 57
    Creating a Link 58
    Linking Excel Data to a PowerPoint Slide 59

Updating Linked Data 64
    Updating Linked Data Automatically 65
    Practice Your Skills 66
    Updating Linked Data Manually 66
    Practice Your Skills 69

Linking a Source Object to Multiple Destination Files 70
    Practice Your Skills 72

Breaking a Link 73
    Practice Your Skills 74

Linking Options 76
    Practice Your Skills 78

Summary 83

Chapter 6: Embedding Data in Office Applications 84

Embedding Objects 86
- Linking versus Embedding: A Clarification 86
- Using the Clipboard to Embed an Object 87
- Embedding Excel Data in a PowerPoint Slide 88

Editing an Embedded Object 90
- Practice Your Skills 93

Using Drag-and-Drop to Embed an Object 94

Creating a New Embedded Object 96
- Practice Your Skills 98

Summary 101

Chapter 7: Examining Office in Greater Detail 104

The Find File Feature 106
- Searching for a File When You Know Its Name 106
- Practice Your Skills 110
- Searching for a File When You Don't Know Its Name 111
- Practice Your Skills 115
- Deleting a File 115
- Practice Your Skills 116

Customizing Office 116
- Customizing the Office Menu 117
- Practice Your Skills 119
- Sizing the Toolbar 119
- Practice Your Skills 121
- Moving the Toolbar 121
- Practice Your Skills 121

    Minimizing the Toolbar 122
    Practice Your Skills 123
    Adding a Button 123
    Removing a Button 124
    Practice Your Skills 125
    Making the Toolbar Invisible 125
    Practice Your Skills 125

Summary 126

Chapter 8: Using One Application to Access Others 128

Creating an Excel Worksheet in Word 130
    Editing the Worksheet 133
    Practice Your Skills 134
    Moving the Worksheet 135

Creating an Excel Worksheet in PowerPoint 136
    Moving and Sizing the Worksheet 137
    Editing the Worksheet 137
    Practice Your Skills 137

Creating a Word Table in PowerPoint 139
    Editing the Table 141
    Practice Your Skills 141

Summary 143

Chapter 9: Additional Office Techniques 146

Making a PowerPoint Presentation from a Word Outline 148
    Practice Your Skills 153
    Editing the Converted Outline in PowerPoint 154
    Practice Your Skills 154

Making a Word Document from PowerPoint Text 156
    Editing the Converted Text in Word 160
    Practice Your Skills 160

Changing the Default Position of the Office Toolbar 160
    Practice Your Skills 163

Summary 163

Chapter 10: Working with Microsoft Mail 166

An Important Note on Installing Microsoft Mail 168

Starting Microsoft Mail 168
    Starting Mail Manually 168
    Starting Mail Automatically 169

Reading an Inbox Message 170

Deleting an Inbox Message 171
    The Metaphysics of Deletion 173

Creating and Sending a Message 173
    Opening a Send Note Form 173
    Addressing the Message 173
    Specifying the Message Subject 176
    Writing the Message 176
    Setting the Send Options 177
    Sending the Message 177

Working with Folders 178
    Permanent Folders 178
    Opening an Existing Folder 178
    Creating a New Folder 178
    Deleting a Folder 180

Forwarding a Message 180

Replying to a Message 181

Using Mail to Share Files 182
    Sending a File by Attaching It to a Message 182
    Sending a File from Its Source Application 184

Summary 187

Appendix A: Installing Microsoft Office 4.2 188

Who This Appendix Is For 190

Installation Prerequisites 190

Installation Options 191

Installing Office 4.2 on Your Computer 191

Modifying Your Office Setup 192

Appendix B: Sharing Information on a Network 194

Overview 196

Network-Navigating Prerequisites 196

Sharing Office Files on a Network 196
    Opening a Shared File 196
    Protecting Shared Information 197
    Sharing Files with Different Formats 198

Index 199

INTRODUCTION

Welcome to *PC Learning Labs Teaches Microsoft Office 4.2,* a hands-on instruction book that will quickly make you a proficient Microsoft Office user. And congratulations on choosing Microsoft Office 4.2, a robust integrated working environment that will vastly simplify and increase your overall computer productivity.

We at PC Learning Labs believe this book to be a unique and welcome addition to the teeming ranks of "How To" computer publications. Our instructional approach stems directly from over a decade of successful teaching in a hands-on classroom environment. Throughout the book, we combine theory with practice by presenting new techniques and then applying them in hands-on activities. These activities use specially prepared sample Office files, which are stored on the enclosed Data Disk.

Unlike a class, this book allows you to proceed at your own pace. And we'll be right there to guide you along every step of the way, providing landmarks to help you chart your progress and hold to a steady course.

When you're done working your way through this book, you'll have a solid foundation of skills in

- Using and customizing your Office Manager toolbar
- Getting on-line Help for selected Office Manager topics
- Sharing data among your Office applications (copying, linking, and embedding)
- Working with Microsoft Mail

WHO THIS BOOK IS FOR

This book is for you if

- You are a beginning Office user.

- You are competent (or at least familiar) with the trio of Office applications—Excel 5.0, PowerPoint 4.0, and Word 6.0.

Unlike most other books on Office, we do not show you how to perform standard Excel, PowerPoint, or Word tasks; we take it for granted that you know this already. Instead, we concentrate on teaching you how to use Office to *integrate* these applications: how to move fluently and share data among them.

HOW TO USE THIS BOOK

You can use this book as a learning guide, a review tool, and a quick reference.

AS A LEARNING GUIDE

Each chapter covers one broad topic or set of related topics. Chapters are arranged in order of increasing proficiency; skills you acquire in one chapter are used and elaborated on in later chapters. For this reason, you should work through the chapters in sequence.

Each chapter is organized into explanatory topics and step-by-step activities. Topics provide the theory you need to master Office; activities allow you to apply this theory to practical, hands-on examples.

You get to try each new skill on a specially prepared sample Office file stored on the enclosed Data Disk. This saves you typing time and allows you to concentrate on the technique at hand. Through the use of sample files, hands-on activities, illustrations that give you feedback at crucial steps, and supporting background information, this book provides you with the foundation and structure to learn Microsoft Office 4.2 quickly and easily.

AS A REVIEW TOOL

Any method of instruction is only as effective as the time and effort you are willing to invest in it. For this reason, we strongly encourage you to spend some time reviewing the book's more challenging topics and activities.

AS A QUICK REFERENCE

General procedures—such as how to start Office or how to link data between two files—are presented as a series of bulleted steps; you can find these bullets (•) easily by skimming through the book. Bulleted procedures can serve as a handy reference.

At the end of every chapter, you'll find a quick reference that lists the mouse/keyboard actions needed to perform the techniques introduced in that chapter.

WHAT THIS BOOK CONTAINS

This book contains the following 10 chapters:

Chapter 1:	First Things First
Chapter 2:	A Quick Tour of Microsoft Office Manager
Chapter 3:	Getting Help from the Office Manager
Chapter 4:	Copying and Pasting Data between Applications
Chapter 5:	Linking Data to Office Applications
Chapter 6:	Embedding Data in Office Applications
Chapter 7:	Examining Office in Greater Detail
Chapter 8:	Using One Application to Access Others
Chapter 9:	Additional Office Techniques

Chapter 10:   Working with Microsoft Mail

In addition, there are two appendixes:

Appendix A: Installing Microsoft Office 4.2

Appendix B: Sharing Information on a Network

To attain full Office fluency, you should work through all ten chapters. The appendixes are optional.

SPECIAL LEARNING FEATURES

The following features of this book will facilitate your learning:

- Carefully sequenced topics that build on the knowledge you've acquired from previous topics
- Frequent hands-on activities that sharpen your Office skills
- Numerous illustrations that show how your screen should look at key points during these activities
- The Data Disk, which contains all the files you will need to complete the activities (as explained in the next section)
- Easy-to-spot, bulleted procedures that provide the general, step-by-step instructions you'll need to perform Office tasks
- A quick reference at the end of each chapter, listing the mouse/keyboard actions needed to perform the techniques introduced in the chapter

THE DATA DISK

One of the most important learning features of this book is the Data Disk, the 3½-inch floppy disk that accompanies the book. This disk contains the Office files you'll retrieve and work on throughout the book.

To perform the activities in this book, you will first need to create a work directory on your hard disk, as explained in Chapter 1's "Creating Your Work Directory." You'll then copy the files from the Data Disk to your work directory. This directory will also hold all the Office files that you will be creating, editing, and saving during the course of this book.

WHAT YOU NEED TO USE THIS BOOK

To run Microsoft Office 4.2 and complete this book, you need a computer with a hard disk and at least one floppy-disk drive, a monitor, a keyboard, and a mouse (or equivalent tracking device). Microsoft Office 4.2 must be installed on your computer, either Standard or Professional edition. For help installing, see Appendix A.

COMPUTER AND MONITOR

You need an IBM or IBM-compatible personal computer and monitor that are capable of running Microsoft Windows version 3.1 (or later). A 386-based system is technically sufficient, but both Windows and Office will run somewhat slowly on it; therefore, we recommend that you use a 486 or higher computer.

You need a hard disk which has at least 5 megabytes (5,000,000 bytes) of free storage space *after* Microsoft Office 4.2 has been installed on it.

Finally, you need a VGA (or higher resolution) video card and monitor to display Windows and Office at their intended screen resolution. (**Note:** The Office screens shown in this book are taken from a VGA monitor; depending on your monitor type, your screens may look slightly different.)

KEYBOARD

IBM-compatible computers come with various styles of keyboards; these keyboards function identically but have different layouts. Figures I.1, I.2, and I.3 show the three main keyboard styles and their key arrangements.

Figure I.1 **IBM PC–style keyboard**

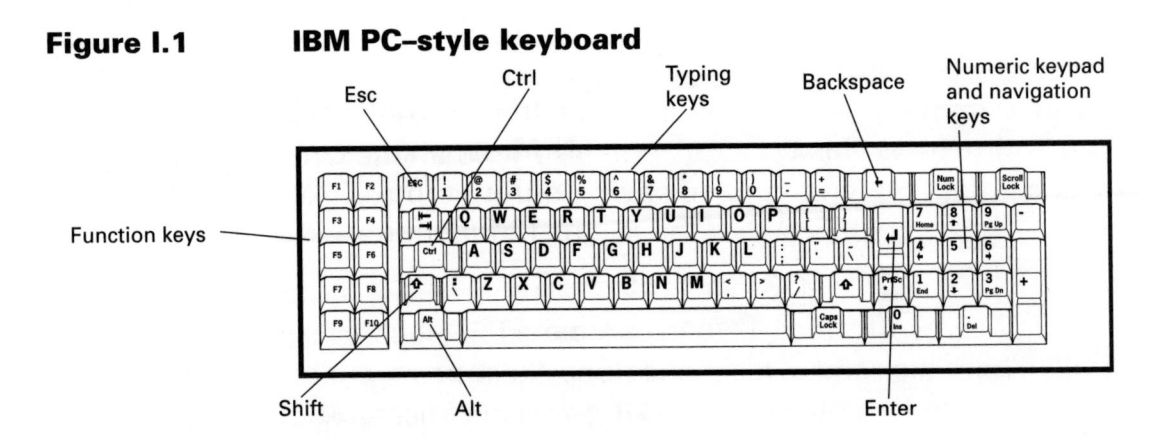

Figure I.2 **XT/AT–style keyboard**

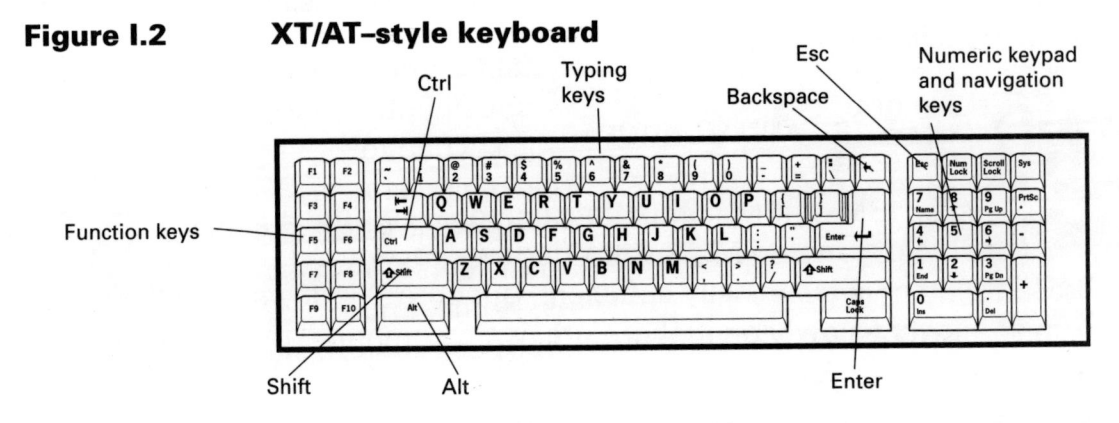

Figure I.3 **The 101-key Enhanced Keyboard**

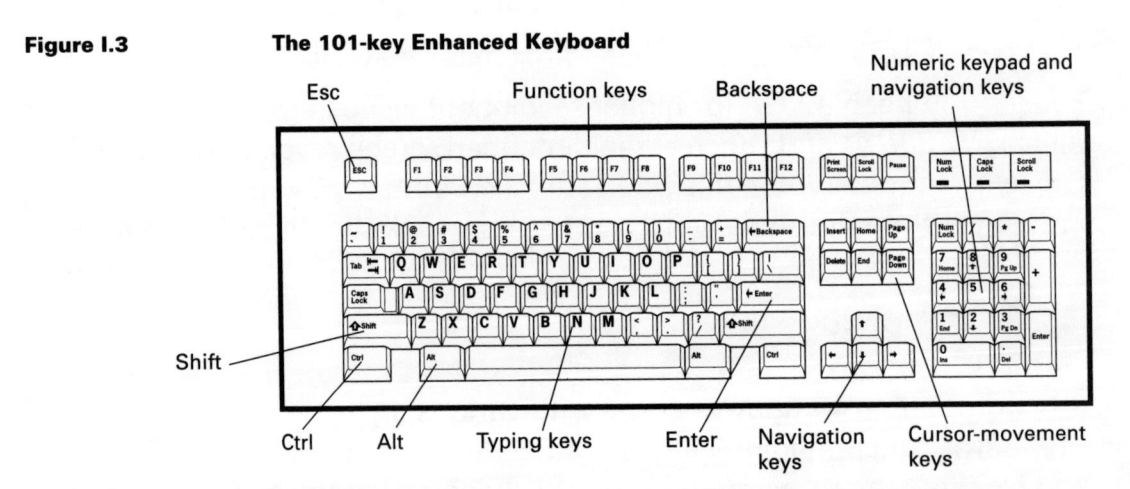

Office uses all main areas of the keyboard:

- The *function keys*, which enable you to access Office's special features. On the PC-, XT-, and AT-style keyboards, there are ten function keys at the left end of the keyboard; on the 101-key Enhanced Keyboard there are 12 function keys at the top of the keyboard.

- The *typing keys*, which enable you to enter letters, numbers, and punctuation marks. These keys include the Shift, Ctrl, and Alt keys, which you need to access several of Office's special features. The typing keys are located in the main body of all the keyboards.

- The *numeric keypad*, which enables you either to enter numeric data or to navigate through a document. When *Num Lock* is turned on, you use the numeric keypad to enter numeric data, just as you would on a standard calculator keypad. When Num Lock is turned off, you use the numeric keypad to navigate through a document by using the cursor-movement keys: Up, Down, Left, and Right Arrows; Home, End, PgUp (Page Up), and PgDn (Page Down). To turn Num Lock on/off, simply press the Num Lock key. To enter numeric data when Num Lock is off, use the number keys in the top row of the typing area.

- The *cursor-movement keypad*, which is available only on the Enhanced Keyboard, enables you to navigate through a document by using the Home, End, Page Up, and Page Down keys. The cursor-movement keypad works the same when Num Lock is turned on or off. This enables you to use the numeric keypad for numeric data entry (that is, to keep Num Lock on) and still have access to cursor-movement keys.

MOUSE OR EQUIVALENT TRACKING DEVICE

You need a mouse or equivalent tracking device (a trackball, for example) to work through the activities in this book. Any standard PC mouse or tracking device will do.

Note: Throughout this book, we direct you to use a mouse. If you have a different tracking device, simply use your device to perform all the mousing tasks: pointing, clicking, dragging, and so on.

CHAPTER 1: FIRST THINGS FIRST

Conventions Used
in This Book

Creating Your
Work Directory

Before You
Proceed Further

The hands-on activities in this book are your key to learning Microsoft Office 4.2 quickly and thoroughly. To perform these activities, you must first

- Familiarize yourself with the book's conventions
- Create a work directory in which you store the practice files from the accompanying Data Disk

To meet these requirements, you must work diligently through this entire chapter. In Chapter 2, you'll begin learning the nuts and bolts of Microsoft Office.

CONVENTIONS USED IN THIS BOOK

The following conventions used in this book will help you learn Microsoft Office 4.2 easily and efficiently.

- Each chapter begins with a short introduction and ends with a summary that includes a quick-reference guide to the techniques introduced in that chapter.

- Main chapter topics (large, capitalized headings) and subtopics (headings preceded by a cube) explain Office features.

- Hands-on activities allow you to practice using these features.

- In the activities, keystrokes, menu choices, and anything you are asked to type are printed in boldface. Here's an example from Chapter 2:

    2. Click (use your left mouse button) on **Customize** to open the Customize dialog box.

- Activities adhere to a *cause-and-effect* approach. Each step tells you what to do (cause) and then what will happen (effect). From the preceding example,

    Cause: Click on the **Customize** command.

    Effect: The Customize dialog box is opened.

- A plus sign (+) is used with the Shift, Ctrl, and Alt keys to indicate a multikey keystroke. For example, "press Ctrl+V" means "Press and hold down the Ctrl key, press the letter V, and then release both keys."

- To help you distinguish between steps presented for reference purposes (*general procedures*) and steps you should carry out at your computer as you read (*specific procedures*), we use the following system:

    - A bulleted step, like this, is provided for your information and reference only.

    1. A numbered step, like this, indicates one in a series of steps that you should carry out in sequence at your computer.

CREATING YOUR WORK DIRECTORY

Throughout this book, you will be creating, editing, and saving several text and graphics files. To keep these files together, you need to create a work directory for them on your hard disk. This directory will also hold the practice files contained on the enclosed Data Disk.

Follow these steps to create your work directory:

1. If Microsoft Office 4.2 is not currently installed on your computer, please install it now, before proceeding any further.

2. If you have 5,000,000 or more free bytes on the hard disk where you want to create your work directory, skip the rest of this step. If not, delete enough files from your hard disk to increase its free-byte total to at least 5,000,000. Otherwise, you won't be able to create your work directory and perform the hands-on activities in this book (while still maintaining an adequate amount of free hard-disk space). Make sure you back up all your important files before deleting them!

3. Start **Windows**, and insert the **Data Disk** (from the back of this book) in the appropriate drive.

4. Activate **Program Manager**. If your Program Manager is running as an icon, double-click on it to restore it to a window.

5. Choose **File, Run** from the menu bar to open the Run dialog box. Enter a command of the form

    ```
    fdrive:install hdrive: offwork
    ```

    where *fdrive* is the letter of the floppy-disk drive holding the Data Disk, and *hdrive* is the letter of the hard-disk drive on which you want to create your work directory. (Make sure to type a space before *hdrive*: and *offwork*.)

    For example, if the Data Disk is in drive A and you're creating your work directory on drive C, you'd enter

    ```
    a:install c: offwork
    ```

6. If all goes well, the message

    ```
    Work directory under construction.
    Please wait ......................
    ```

will appear, followed by a list of files being copied. And when the procedure is complete, the message

```
Work directory successfully completed!
```

will appear, followed by a line reporting the name of your work directory (c:\offwork, for example). If these messages appear, skip directly to the Note following the next step.

7. If all does not go so well, one of two error messages will appear. The first is

```
Installation failed! c: drive does not exist.
Reenter the INSTALL command using the
correct drive.
```

(Your drive letter may be different.) This message indicates that the hard drive you specified in your step 5 command does not exist on your computer. If you get this message, simply repeat step 5, making sure to specify the correct letter of your hard drive.

The second error message is

```
Installation failed! c:\offwork directory
already exists.
Reenter the INSTALL command using a
different work directory name.
```

(Your drive letter and/or directory name may be different.) This message indicates that a directory with the same name as your proposed work directory (OFFWORK) already exists on your specified hard disk. If this happens, repeat step 5, specifying a new work directory name of your choice instead of *offwork*. The name can be up to eight letters long; do not include spaces, periods, or punctuation marks.

Note: The hands-on activities in this book assume that your work directory is on drive C and is named OFFWORK. If you specified a different hard-disk drive or a different directory name, please remember to substitute this drive and/or name whenever we mention drive C or OFFWORK.

BEFORE YOU PROCEED FURTHER

The activities within each remaining chapter proceed sequentially. In many cases, you cannot perform an activity until you've performed one or more of the activities preceding it. For this reason, we recommend that you allot enough time to work through an entire chapter in one continuous session. Feel free to take as many breaks as you need: Stand up, stretch, take a walk, relate an amusing anecdote to a friend, drink some valerian-and-passionflower tea. Don't try to absorb too much information at any one time. Studies show that people assimilate and retain information most effectively when it is presented in digestible chunks and followed by a liberal amount of hands-on practice.

In the next chapter, we'll take you on a whirlwind tour of Microsoft Office Manager. You'll learn how to start and exit Office Manager, issue Office commands, and start, switch, and exit Office applications.

Good learning and...*bon voyage!*

CHAPTER 2: A QUICK TOUR OF MICROSOFT OFFICE MANAGER

Issuing Office Commands

Starting Office Automatically

Starting Office Applications

Switching between Running Office Applications

A Note on Office's Memory Requirements

Exiting Office Applications

Exiting Office

Starting Office Manually

Now that you've studied our conventions and created your OFFWORK work directory—you *did* do both of these things, right?—you can begin to explore Microsoft Office Manager (henceforth referred to simply as *Office*). In this chapter, we'll take you on a tour of Office and show you how to navigate its wide waters.

When you're done working through this chapter, you will know

- How to issue Office commands
- How to start Office applications
- How to switch between running Office applications
- How to exit Office applications
- How to exit Office
- How to manually start Office

ISSUING OFFICE COMMANDS

You can use any of the following to issue Office commands:

- The Office toolbar
- The Office menu
- The Office shortcut menu

Let's examine these one by one.

THE OFFICE TOOLBAR

The *Office toolbar* is a set of buttons grouped together in an on-screen toolbar. Each button represents an executable application. For example, the five buttons in the Office toolbar shown in Figure 2.1 represent the five listed applications. You use the Office toolbar to start applications and to switch between running applications.

Figure 2.1   **The Office toolbar**

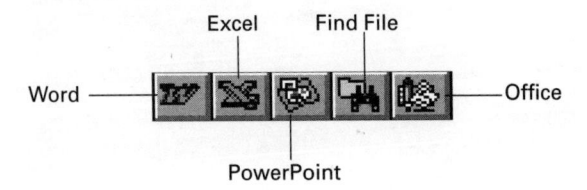

Word — Excel — PowerPoint — Find File — Office

THE OFFICE MENU

The *Office menu* is a set of commands grouped together in a drop-down menu. As shown in the Office menu in Figure 2.2, these commands allow you to start applications, switch between running applications, customize Office, change Office's setup, un-install Office, get on-line Office help, and exit Office.

Figure 2.2 **The Office menu**

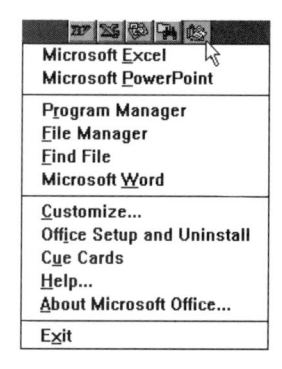

```
Microsoft Excel
Microsoft PowerPoint

Program Manager
File Manager
Find File
Microsoft Word

Customize...
Office Setup and Uninstall
Cue Cards
Help...
About Microsoft Office...

Exit
```

To open the Office menu,

- Click on the *Microsoft Office* button in the Office toolbar (as shown in Figure 2.1).

Note: When we want you to click the *left mouse button*, we'll simply say "click." When we want you to click the *right mouse button*, we'll say "click the right mouse button."

THE OFFICE SHORTCUT MENU

The *Office shortcut menu* is a set of shortcut commands grouped in a menu. As shown in the Office shortcut menu in Figure 2.3, these commands allow you to customize Office, change the size of the Office toolbar buttons, minimize the Office toolbar to an icon, and get on-line Office help.

To open the Office shortcut menu,

- Click the *right mouse button* anywhere on the Office toolbar.

Figure 2.3   **The Office shortcut menu**

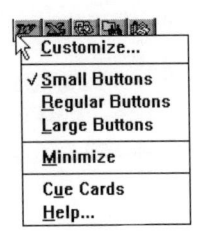

STARTING OFFICE AUTOMATICALLY

By default, Office is set to start automatically when you start Windows. However, since Office is a customizable program, this may *not* happen on your computer. If Office does not start automatically when you start Windows, you'll have to start it manually (as described in step 2 of the following activity).

Let's start Office and get some hands-on experience using its toolbar and menus to issue commands:

1. If you have not created your OFFWORK work directory, please do so before proceeding any further. You'll find instructions in Chapter 1's "Creating Your Work Directory."

2. Start **Windows**. If Office does *not* start automatically, start it manually (by double-clicking on the **Microsoft Office** program icon, which is stored in the Microsoft Office group in Program Manager).

3. If any applications other than Office and Program Manager are running, please terminate them. We want to start with a clean slate.

4. Observe your Office toolbar. It should match (or resemble) the toolbar shown in Figure 2.1. If, instead, your Office toolbar is running as an icon—as shown in Figure 2.4—double-click on it to restore it to a toolbar.

Figure 2.4   **The Office toolbar running as an icon**

STARTING OFFICE AUTOMATICALLY • 11

Since the Office toolbar is customizable, your toolbar may differ quite a bit from ours. Let's take a moment to make our toolbars match, or at least closely resemble each other:

1. Click your **right mouse button** anywhere on the **Office toolbar** to open its shortcut menu (as shown previously in Figure 2.3).

2. Click (your **left mouse button**) on **Customize** to open the Customize dialog box.

3. Click on the **View** tab to display the View options. Under Toolbar Button Size, select **Small Buttons**. Make sure that the following check boxes are checked (to *check* a check box, click on it until an X appears):

   ```
   Toolbar Is Always Visible
   Show ToolTips
   ```

   Do *not* uncheck any additional check boxes that may be checked.

4. Click on the **Toolbar** tab to display the Toolbar options. Make sure that the following check boxes are checked:

   ```
   Microsoft Word
   Microsoft Excel
   Microsoft PowerPoint
   Find File
   ```

   Again, do *not* uncheck any additional check boxes that may be checked.

5. Click on the **Menu** tab to display the Menu options. Make sure that the following check boxes are checked:

   ```
   Microsoft Excel
   Microsoft PowerPoint
   Program Manager
   File Manager
   Find File
   Microsoft Word
   Office Setup and Uninstall
   ```

   Once again, do *not* uncheck any additional check boxes.

6. Click on **OK** to accept your settings and close the Customize dialog box. Your Office toolbar should now match (or closely resemble) that shown in Figure 2.1. Your toolbar may have

more than five buttons, or your buttons may be arranged differently from those in Figure 2.1. If so, don't worry; this won't impair your ability to perform the book's hands-on activities.

On with the show:

1. Point to—but *don't* click on—the Office toolbar button that shows a slanted *W*. After a moment, the ToolTips feature engages and the button's name, "Microsoft Word," is displayed (see Figure 2.5).

Figure 2.5 **The ToolTips feature in action**

2. Use this technique to identify your remaining toolbar buttons. (Remember to point, not click!) The ToolTips feature is particularly useful when you're working with small toolbar buttons whose pictures are not always instantly recognizable.

3. Click on the **Microsoft Office** button to display its drop-down menu, as shown previously in Figure 2.2. (Your menu may not match ours.) This menu contains commands for starting applications, switching between running applications, customizing Office, changing Office's setup, uninstalling Office, getting on-line Office help, and exiting Office.

4. Click on **About Microsoft Office** to open a dialog box showing your Office version number and licensing information, and your computer system's statistics. Click on **OK** to close this dialog box.

5. Now click your **right mouse button** anywhere on the **Office toolbar** to open its shortcut menu. Note that several commands are the same as those in the toolbar's drop-down menu (Customize, Cue Cards, and Help). As you no doubt already know, Microsoft programs almost always give you two (or more!) methods for issuing the same command.

6. Click on **Minimize** to shrink your Office toolbar to an icon. Some users prefer to run the Office toolbar as a toolbar that remains constantly on screen (in the upper-right corner), even when other applications are running. Others find this arrangement too busy visually, and prefer to run the toolbar as an icon, double-clicking on it (or Alt+Tabbing to it) when necessary to restore it to a toolbar. In this book, we'll run the Office toolbar as a toolbar. When you're done with the book, feel free to run the Office toolbar as an icon.

7. Double-click on the **Microsoft Office** icon to restore it to a toolbar.

STARTING OFFICE APPLICATIONS

Starting Office applications is a breeze. You can use the Office toolbar or the Office menu to do it. To use the toolbar to start an application,

- Click on the desired toolbar button.

To use the Office menu to start an application,

- Click on the *Microsoft Office* button to open the Office menu.
- Choose the desired application in this menu.

You can also use all of the standard Windows methods for starting your applications: double-clicking on the application's program icon in Program Manager; pressing the application's shortcut key (provided that you specified a shortcut key for the application's program icon); double-clicking on the application's .EXE file in File Manager; or placing a copy of the application's program icon in the StartUp group in Program Manager.

Let's start some Office applications:

1. Click on the **Microsoft Word** button in the Office toolbar to start Word. (If you need help finding this button, use Tool-Tips.) Maximize the Microsoft Word application window, if necessary.

2. Note that the Office toolbar remains on screen, and that it fits neatly within Word's title bar without overlapping the Minimize or Maximize/Restore buttons. That's the advantage to displaying the Office toolbar with small buttons. When you display it with regular or large buttons, the toolbar no

longer fits within the current application's title bar. (More on this in Chapter 7.)

3. Click on the **Microsoft Office** button to open the Office menu.

4. Choose **Microsoft Excel** from this menu to start Excel. Maximize the Excel application window, if necessary. Note that the Office toolbar remains visible, ready to do your bidding.

PRACTICE YOUR SKILLS

1. Use the Office toolbar to start **Microsoft PowerPoint**.
   Note: If you have insufficient memory to run Word, Excel, and PowerPoint simultaneously, sneak a look at the upcoming section, "A Note On Office's Memory Requirements."

SWITCHING BETWEEN RUNNING OFFICE APPLICATIONS

Switching between running applications is just as easy as starting applications. To use the toolbar to switch to a running application,

- Click on the desired toolbar button.

To use the Office menu to switch to a running application,

- Click on the *Microsoft Office* button to open the Office menu.
- Choose the desired application from this menu.

Once again, you can also use the standard Windows methods to switch between running Office applications: pressing Alt+Tab; or pressing Ctrl+Esc to display the Task List, selecting the application, and clicking on Switch To.

Let's practice using the toolbar and the menu to switch between our running applications:

1. Use the Office toolbar to switch to the following programs:

   ```
   Microsoft Word
   Microsoft Excel
   Microsoft PowerPoint
   ```

2. Repeat the previous step, this time using the Office menu.

What's the verdict: Are you a toolbar person or a menu person?

SWITCHING BETWEEN RUNNING OFFICE APPLICATIONS • 15

PRACTICE YOUR SKILLS

1. Switch to **Word**, and open the document file **herbs.doc** from your OFFWORK work directory, as shown in Figure 2.6. This document contains the Herbal Manifesto of Rick and Nancy's Herbal Emporium (a progressive company you'll see lots of in these first few chapters).

Figure 2.6 **In Word, HERBS.DOC's Herbal Manifesto**

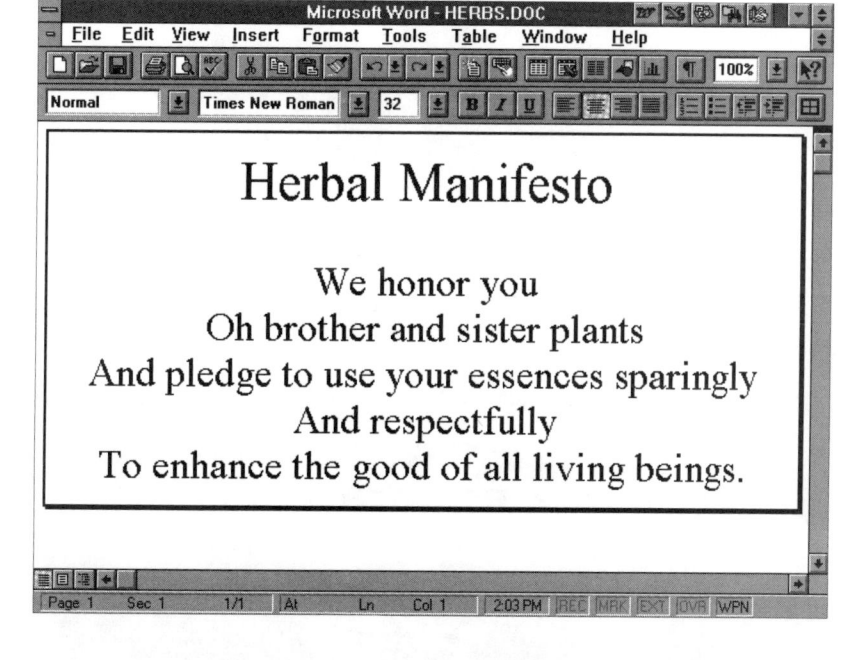

> Herbal Manifesto
>
> We honor you
> Oh brother and sister plants
> And pledge to use your essences sparingly
> And respectfully
> To enhance the good of all living beings.

2. Switch to **Excel**, and open the workbook file **herbs.xls** from your OFFWORK directory. This workbook contains data on several herbs sold in Rick and Nancy's Emporium. Press **PgDn** to display a wholesale/retail cost chart for these herbs, as shown in Figure 2.7.

3. Switch to **PowerPoint**, and open the presentation file **herbs.ppt** from OFFWORK. This presentation—once again, a product of Rick and Nancy's delightful Emporium—explores the pros and cons of adopting a planetary approach to herbal-formula creation. Take a quick look at the presentation's nine slides. When you're done, display the **Herbal Manifesto** on slide 2, as shown in Figure 2.8.

16 • CHAPTER 2: A QUICK TOUR OF MICROSOFT OFFICE MANAGER

Figure 2.7 **In Excel, HERBS.XLS's Wholesale/Retail Cost chart**

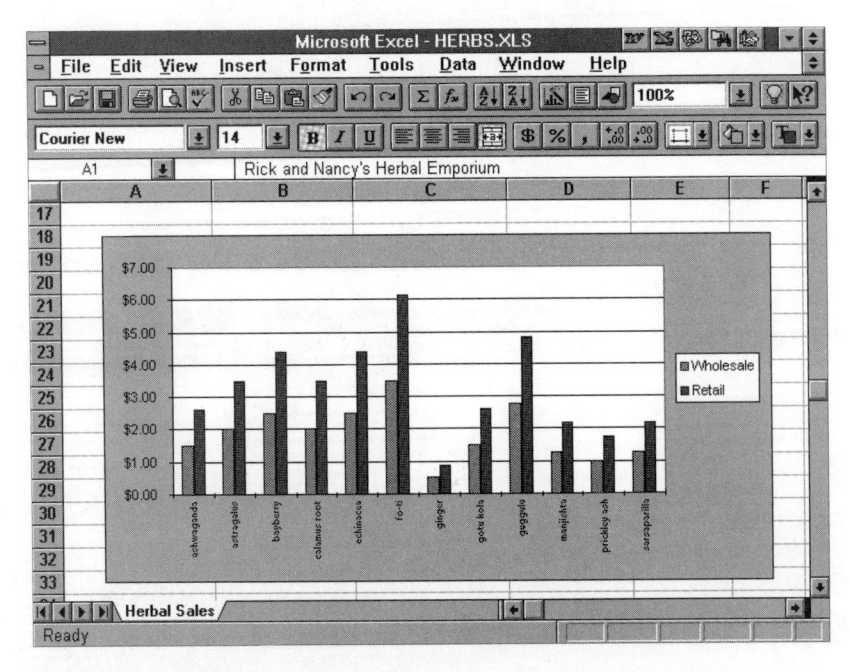

Figure 2.8 **In PowerPoint, HERBS.PPT's Herbal Manifesto**

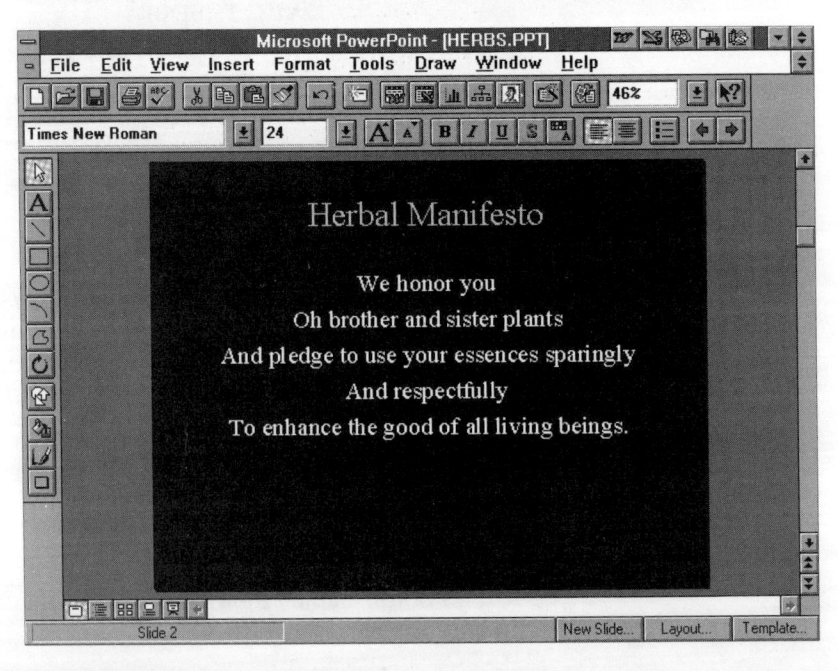

A NOTE ON OFFICE'S MEMORY REQUIREMENTS • 17

4. Switch to **Word**. Compare its Herbal Manifesto with the Manifesto on slide 2 of the PowerPoint presentation. They are identical, except for some minor formatting differences.

5. In PowerPoint, display the **Wholesale/Retail Cost of Herbs** chart on slide 9, as shown in Figure 2.9. Compare it to the chart in Excel. Once again, they are practically identical.

Figure 2.9   **HERBS.PPT's Wholesale/Retail Cost chart**

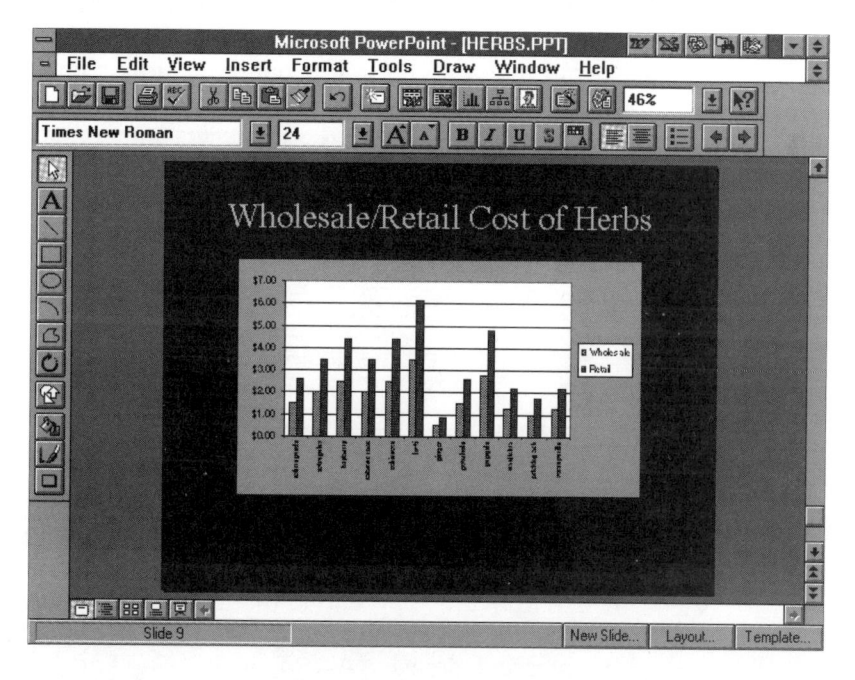

The fact that these three files contain certain identical elements (the Herbal Manifesto and/or the Wholesale/Retail chart) points to an essential feature of Office: the ability to share data among several applications. Rather than create the Manifesto and chart twice—once for each file in which they appear—we created them *once* in Word and Excel and then *copied* them to the PowerPoint file. You'll learn how to do this in Chapter 4.

A NOTE ON OFFICE'S MEMORY REQUIREMENTS

It takes RAM to run a program (you knew that!). It takes even more RAM to run several programs at once (which is what you're doing when you run two or more Office applications). Depending on your computer's memory configuration, you may not always have enough free RAM to be able to perform a certain step in a hands-on activity. For example, you may not have been able to open all three of the files in the previous activity at once. For all we know, you may not even have been able to run Word, Excel, and PowerPoint simultaneously!

We've tried to limit your RAM requirements throughout this book. Chances are you'll be fine. If, however, you should run into a memory snag, simply work around it as best you can. You may need to skip a step, or perform some steps out of sequence. Use your ingenuity! If things get really ugly, think seriously about increasing your system RAM. Office's *raison d'être* is to integrate several applications: It only makes sense that you have enough RAM to do this properly.

EXITING OFFICE APPLICATIONS

To use the Office toolbar to exit (terminate) a running application,

- Alt+click on the desired toolbar button. (That is, hold down the *Alt* key and click on the toolbar button.)
  Note: You cannot use this method to exit Find File. You must, instead, click on the Close button in the Find File dialog box, or double-click on its Control-menu box.

You cannot use the Office menu to exit a running application. You can, however, use the standard Windows methods: choosing File, Exit from the application's menu bar; double-clicking on the application's Control-menu box; choosing Close from the application's Control menu; pressing Alt+F4; or choosing End Task from the Task List.

PRACTICE YOUR SKILLS

1. Use the Alt+click Office toolbar method to exit **Microsoft Word** and **Microsoft Excel**.

2. Use your favorite standard method to exit **Microsoft PowerPoint**.

EXITING OFFICE

To use the Office menu to exit Office,

- Choose *Exit* from the Office menu.

  You cannot use the Office toolbar to exit Office. You can, however, choose End Task from the Task List.

PRACTICE YOUR SKILLS

1. Use the Office menu to exit Office. Note that the Office toolbar disappears.

STARTING OFFICE MANUALLY

Chances are your Office starts automatically when you start Windows. Even so, you may occasionally need to start Office manually. Let's say you exited Office without exiting Windows (which is, in fact, what you just did). If you decided to use Office again, you could exit Windows and then restart it (boo!). Or, you could simply restart Office manually (hooray!), as follows:

- Double-click on the *Microsoft Office* program icon.

  This icon is normally stored in the Program Manager group *Microsoft Office*, as shown in Figure 2.10. Depending on how your Program Manager is set up, however, your Office icon may be stored in a different group (in which case you'll have to do some reconnaissance work to find it).

PRACTICE YOUR SKILLS

1. Restart **Office** manually. The Office toolbar should reappear.

SUMMARY

In this chapter, you learned how to issue Office commands, start Office applications, switch between running Office applications, exit Office applications, exit Office, and manually start Office.

Figure 2.10   **The Microsoft Office program icon**

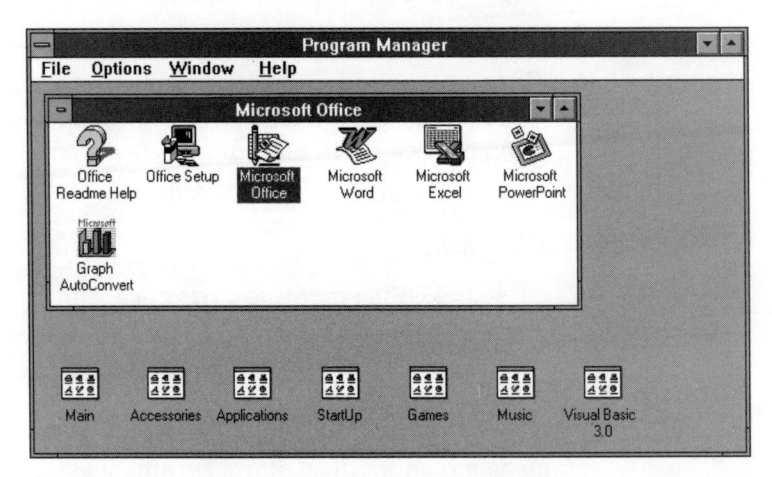

Here's a quick reference for the techniques you learned in this chapter:

Desired Result	How to Do It
Issue Office commands	Use Office toolbar, Office menu, or Office shortcut menu
Open Office menu	Click on **Microsoft Office** button in Office toolbar
Open Office shortcut menu	Click **right mouse button** anywhere on **Office toolbar**
Use Office toolbar to start application	Click on desired toolbar button
Use Office menu to start application	Click on **Microsoft Office** button to open Office menu; choose desired application from menu
Use Office toolbar to switch to running application	Click on desired toolbar button

Desired Result	How to Do It
Use Office menu to switch to running application	Click on **Microsoft Office** button to open Office menu; choose desired application from menu
Use Office toolbar to exit running application	**Alt+click** on desired toolbar button
Use Office menu to exit Office	Choose **Exit** from Office menu
Start Office manually	Double-click on **Microsoft Office** program icon (in Program Manager)

In the next chapter, you'll learn how to gain access to the Office Help system, how to get general and dialog-box help, and how to get help about individual applications. You'll also learn to use Office Cue Cards for step-by-step help.

A NOTE ON HOW TO PROCEED

If you wish to break off here, please do so. If you feel energetic and wish to press onward, proceed enthusiastically to the next chapter. Remember to allot enough time to work through an entire chapter in one sitting!

CHAPTER 3: GETTING HELP FROM THE OFFICE MANAGER

The Office Help System

Using Office Cue Cards for Step-by-Step Help

Each Office application has its own Help menu, through which you can gain access to information about that application. However, you can also use Office's Help system to learn about these same applications. More importantly, Office's Help system can provide you with valuable information about Office itself and its uses.

When you're done working through this chapter, you will know

- How to gain access to the Office Help system
- How to get general help
- How to get dialog-box help
- How to get help about individual applications
- How to use Office Cue Cards for step-by-step help

THE OFFICE HELP SYSTEM

Just as each Office application contains its own Help system, so, too, does Office. Because you can also use Office to get help about its component applications (Word, Excel, and PowerPoint), Office's Help system functions, in a way, as a kind of metahelp system.

A note to veteran Help users: If you're an old hand at using help systems, some of the information that follows might be old hat to you. But please be patient. Very shortly, we'll use this information to gain access to some of the deeper realms of Office Help, within which you might someday find your salvation.

As with the Help systems in Office's individual applications, you can use Office's Help system to get information about Office—commands, concepts, procedures, and so on—at any point during a work session. It might be helpful to think of Help as a very knowledgeable tech-support person sitting in the background and waiting patiently to answer your questions.

You can use Help to get both *general* help and *dialog-box* help. General help provides information on a vast array of Office topics. For example, let's say you forgot the function of one of the commands in the Office menu; you could refresh your memory by running Help and viewing the *Reference Information* topic. Dialog-box help provides you with information about the dialog box that is currently active. For example, let's say that you opened the Customize dialog box (which you'll learn more about in Chapter 7) and wanted to learn about one of its available commands. In this case, you could run Help directly from the opened dialog box to get the information you desire.

THE OFFICE HELP SYSTEM • 25

GENERAL HELP

To get general Office help:

- Click on the *Office* button to open the Office menu.
- Choose *Help* to open the Help Contents window.
- To view the Help window for an underlined topic, click on the topic.
- To search for a topic you want help with:
  - Click on the *Search* button.
  - Locate the desired search word by typing the initial part of the word or by scrolling through the search-word list.
  - Double-click on the desired search word to show its associated topics.
  - Double-click on the desired topic to view its Help window.
- To view previous Help windows, click on the *Back* button.
- To view the Contents window, click on the *Contents* button.
- To display the Windows Help History box, which displays, in reverse chronological order, the names of the Help windows you've thus far opened during the current Help session, click on the *History* button.
- To reopen a Help window whose name is displayed in the Windows Help History box, double-click on the desired window name.

Let's get general Help for some of the topics that we'll cover later in this book:

1. Click on the **Office** button in the Office toolbar to open the Office menu. Then choose **Help** from the menu (click on it). The Help Contents window is displayed.

2. Maximize the Help Contents window, and compare your screen to Figure 3.1. The underlined items in this window are Office Help's main topics. Below the menu bar, notice the four buttons: *Contents, Search, Back,* and *History.*

3. Examine the available Help topics. Under the various topics are brief descriptions of each. Use the vertical scroll bar to scroll through the window. Then scroll back up to the first topic.

Figure 3.1   **The Help Contents window**

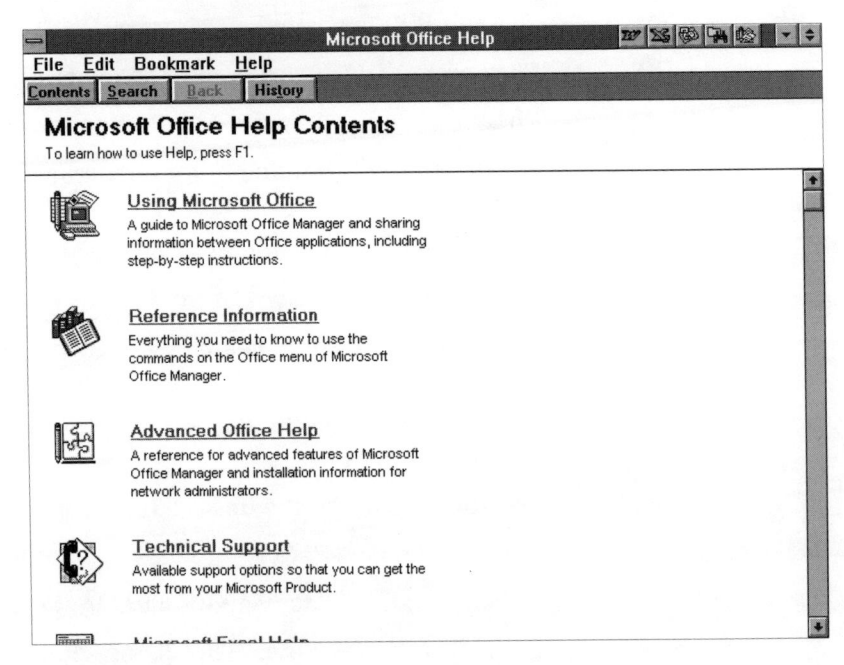

[Screenshot of Microsoft Office Help window showing Contents with topics: Using Microsoft Office, Reference Information, Advanced Office Help, Technical Support, Microsoft Excel Help]

4. Place the mouse pointer over the underlined Help topics. Notice that the pointer changes to a pointing hand. In any Help window, clicking on a highlighted (green on a color monitor) and underlined heading or term tells Help to display information specific to it.

5. Click on the second topic in the Help Contents window, **Reference Information**. The topic is now displayed in the Help window (see Figure 3.2). Notice that Reference Information has now been further subdivided into two subtopics. Under these subtopics appear more headings.

6. Under Command Reference Information, click on **Find File** to display information in the Help window about the Find File command. Take a brief look at the current contents of the Help window (see Figure 3.3). (There's no need to digest the information we're viewing now. We simply want to give you an idea of the structure of the Help system and of the many layers that a Help topic can contain.)

Figure 3.2   **The Reference Information Help topic**

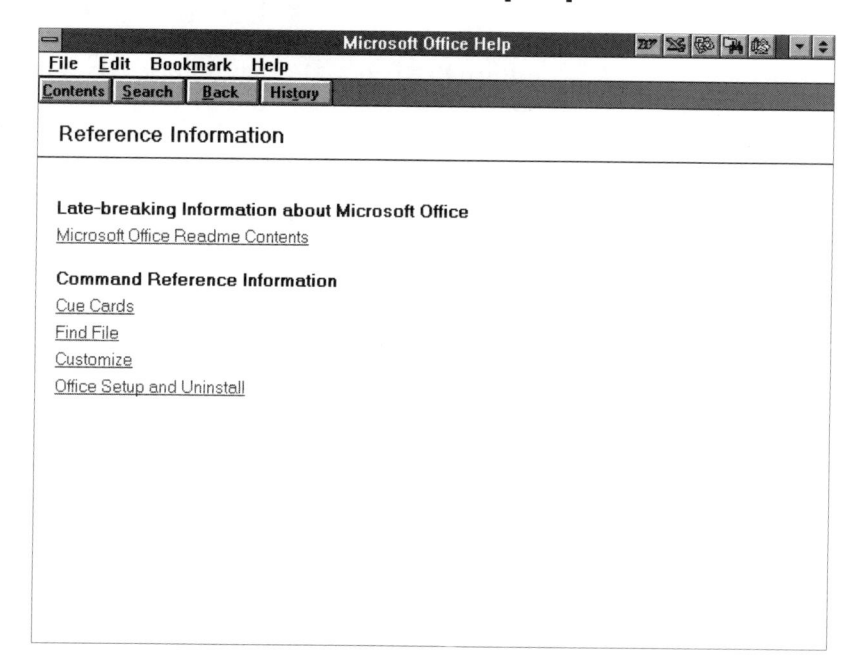

```
─────────────────────────── Microsoft Office Help ───────────────────────────
 File  Edit  Bookmark  Help
 Contents  Search   Back   History
─────────────────────────────────────────────────────────────────────────────
 Reference Information


 Late-breaking Information about Microsoft Office
 Microsoft Office Readme Contents

 Command Reference Information
 Cue Cards
 Find File
 Customize
 Office Setup and Uninstall
```

Figure 3.3   **Help on the Find File command**

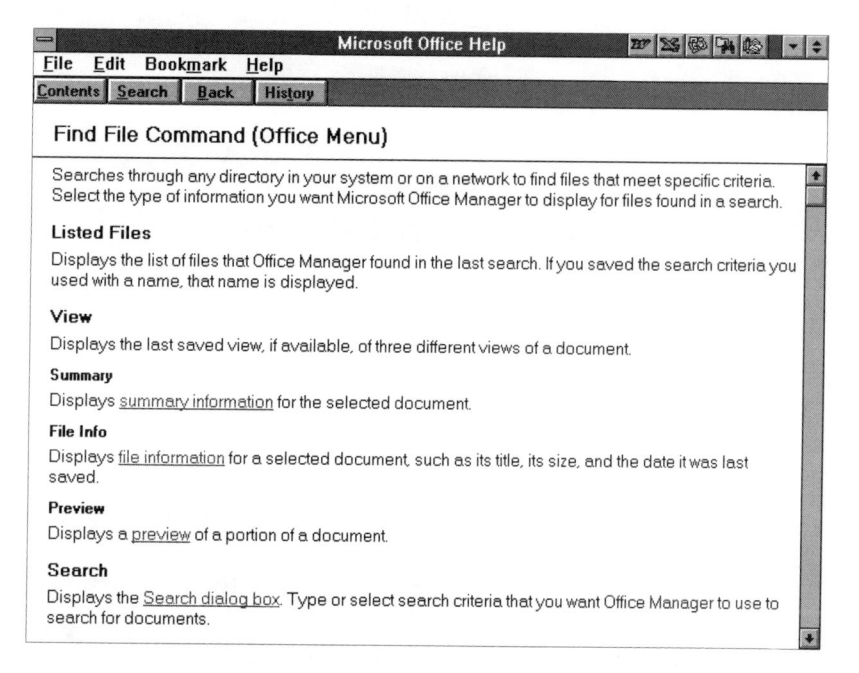

```
─────────────────────────── Microsoft Office Help ───────────────────────────
 File  Edit  Bookmark  Help
 Contents  Search   Back   History
─────────────────────────────────────────────────────────────────────────────
 Find File Command (Office Menu)

 Searches through any directory in your system or on a network to find files that meet specific criteria.
 Select the type of information you want Microsoft Office Manager to display for files found in a search.

 Listed Files
 Displays the list of files that Office Manager found in the last search. If you saved the search criteria you
 used with a name, that name is displayed.

 View
 Displays the last saved view, if available, of three different views of a document.

 Summary
 Displays summary information for the selected document.

 File Info
 Displays file information for a selected document, such as its title, its size, and the date it was last
 saved.

 Preview
 Displays a preview of a portion of a document.

 Search
 Displays the Search dialog box. Type or select search criteria that you want Office Manager to use to
 search for documents.
```

7. Under View are three subheadings: *Summary, File Info*, and *Preview*. In the sentence under the Summary subheading, click on the underlined term **summary information** to display information about the Summary View option of the Find File command (see Figure 3.4). We've seen enough of this.

Figure 3.4 **The Summary View Help topic**

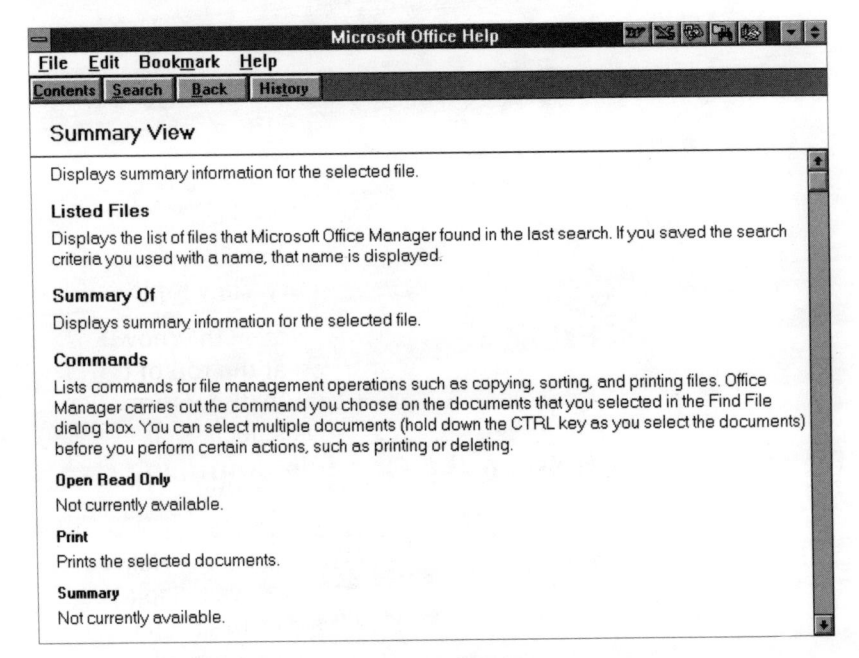

![Screenshot of Microsoft Office Help window showing the Summary View topic, with sections for Listed Files, Summary Of, Commands, Open Read Only, Print, and Summary.]

8. Click on the **Back** button (below the menu bar). This takes us back to the previously displayed Help information about the Find File command. One of the handy features of the Help system is its memory of what Help information you've displayed during the current Help session. We'll see a more dazzling example of this shortly.

9. Click on the **Contents** button. The Help Contents window (the one we first opened) is once again displayed.

10. Click on the **History** button. The Windows Help History box is displayed (see Figure 3.5). This box lists all the topics that have been displayed in the Help window during this Help

session, from the latest to the earliest. Notice that Find File is selected in the box, indicating that it was the topic displayed before the Help Contents information.

Figure 3.5   **The Windows Help History box**

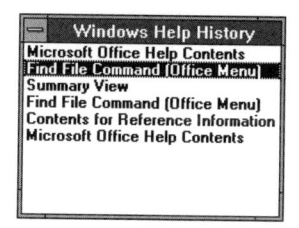

```
Windows Help History
Microsoft Office Help Contents
Find File Command (Office Menu)
Summary View
Find File Command (Office Menu)
Contents for Reference Information
Microsoft Office Help Contents
```

11. In the Windows Help History box, double-click on **Summary View**. The Summary View topic is once again displayed.

12. Click on **History**. Notice that now Summary View (the current topic) is displayed at the top of the list and that Microsoft Office Help Contents (the information displayed before Summary View) is selected.

13. Double-click on the Windows Help History box's **Control-menu box** to close it.

14. Now click on **Back**. Because Help remembers that the Help Contents information was displayed immediately before the Summary View topic, the Help Contents information is once again displayed.

Now, let's say that you want information on starting Office applications. You could use the Help Contents window to find the general topic, and then gradually narrow your search through the various layers of Help. More expediently, you could use the Search feature to look up information about starting office applications. Let's do so now:

1. In the Help Contents window, click on **Search** to open the Search dialog box (see Figure 3.6). Near the top of the dialog box, you are instructed to

    Type a word, or select one from the list.

    Notice the blinking insertion point in the text box below it.

Figure 3.6   **The Search dialog box**

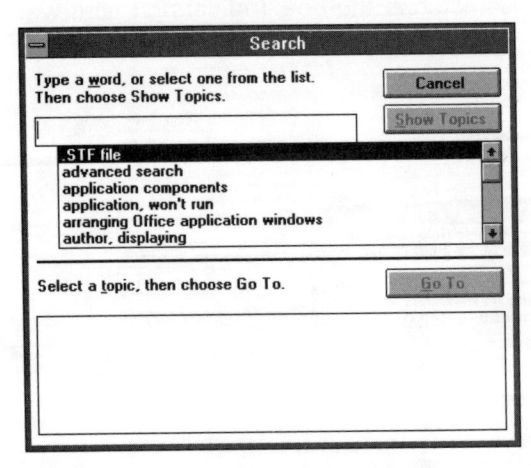

2. Begin typing the word **starting** while you watch the list of subjects. The smart little Help system scrolls through the list of subjects, trying to match the word you are typing. In this case, by the time you type the first *t* in *starting*, the topic *starting Office applications* is found and selected in the list (pretty neat, huh?).

3. Click on the **Show Topics** button to display any topics that the Help system might contain that are related to the selected subject. In the list box at the bottom of the dialog box, one such topic has been found: *Starting Applications and Working with Application Windows* (see Figure 3.7). Notice the instruction above this list box:

   ```
   Select a topic, then choose Go To.
   ```

   In this case, since there's only one topic, it's already selected.

4. Click on the **Go To** button to display the topic in the Help window. Skim the displayed topic (there won't be a test on this information). Under the heading *To arrange two application windows on your desktop using Office Manager* (you'll need to scroll), notice that there are two words highlighted and underscored with dashed lines: *tiled* and *desktop*.

THE OFFICE HELP SYSTEM • 31

Figure 3.7 **The desired topic selected in the Search dialog box**

[Search dialog box showing "starting Office applications" typed in the search field, with a list of topics below including "starting Office applications" highlighted, "stopping Office applications", "subject files", "Summary tab, Find File command (Office menu)", "summary view", "Summary View command (Office menu)". Below is "Starting Applications and Working with Application Windows" selected. Buttons shown: Close, Show Topics, Go To.]

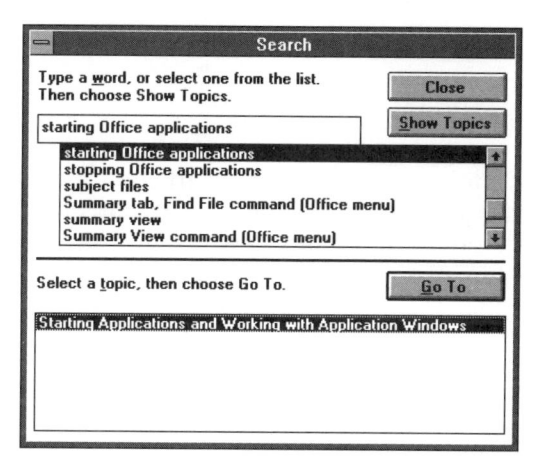

5. Place your mouse pointer over the highlighted words *tiled* and *desktop*. Notice that the phantom pointing hand once again appears. As was true earlier when you placed the mouse pointer over an underlined topic, here too you're being informed that clicking on these words will provide you with yet more information.

6. Click on the word **tiled**. Voilà! Help displays a definition of the word in a little box (see Figure 3.8). Help includes a glossary of such terms; whenever you click on one, its definition is displayed. Just remember that these terms are always underscored by a dashed line.

Figure 3.8 **Displaying definitions of highlighted terms in Help**

> tile
> A way of arranging active windows so that no windows overlap and all windows are visible.

PRACTICE YOUR SKILLS

1. Display and read the definition of the term *desktop*. Then remove it from view.

2. Try using the Search feature to look up a topic or two that might interest you.

3. When you're tired of searching, return to the Help Contents window. (**Hint:** Click on the **Contents** button; it's the fastest method.)

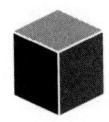

EXITING HELP

You exit Help using one of the same methods you would use to close any application. (In this way, it helps to think of the Help system as a separate program—which, in fact, it is.) To exit Help, simply double-click on the Help window Control-menu box, or choose File, Exit from the Help menu bar.

Note: It is not necessary to return to the Help Contents window before you exit Help. You can exit from anywhere within the system. However, it's always a good idea to close any dialog boxes before you attempt to exit, as some of these will remain open even after the Help system is closed—for example, the Windows Help History box. There's no danger in this; it's just that leaving programs running unnecessarily will clutter your desktop and take up memory.

Let's exit the Help system:

1. Double-click on the Help window's **Control-menu box** to exit Help.

PRACTICE YOUR SKILLS

1. Run **Help**.
2. Feel free to explore the Help system's cavernous recesses.
3. Once again, practice using the Search feature. (It will no doubt come in handy someday.)
4. When you've completed your whirlwind tour of the Help universe, exit Help.

DIALOG-BOX HELP

Now that you know how to get general help, let's find out how to get its counterpart, dialog-box help. Dialog-box help is specific to the dialog box which is open; this saves you the time of digging through general help to eventually uncover the same information.

THE OFFICE HELP SYSTEM • 33

To get dialog-box help:

- Open the desired dialog box.
- Click on the *Help* button, or press *F1*.

In the following exercise, we're going to take a brief look at the Find File dialog box. At this point, it's not necessary to know anything about this dialog box and its function. We'll take a much closer look at the Find File feature in Chapter 7.

Let's get some dialog-box help:

1. In the Office toolbar, click on the **Find File** button. The Search File dialog box is displayed (see Figure 3.9). As you might have guessed, this dialog box is primarily used to search for files. Notice the Help button. **Note:** The first time you click on Find File, the Search dialog box is displayed. Subsequent times, the Find File dialog box will open.

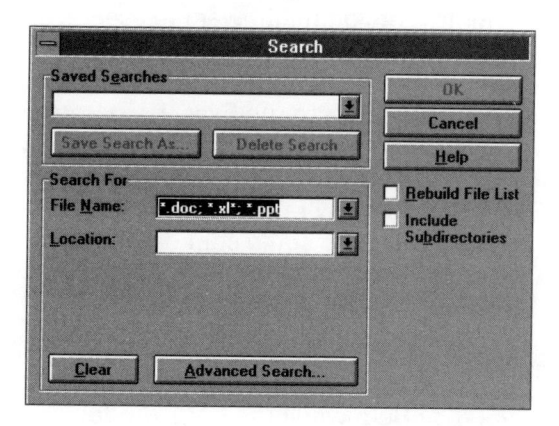

Figure 3.9   **The Search dialog box**

2. Click on **Help**. Eureka! The Help window opens, and the Search dialog box is displayed. You might have recognized this topic from our tour of general help. With this example, you can see the innate beauty of dialog-box help: With one command, you are able to move quickly to the pertinent topic, instead of first sifting through screens of information.

3. Exit Help.

4. In the Search dialog box, click on **Cancel** to close it.

PRACTICE YOUR SKILLS

1. From the Office menu (click on the **Office** button), choose **Customize** to open the Customize dialog box.
2. Get help for this dialog box. If you want, you can read through the topic.
3. Exit Help.
4. Close the Customize dialog box *without* making any changes. (**Hint:** Click on **Cancel**.)

GETTING HELP ON INDIVIDUAL APPLICATIONS

Earlier, when we were looking at the Office Help Contents window, you might have noticed that you could get further help on the individual Office applications. Clicking on any of these topics opens the actual Help file of that application; though you start out in Office Help, you are, in effect, catapulted into the Help program of that application.

The only time that you might want to access, say, Excel Help from Office Help is if you are not currently running Excel, yet you wish to glean some information about it. If you are running Excel, it generally makes more sense to run Excel Help from Excel. In this chapter, we have been focusing on the Office Help system, and we assume that you are familiar with the Help systems of Excel, Word, and PowerPoint. At any rate, their structures are so similar to that of Office Help, that you could confidently apply the techniques you've learned here to the Help system of any Office application.

USING OFFICE CUE CARDS FOR STEP-BY-STEP HELP

When you use Help while the Help window is active, the Help window supersedes any other window. So if, for example, the Excel Help window is active on your screen, you cannot access Excel commands without first activating the Excel application window (and thereby deactivating the Help window). Needless to say, this can make the task of using Help for step-by-step instruction quite cumbersome. But read on....

The *Cue Cards* feature does provide you with step-by-step instruction, enabling you to learn about Office concepts and procedures

USING OFFICE CUE CARDS FOR STEP-BY-STEP HELP • 35

as you go. In addition, you can access the Office Help system directly from Cue Cards. To display Cue Cards, simply choose Cue Cards from the Office menu. When you're done using Cue Cards, double-click on the Cue Cards Control-menu box to close them.

Let's use Cue Cards to display information about switching between applications:

1. In the Office menu, choose **Cue Cards** to display the Microsoft Office Cue Cards dialog box (see Figure 3.10). Take a moment to read the contents of the dialog box. Notice that it contains a number of topics, with buttons to the left of each. The topic that would seem to cover switching between applications should be the first one.

Figure 3.10   **The Microsoft Office Cue Cards dialog box**

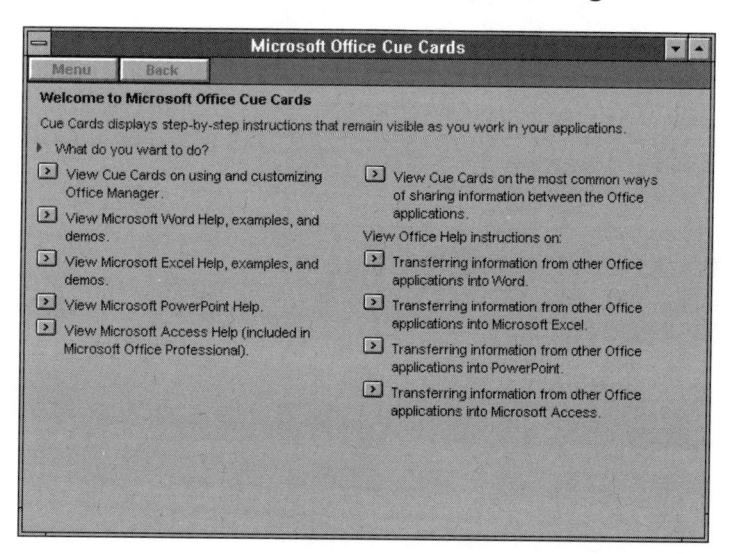

2. Click on the **>** button next to *View Cue Cards on using and customizing Office Manager*. Momentarily, a list of topics is displayed; these topics are all related to using and customizing Office. Notice that the Cue Cards dialog box is now set off out of the way, toward the right edge of the screen. Take a moment to read through this Cue Card. The second choice is definitely the one we want.

36 • CHAPTER 3: GETTING HELP FROM THE OFFICE MANAGER

3. Click on the **>** button next to *Switch applications using Office Manager*. That's it! This Cue Card zeroes in on our topic; take a moment to read it. Notice that the Cue Card gives you a couple of methods for performing the procedure (see Figure 3.11).

Figure 3.11 **Using the Cue Cards feature to learn how to switch between Office applications**

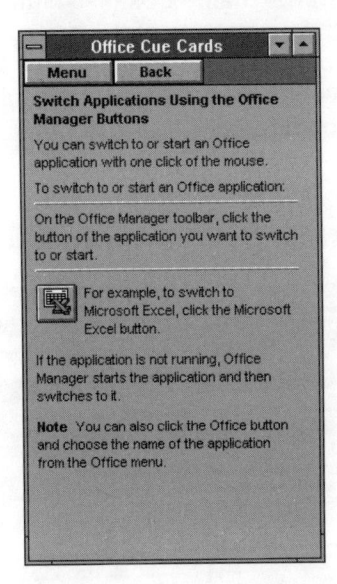

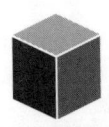

PRACTICE YOUR SKILLS

Use your Help/Cue Cards knowledge to do the following:

1. Return to the previous Cue Card, the Cue Cards "menu." (**Hint:** Notice the **Back** button.)

2. Display a Cue Card that tells you how to exit Office.

3. Take a self-guided tour through the realm of Cue Cards.

4. Return to the Cue Cards menu. (**Hint:** Notice the **Menu** button.)

5. Exit the Cue Cards feature. (**Hint:** Don't forget the **Control-menu box**!)

SUMMARY

In this chapter, you learned how to get general and dialog-box help, how to navigate through the Office Help system, and how to display the definitions of key terms in Help. You also learned how to get specialized help by using the Office Cue Cards feature.

Here's a quick reference for the Office techniques you learned in this chapter:

Desired Result	**How to Do It**
Run Office Help	Click on **Office** button to open Office menu, choose **Help** to open Help Contents window, click on underlined topic
Search for Help topic	In Help window, click on **Search** button, locate desired search word by typing initial part of word or by scrolling through search-word list, double-click on desired search word to show its associated topics, double-click on desired topic to view its Help window
View previous Help windows	Click on **Back** button
View Help Contents window	Click on **Contents** button
Display Windows Help History box	Click on **History** button
Reopen Help window whose name is displayed in Windows Help History box	Double-click on desired window name
Exit Help	Double-click on Help window **Control-menu box**
Run dialog-box Help	Open desired dialog box; click on **Help** button, or press **F1**
Display Cue Cards	Choose **Cue Cards** from Office menu

Desired Result	How to Do It
Select Cue Cards topic	Click on **>** button next to desired topic
Display previous Cue Card	Click on **Back**
Return to Cue Cards menu	Click on **Menu**
Exit Cue Cards	Double-click on Cue Cards dialog box **Control-menu box**

In the next few chapters, you will begin to learn how to exchange data between applications. In Chapter 4, you will learn how to cut, copy, and paste data between applications using the Windows Clipboard.

CHAPTER 4: COPYING AND PASTING DATA BETWEEN APPLICATIONS

Cut, Copy, and Paste

Using the Cut and Paste Commands

Using the Copy and Paste Commands

In Chapter 2, you learned how to run more than one Office application at a time and switch between them. However, the real beauty of Office lies in its ability to take advantage of several methods of transferring data from one application to another.

We'll examine these methods in detail in this portion of the book. In this chapter, we'll take a look at one of these methods, which encompasses three important procedures: cutting, copying, and pasting.

When you're done working through this chapter, you will know

- How to *cut* data from a file in an application
- How to *paste* the data to one or more other applications
- How to *copy* data to one or more other applications
- How to modify copied data

CUT, COPY, AND PASTE

In your exploration of individual Office applications, you've no doubt noticed that they share many features. These features include a few of the same toolbar buttons and menus. Having similar features and commands in different applications obviously can make it easier for you to switch between applications without becoming confused about their availability and function.

One example of a menu that contains some choices that are common to all Office—indeed, to all Windows-based—applications is the Edit menu. Figure 4.1 shows Word's Edit menu. Furthermore, three Edit menu choices common to Windows-based applications are *Cut, Copy,* and *Paste*. These are also the most commonly used commands in the Edit menu. Because of this, Cut, Copy, and Paste are also available in the standard toolbars of every Office application (see Figure 4.2).

Figure 4.1   **Word's Edit menu**

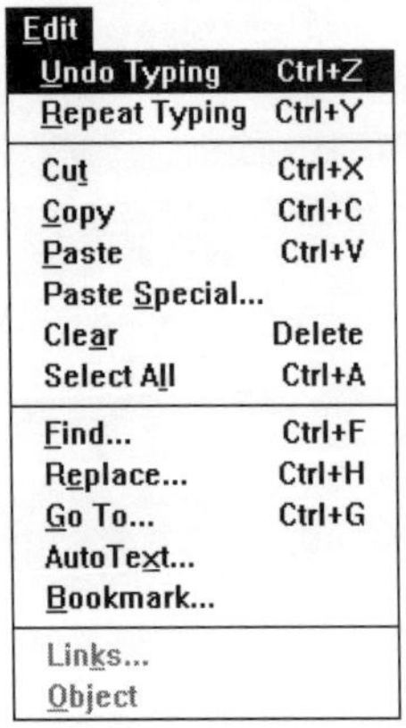

Edit	
Undo Typing	Ctrl+Z
Repeat Typing	Ctrl+Y
Cut	Ctrl+X
Copy	Ctrl+C
Paste	Ctrl+V
Paste Special...	
Clear	Delete
Select All	Ctrl+A
Find...	Ctrl+F
Replace...	Ctrl+H
Go To...	Ctrl+G
AutoText...	
Bookmark...	
Links...	
Object	

Figure 4.2   **The Cut, Copy, and Paste toolbar buttons**

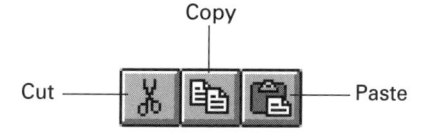

In the next section, we'll take a look at how to use these commands and exactly what they do, but first we need to step outside the bounds of Office and tell you about the Windows Clipboard, the feature these commands use.

THE WINDOWS CLIPBOARD

The Windows Clipboard is actually a sophisticated program, though you don't need to run it in the same way you would run a program such as Word or Excel. When you use the Cut or Copy command, the application you are using activates the Clipboard by sending data to it; when you use the Paste command, the application retrieves data from the Clipboard. The Cut command *removes* selected data from the file you are working in and places it on the Clipboard. The Copy command *copies* the selected data to the Clipboard, keeping the original intact. The Paste command places a copy of the Clipboard contents at the position of the insertion point or selected data.

Note: The Clipboard serves as a *temporary* storage area for the information you are copying or moving. Data moved or copied to the Clipboard will remain there only until the next time you use Cut or Copy—or until you exit Windows.

USING THE CUT AND PASTE COMMANDS

As you can see, the Cut and Paste commands go hand-in-hand. When you cut something from a file, you do it with the intention of pasting it somewhere else.

Note: Casual users will sometimes use the Cut command to delete selected data; however, we recommend that you don't acquire this habit. Remember that whenever you remove data to the Clipboard, you obliterate the previous contents of the Clipboard.

44 • CHAPTER 4: COPYING AND PASTING DATA BETWEEN APPLICATIONS

To use the Cut and Paste commands:

- In the source application, select the data you wish to remove to the Clipboard.
- Click on the *Cut* button in the toolbar of the source application. (You can, of course, use the Edit menu instead; use whichever technique works best for you. However, for the sake of brevity, we'll use the toolbar.)
- Open the destination file in the desired application.
- In the destination application, place the insertion point in, select, or display the location to which you wish to place the cut data.
- Click on the *Paste* button.

MOVING WORD TEXT TO A POWERPOINT SLIDE

Let's begin our paste-fest by moving data from a Word document to a PowerPoint presentation:

1. Run **Word** (click on the **Word** button in the Office toolbar).
2. In the OFFWORK directory, open the Word file **cut.doc**.
3. Run **PowerPoint** (click on the **PowerPoint** button in the Office toolbar).
4. In the OFFWORK directory, open the PowerPoint file **paste.ppt**.
5. Move through the slides in the presentation. This is essentially the same presentation you opened in Chapter 2. However, notice that slides 2 and 9 are missing some information.
6. Display slide 2 of the presentation. This slide is missing both title and body text (see Figure 4.3).
7. Switch to **Word** (click on the **Word** button). You can see that the CUT.DOC document contains two boxes, each of which contains text. (Depending on how your Word application window is set up, you might need to scroll to view both boxes of text.) We'll move the text in the upper box to slide 2 of PASTE.PPT.
8. In the upper box of text, select the first line of text, **Herbal Manifesto** (see Figure 4.4). This will serve as the title of slide 2.

USING THE CUT AND PASTE COMMANDS • 45

Figure 4.3 **Slide 2 of PASTE.PPT**

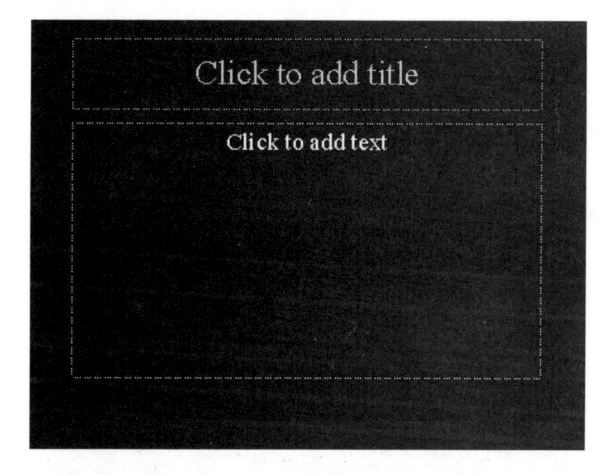

Figure 4.4 **Selecting the text to be moved**

9. With the text selected, click on the **Cut** button in the standard toolbar (see Figure 4.2). The selection has been removed from CUT.DOC and placed on the Windows Clipboard.

10. Switch to **PowerPoint** (click on the **PowerPoint** button). In the title object, which reads

    ```
    Click to add title
    ```

    click to place the insertion point.

46 • CHAPTER 4: COPYING AND PASTING DATA BETWEEN APPLICATIONS

11. Click on the **Paste** button (in PowerPoint's standard toolbar; see Figure 4.2) to paste the text from the Clipboard into the title object. Compare your screen to Figure 4.5.

Figure 4.5   **The cut-and-pasted title**

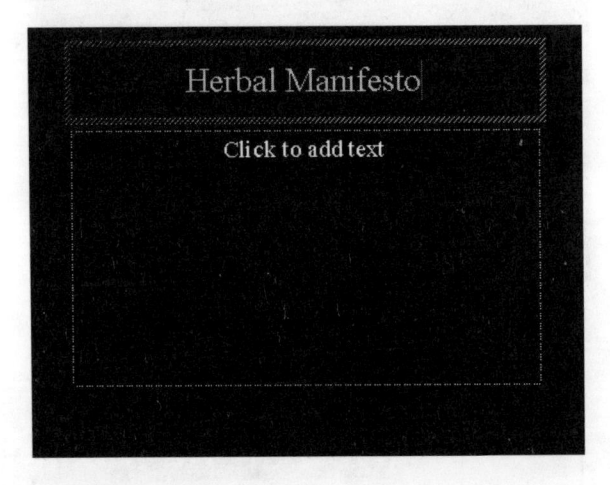

[Slide image showing "Herbal Manifesto" title with "Click to add text" placeholder]

PRACTICE YOUR SKILLS

1. Use the cut-and-paste technique to move the remaining text in the upper box of CUT.DOC to the object in slide 2 that reads

```
Click to add text
```

2. Deselect the objects on slide 2.

3. Save the PowerPoint presentation as **mypaste**, and compare slide 2 to Figure 4.6.

MODIFYING THE MOVED TEXT

Normally, when data is pasted from one Office application to another, the pasted data is converted to a format that the destination application can use. This feature comes in handy; when you wish to edit pasted data, you can use the standard editing techniques normally available in the destination application.

USING THE COPY AND PASTE COMMANDS • 47

Figure 4.6   **The completed slide 2**

> Herbal Manifesto
>
> We honor you
> Oh brother and sister plants
> And pledge to use your essences sparingly
> And respectfully
> To enhance the good of all living beings.

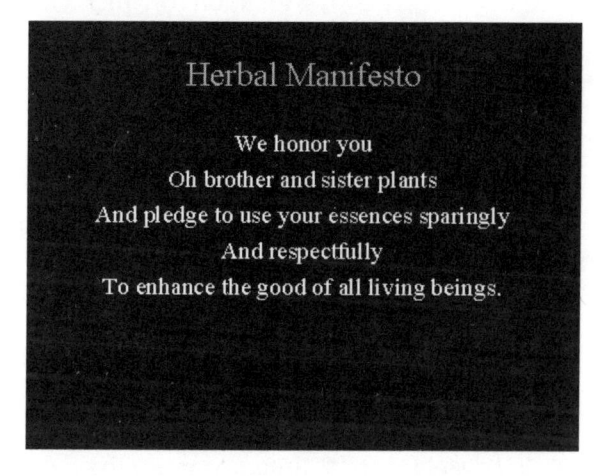

PRACTICE YOUR SKILLS

1. Use standard PowerPoint editing techniques to edit the text in slide 2. (Remember to first click in the desired text object.) Feel free to change the text formatting (the style, size, and font).

2. Save the file (and your masterpiece for posterity).

USING THE COPY AND PASTE COMMANDS

You can see that, while it definitely has its place, using the Cut command has one potential drawback: Once you've cut the selected data, it disappears from the original (source) file. Should you wish to retain the data you want to copy in the source file, then the commands you should use—within the context of cutting, copying, and pasting—are Copy and Paste.

The procedure for using Copy and Paste is as follows:

- In the source application, select the data you wish to copy to the Clipboard.

- Click on the *Copy* button in the toolbar of the source application.

- Open the destination file in the desired application.

- In the destination application, place the insertion point in, select, or display the location to which you wish to place the copied data.
- Click on the *Paste* button.

COPYING EXCEL DATA TO A POWERPOINT SLIDE

Let's copy a chart in an Excel worksheet to our PowerPoint presentation:

1. Display slide 9 of our PASTE.PPT presentation. Notice that it contains only a blank title object.

2. Run **Excel** (click on the **Excel** button in the Office toolbar). If necessary, maximize the Excel Workbook window.

3. In the OFFWORK directory, open the Excel file **copy.xls**. This workbook is similar to the one you opened in Chapter 2. Scroll down to view the chart. We'll *copy* this chart to our PowerPoint slide, because we'd like to keep the original intact in our Excel file.

4. Click on the chart to select it (see Figure 4.7). Notice the selection box and handles bordering the chart. (You can disregard the Chart toolbar, which, by default, opens automatically when you select a chart.)

Figure 4.7   **Selecting the chart to be copied**

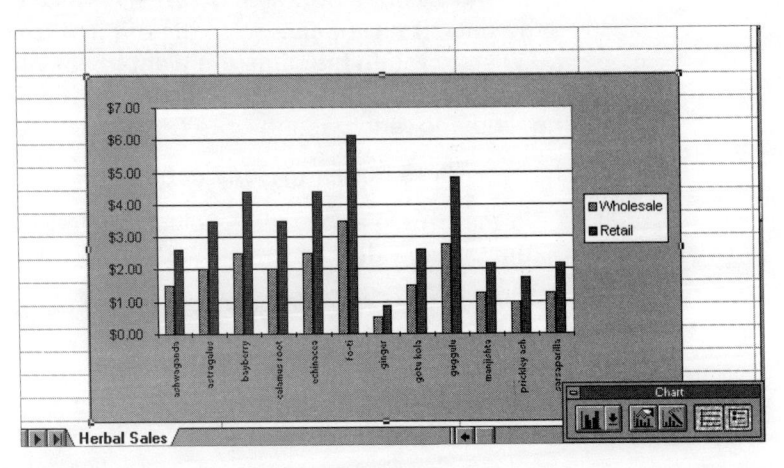

5. With the chart selected, click on the **Copy** button in the Excel standard toolbar (see Figure 4.2). Though nothing much seems to happen, our chart is copied to the Clipboard.

6. Switch to **PowerPoint**, and make sure that slide 9 is displayed. Do *not* select the slide's title object. In PowerPoint, if a slide is displayed without any of its contents being selected, the pasted data will appear in the center of the slide.

7. Click on the **Paste** button (in the PowerPoint standard toolbar). Momentarily, the Excel chart appears in the center of the slide.

8. Proportionally size the chart (press and hold **Ctrl** while you drag a corner handle) to roughly match Figure 4.8.

Figure 4.8   **The copied and sized chart**

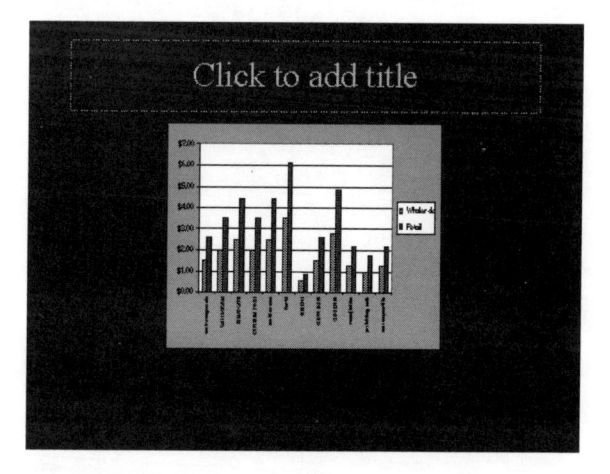

PRACTICE YOUR SKILLS

Let's add the missing title to slide 9:

1. Switch to **Word**.
2. In the document's only remaining box, select the line of text.
3. Copy the selected text to the Clipboard.
4. Switch to **PowerPoint**.

5. On slide 9, click in the title object.
6. Paste the copied text from the Clipboard to the slide.
7. Deselect the title object, and compare your screen to Figure 4.9.
8. Save the PowerPoint file.

Figure 4.9   **The completed slide 9**

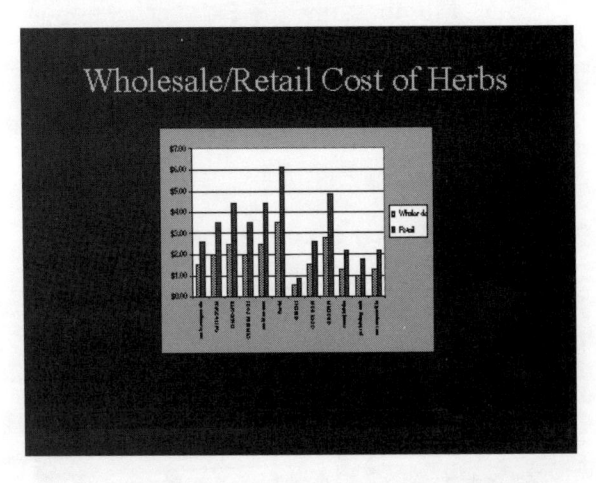

MODIFYING THE COPIED DATA

Let's attempt to edit the data we copied to slide 9 in the previous exercise:

1. On slide 9, click on the title to select it.
2. Use standard PowerPoint text-editing techniques to change *Wholesale/Retail Cost of Herbs* to read **The Cost of Herbs** (see Figure 4.10). As earlier, when we edited text that had been cut and pasted, PowerPoint has converted the pasted text into its own format so that we could edit it.
3. Save the file.
4. Now click on the pasted chart to select it. (Click only once on the chart; do *not* double-click.)

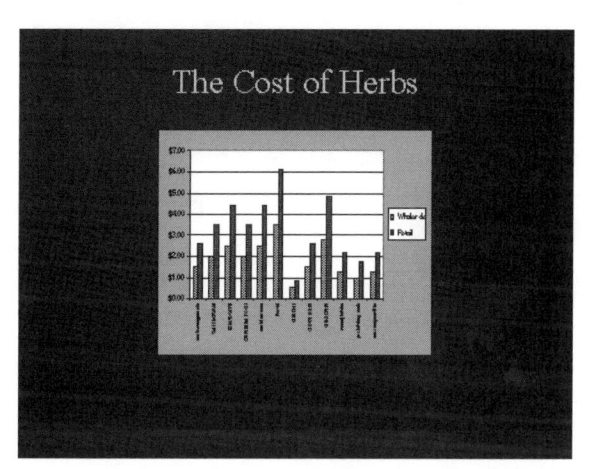

Figure 4.10 **The edited slide title**

5. Attempt to edit elements of the chart; for example, the axes labels or the bars. Notice that you cannot edit the chart using standard PowerPoint editing techniques. When an Office application can't convert pasted data into a format it can use, it automatically *embeds* the data. Embedded data can, in fact, be edited; but that's a topic that we'll have to save until Chapter 6. We've included this aborted attempt to edit an Excel chart in PowerPoint both to make a point and to whet your appetite. The point is that while Cut, Copy, and Paste are useful commands in their own right, there are other methods of transferring data that are much more powerful.

Note: If the upcoming exercise is to work properly, you must proceed directly to the following section.

COPYING DATA TO MULTIPLE APPLICATIONS

In the previous exercise, we edited text that we had copied from our Word document to our PowerPoint slide. Since we pasted that text onto the slide, we have neither cut nor copied any other data—nor have we exited Windows. Therefore, the copied text should still be intact on the Clipboard. As long as data remains on the Clipboard, you can continue to paste it as many times and in as many places as you wish, including in files of more than one application.

PRACTICE YOUR SKILLS

We've already pasted our Clipboard text on a PowerPoint slide. Now, let's paste it in an Excel worksheet:

1. Switch to **Excel**.

2. Display the row of cells directly above the chart.

3. Click on cell **B18** to select it. This is where we'll paste the text.

4. Paste the text in cell B18. (**Hint**: Use the Excel standard toolbar.) Notice that this text is the original version we copied from Word, not the edited version that now exists in PowerPoint.

5. Center the text across columns B through E. (**Hint**: First, select cells **B18:E18**; then, click on the **Center Across Columns** button in the formatting toolbar.)

6. Deselect the range of cells; then compare your screen to Figure 4.11.

Figure 4.11   **The text pasted onto the worksheet**

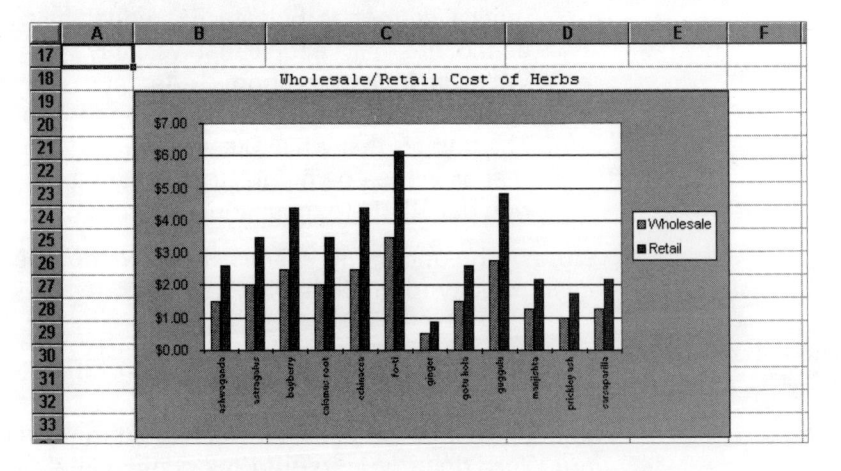

7. Save the Excel file as **mypaste2**. Then close the file.

8. Exit Excel using the Office method. (**Hint**: Press and hold **Alt**, and click on the **Excel** button in the Office toolbar.)

9. If necessary, switch to **PowerPoint**. Then close MYPASTE.PPT without saving your changes.

10. Exit PowerPoint using the Office method.
11. In Word, close CUT.DOC *without* saving your changes.
12. Use whichever method you prefer to exit Word.

SUMMARY

In this chapter, you learned how to use the Cut, Copy, and Paste commands to exchange data between applications. You also learned how to work with pasted text.

Here's a quick reference for the Office techniques you learned in this chapter:

Desired Result	**How to Do It**
Cut and paste data	In source application, select data you wish to move; click on **Cut** button in toolbar of source application; open destination file in desired application. In destination application, place insertion point in, select, or display location to which you wish to paste data; click on **Paste** button
Copy and paste data	In source application, select data you wish to move; click on **Copy** button in toolbar of source application; open destination file in desired application. In destination application, place insertion point in, select, or display location to which you wish to paste data; click on **Paste** button

In the next chapter, you will learn how to use a more powerful tool for transferring data from one application to another: *linking*.

CHAPTER 5: LINKING DATA TO OFFICE APPLICATIONS

Object Linking and Embedding (OLE)

Linking Data

Updating Linked Data

Linking a Source Object to Multiple Destination Files

Breaking a Link

Linking Options

In Chapter 4, you learned how to share data among Office applications by using the Clipboard to cut/copy and paste the data between files. In this chapter, we'll show you another, more sophisticated way of sharing data, *object linking*.

When you're done working through this chapter, you will know

- How to create a link
- How to update a link automatically
- How to update a link manually
- How to link a source object to multiple destination files
- How to break a link

OBJECT LINKING AND EMBEDDING (OLE)

As you learned in Chapter 4, you can use the Clipboard to copy data between applications. When you do this, however, there is no *dynamic connection* between the original data and the copied data. If you revise the original data, and want these same revisions to be applied to the copied data, you must manually recopy the revised data. This two-step process of revision/recopying can grow tiresome, particularly if you go through several rounds of revision.

Office—in conjunction with Windows—provides an ingenious solution to this problem, a procedure called *object linking and embedding*, or *OLE* (pronounced o-LAY). OLE enables you to use the Clipboard not just to copy, but to dynamically connect objects in different applications. An *object* is an element of data, such as a Word table, an Excel chart, or a PowerPoint slide.

Linking connects an object to another *object*. When you create a link to an object, the linked object is *updated* to match any changes you make to the original object. For example, if you created a link in a PowerPoint slide to an Excel chart, then modified the chart in Excel, these same modifications would be applied to your linked chart in PowerPoint.

Embedding connects an object to another *application*. When you embed an object in a file, double-clicking on the embedded object opens it in its application-of-origin, allowing you to edit it. The embedded chart is *not*, however, updated to match changes you make to the original object. For example, if you embedded an Excel chart in a PowerPoint slide, you could edit the embedded PowerPoint chart by double-clicking on it, which would load the chart into Excel, its application-of-origin. If, however, you

LINKING DATA • 57

modified the original Excel chart, these modifications would *not* be applied to your embedded PowerPoint chart.

The terms *source application* and *source file* refer to the application and file in which the *source object*—that is, the original object—resides. The terms *destination application* and *destination file* refer to the application and file in which the linked object or embedded object resides. Figure 5.1 illustrates the differences between copying, linking, and embedding.

Figure 5.1   Copying versus linking versus embedding

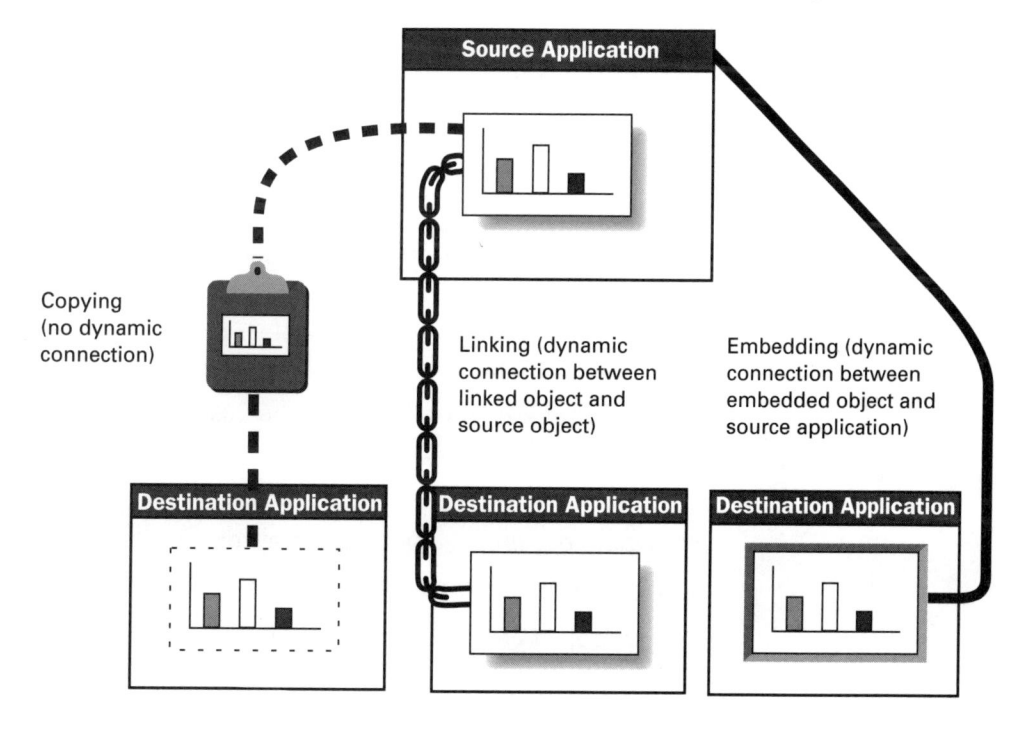

Copying (no dynamic connection)

Linking (dynamic connection between linked object and source object)

Embedding (dynamic connection between embedded object and source application)

LINKING DATA

When you create a link in one file to a source object in another file, you create a *dynamic reference* from the linked object to the source object. The linked object refers to and is dependent on the source object: Whatever changes you make to the source object will be applied to the linked object.

Linking is particularly useful when you need to periodically revise an object that's included in several different files. For example, let's say you created a company logo in Word and needed to include this logo in several Word, Excel, and PowerPoint files. Rather than copy and paste the logo to all these files, you could create a link from the source logo object to each destination file. When you needed to touch up the logo, you could simply revise the source logo and—voilà!—all the linked logos in your various files would automatically be updated to match the revised source logo. Consider the singularly dreary alternative: manually recopying the revised logo to each of your dozens (or hundreds…) of files every time you revised the logo!

CREATING A LINK

To create a link to a source object:

- Activate the source file, and select the source object.
- Copy this object to the Clipboard (by pressing *Ctrl+C*; choosing *Edit, Copy*; or clicking on the *Copy* button in the appropriate toolbar).
- Activate the destination file, and select the place where you want to create your link.
- Choose *Edit, Paste Special* to open the Paste Special dialog box.
- Select the *Paste Link* option.
- In the As list box, select the format (described next) in which you want your linked object to be represented.
- Click on *OK*.

Your linked object can be represented in one of the following formats:

- *Object* This is for a high-resolution, editable graphic. The exact name of this format depends on the source-object type; for example, a *Microsoft Word 6.0 Document Object*.
- *Formatted Text (RTF)* This is for text with font and table formatting—for example, a Word paragraph with 24-point Desdemona text. RTF stands for Rich Text Format.
- *Unformatted Text* This is for plain text with no formatting.

- *Picture* This is for a high-resolution graphic. In contrast to the Bitmap format (see next), Picture takes up less memory and disk space, redraws faster (when your screen is refreshed), and produces a superior printout.

- *Bitmap* This is for a low-resolution graphic. In contrast to Picture, Bitmap takes up more memory and disk space, redraws slower, and produces an inferior printout.

LINKING EXCEL DATA TO A POWERPOINT SLIDE

Enough theory! Let's get our hands dirty.... Here's the plan of action:

- We'll begin by creating a link between a PowerPoint slide and an Excel chart.

- Then we'll explore this link from every angle, delving deeply into its nethermost mysteries.

- Once you've gotten the feel for linking, we'll present you with a table listing all the types of objects that can be linked among Office applications.

- We'll end the chapter by having you create several of these links.

As promised, our first link will be between a PowerPoint slide and an Excel chart. To create this link, we'll follow the general procedure outlined under the previous heading, "Creating a Link." Here goes:

1. Start **Windows**. If Office does *not* start automatically, start it manually.

2. Start **Excel** and **PowerPoint**. If any applications other than Office, Program Manager, Excel, and PowerPoint are running, please exit them.

3. In PowerPoint, open the file **SOUND.PPT** from your OFFWORK directory, as shown in Figure 5.2. SOUND.PPT is the destination file in our linking procedure; it's where you'll create your link.

4. Display slide **2** of this two-slide presentation. You'll create your link to an Excel chart here.

5. In Excel, open the file **SOUND.XLS** from your OFFWORK directory, as shown in Figure 5.3. SOUND.XLS is the source file in our linking procedure; it contains the source object (a chart, in this case) to which you'll create your link.

60 • CHAPTER 5: P LINKING DATA TO OFFICE APPLICATIONS

Figure 5.2   **Opening SOUND.PPT in PowerPoint**

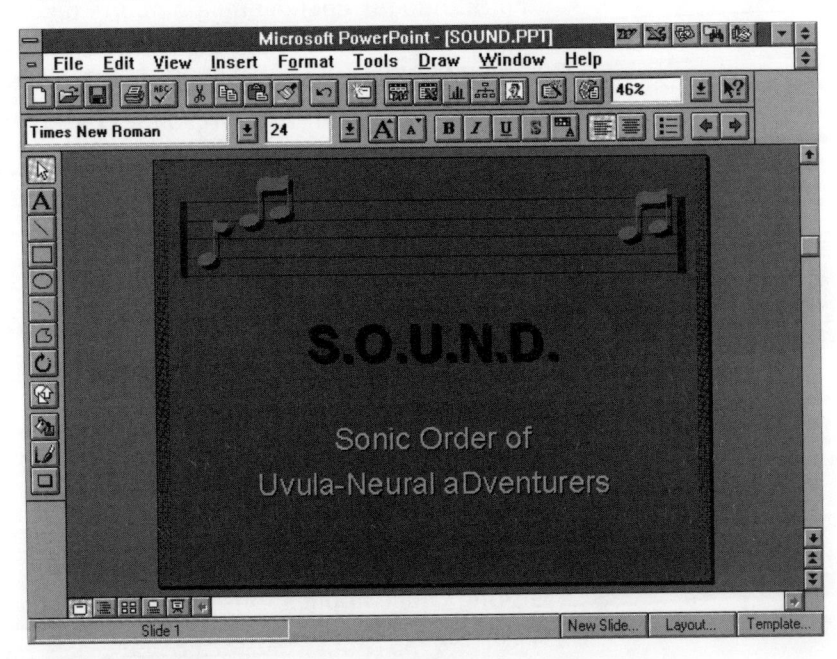

Figure 5.3   **Opening SOUND.XLS in Excel**

LINKING DATA • 61

6. Take a moment to page through the SOUND.XLS workbook. It contains six worksheets. The first five—Germany, Lithuania, and so on—contain relevant data on different countries' S.O.U.N.D. members. The sixth worksheet—Events—is blank; it will eventually contain data on upcoming S.O.U.N.D. events.

7. Activate the **Lithuania** worksheet. Scroll down to view the entire *Lithuanian Energetic (Yin/Yang) Profiles* chart, as shown in Figure 5.4. This 3-D bar chart depicts the energetic profiles of Lithuania's four S.O.U.N.D. members, as measured in Yin/Yang index units of 0 ("absolute" Yin) to 10 ("absolute" Yang).

Figure 5.4   **The Lithuanian Energetic (Yin/Yang) Profiles chart**

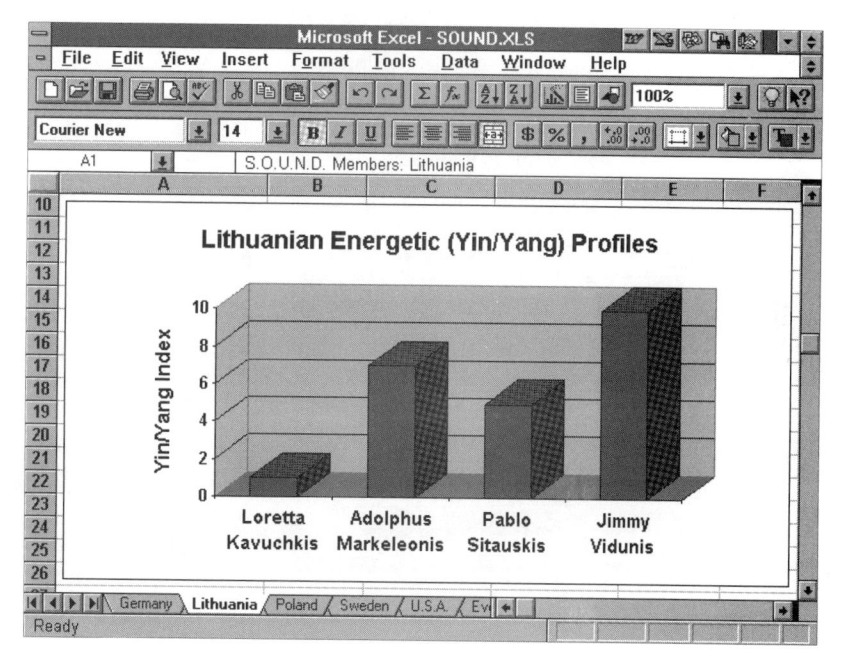

8. Select this all-important chart (by clicking once on it), and then copy it to the Clipboard (by pressing **Ctrl+c** or clicking on the **Copy** button in the standard toolbar).

9. Switch to **PowerPoint**. Verify that slide 2 is displayed (in Slide view).

62 • CHAPTER 5: P LINKING DATA TO OFFICE APPLICATIONS

10. Choose **Edit, Paste Special** to open the Paste Special dialog box, as shown in Figure 5.5. Let's investigate the contents of this very powerful dialog box:

    Source This line shows the source file from which the current Clipboard object was copied.

    Paste This button pastes the Clipboard object into the slide without creating a link to the source object.

    Paste Link This button pastes the Clipboard object into the slide and creates a link to the source object.

    As This list box lists the various formats in which the current Clipboard object can be pasted or paste-linked into the slide. For example, the Excel chart in your Clipboard can be pasted either as a Microsoft Excel 5.0 chart object or as a picture.

    Display As Icon This check box displays the Clipboard object as an icon in the slide.

    Change Icon This button only appears when you check the Display As Icon check box. Clicking on it opens the Change Icon dialog box, which allows you to select the icon you want to display in the slide.

Figure 5.5   **The very powerful Paste Special dialog box**

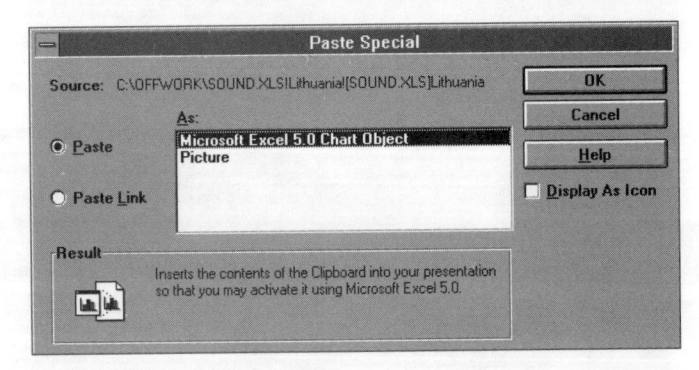

11. Select the **Paste Link** option. Note that the Picture format in the As list box disappears. You can only paste-link the Excel chart in your Clipboard as a Microsoft Excel 5.0 chart object.

12. Click on **OK**, and observe the results, as shown in Figure 5.6.

LINKING DATA • 63

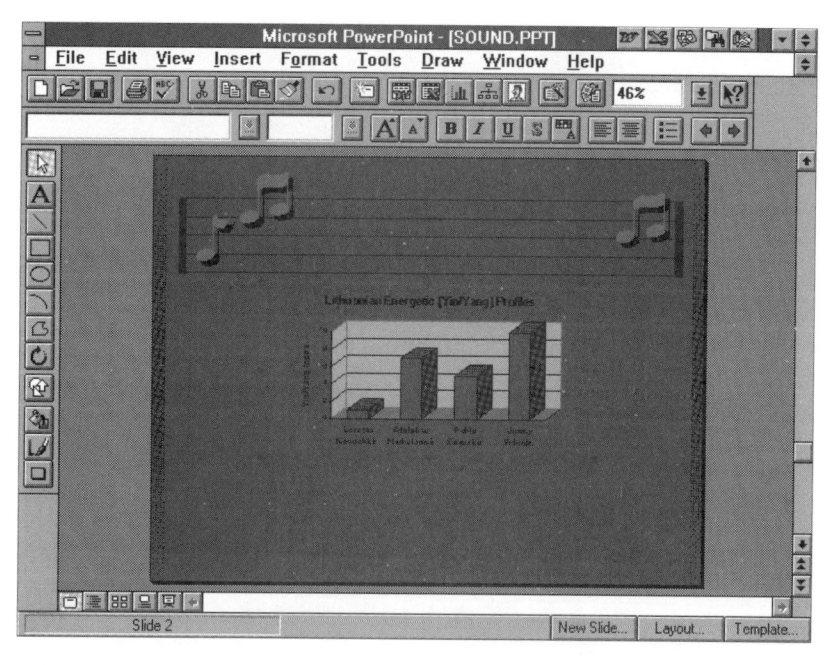

Figure 5.6   **Linking an Excel chart to a PowerPoint slide**

Alas, our linked chart object is too small for the slide. Let's use the Scale command to enlarge the chart proportionally:

1. If your linked chart object is not selected, select it now. Choose **Draw, Scale** to open the Scale dialog box.

2. Check **Best Scale For Slide Show**, and click on **OK**. There, that's better. Now all we have to do is center the chart within the slide.

3. Press **Down Arrow** ten times and **Left Arrow** twice to nudge the chart into proper position.

4. Click on the **Slide Show** button (located at the bottom of the PowerPoint application window, directly to the left of the Left Scroll arrow) to display the slide in its full glory. Your screen should match Figure 5.7.

Figure 5.7   **Scaling and centering the linked chart object**

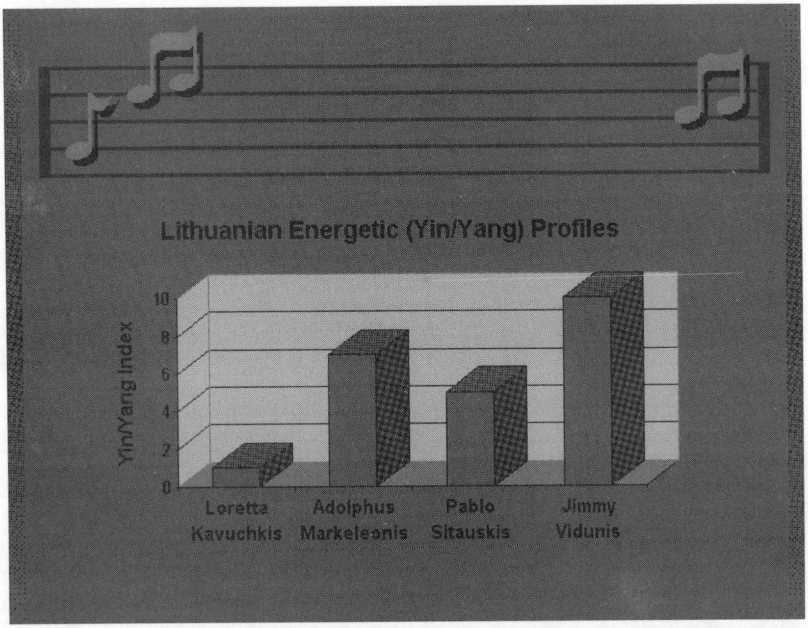

UPDATING LINKED DATA

Linking establishes a dynamic connection between the source object and the linked object. When you modify the source object, the linked object is modified to match the source object. This process—called *updating linked data* or simply *updating a link*—is the main advantage of linking over pasting and embedding. Neither pasting nor embedding establishes a dynamic connection between the source object and the pasted or embedded object; the changes you make to the source object are not reflected in the pasted or embedded object.

Office applications provide two options for updating linked data:

- When you specify *automatic updating* for a linked object, it is updated automatically when you modify the source object.

- When you specify *manual updating* for a linked object, it is updated only when you issue an Update Now command.

Let's take a closer look at these two link-updating options.

UPDATING LINKED DATA AUTOMATICALLY

The advantage to specifying automatic updating for a linked object is that it automates the updating process. Whenever you change the source object, the linked object will be updated to match it, without your having to issue any Update commands. This is useful when you need your linked object to always match the current status of your source object—for example, when preparing up-to-the-minute status reports of a spreadsheet that you revise several times daily.

When you create a link, your linked object is set by default to update automatically. If, however, you've turned off automatic updating for the object—by specifying manual updating instead—here's how you'd turn automatic updating back on:

- Select the linked object.
- Choose *Edit, Links* to open the Links dialog box.
- In the Update field at the bottom of the dialog box, select *Automatic*. (If the Locked check box is checked, you'll have to uncheck it to select the Automatic updating option.)
- Click on *OK* or *Close*.

Note: In certain situations, automatic links will not update immediately after you change the source object. To force an automatic link to update, either perform a manual update (as discussed in the next section), or close the destination file (the site of the link) and then reopen it.

Prepare to experience the keen thrill of automatic updating:

1. Switch to **Excel**. In the Lithuania worksheet, change the Yin/Yang index of Loretta Kavuchkis (in cell E5) from 1 to **4**. Verify that this change is reflected in the Lithuania worksheet chart.

2. Now switch to **PowerPoint**. (You should still be in Slide Show view.) Note that the Loretta Kavuchkis bar now reads 4. Your linked chart object has been automatically updated!

PRACTICE YOUR SKILLS

1. In the Lithuania worksheet, make the following Yin/Yang index changes:

Adolphus Markeleonis	5
Pablo Sitauskis	6
Jimmy Vidunis	7

2. Verify that these changes are reflected both in the Lithuania worksheet chart, and in the PowerPoint linked chart object (as shown in Figure 5.8.)

Figure 5.8 **Automatically updating the linked chart object**

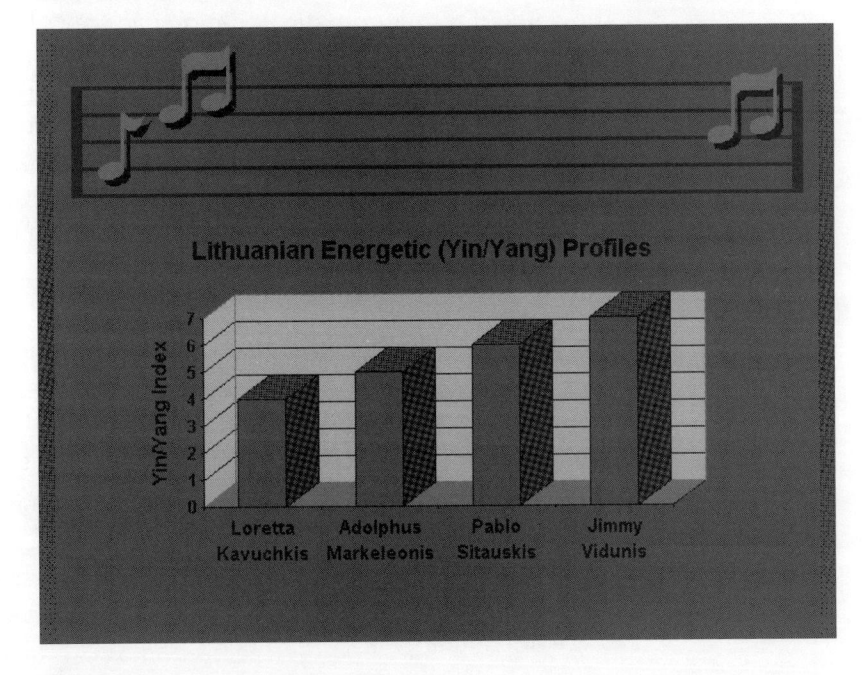

UPDATING LINKED DATA MANUALLY

The advantage to specifying manual updating for a linked object is that it gives you the option of keeping the linked object independent from its source object. When you change the source object,

UPDATING LINKED DATA • 67

the linked object will be updated *only if* you specify so. This is useful when you need to change the source object constantly, but only want to change the linked object periodically—for example, when preparing weekly status reports of a spreadsheet that you revise several times daily.

Manual updating can also be a timesaving device. When you open a file that contains automatic links, the links are updated before the file is displayed. Depending on the number of links and the speed of your hard disk (or your network server, if your source objects are stored there), this process may take an annoyingly long time. When you specify manual updating, however, you can open the file without having its links automatically updated, thus saving time.

To specify that a linked object be updated manually,

- Select the linked object.
- Choose *Edit, Links* to open the Links dialog box.
- In the Update field at the bottom of the dialog box, select *Manual*. (If the Locked check box is checked, you'll have to uncheck it to select the Manual updating option.)
- Click on *Close* or *OK*.

To manually update a linked object by using the menu,

- Select the linked object.
- Choose *Edit, Links* to open the Links dialog box.
- Click on *Update Now*.
- Click on *OK*.

To manually update a linked object by using the keyboard,

- Select the linked object.
- Use the appropriate keyboard shortcut:
  - In Word, press *F9*.
  - In PowerPoint, press *Ctrl+Shift+F7*.

You cannot manually update a linked object in an Excel source file by using the keyboard. You must use the Edit, Links menu command.

To manually update a linked object by using a *shortcut menu*, rather than a normal drop-down menu,

- Select the linked object.

- Click the *right mouse button* on the linked object to open a shortcut menu.
- Choose *Update Links* from this menu.

Note: In certain situations, manual links will not update when you perform the above procedure. To force a manual link to update, close the destination file (the site of the link), and then reopen it.

Let's change our automatic link to a manual link, and then practice updating it:

1. In PowerPoint, change to **Slide view**, and select the **linked chart object** on slide 2.
2. Choose **Edit, Links** to open the Links dialog box, as shown in Figure 5.9. Lean back and peruse its exciting contents:

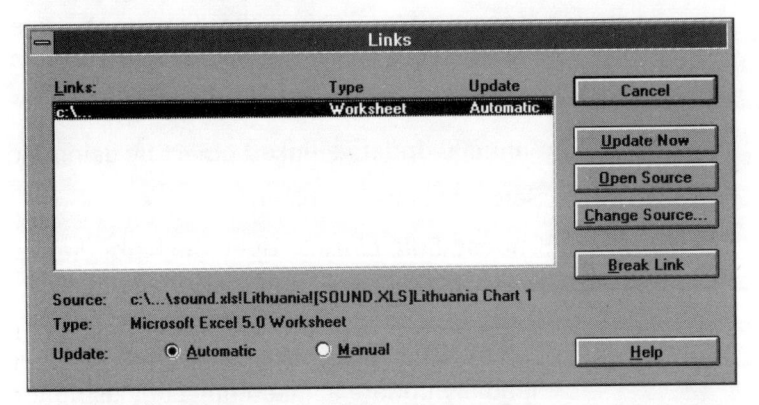

Figure 5.9   **The Links dialog box**

Links This list box lists all the presentation's linked objects. The Links column shows the source file to which the object is linked (see the following Note), the Type column shows the source-file type (worksheet, document, and so on), and the Update column shows whether the link is automatic or manual.

Note: In Figure 5.9, the Links column of the Links list box shows *c:\...*, indicating that the full path name of the source file is too long to fit in the allotted space. The full path name is listed in the Source line.

Source This line shows the source object of the selected linked object. This is an elaboration of the Links entry in the Links list box.

Type This line shows the type of the selected linked object. This is an elaboration of the Type entry in the Links list box.

Update This line shows the type of updating for the selected linked object, *Automatic* or *Manual*.

Update Now This button updates the linked object.

Open Source This button opens the source object in its application-of-origin, allowing you to modify it.

Change Source This button redirects the link to a new source file. You typically use this to maintain the link to a renamed or relocated source file.

Break Link This button *permanently* cancels the link to the source object and converts the linked object to a PowerPoint picture. Keep in mind that once you break a link, you cannot restore it (except by re-creating the link from scratch).

3. Select the **Manual** updating option, and click on **Close**.

4. Switch to **Excel**. In the Lithuania worksheet, change the Yin/Yang index of Loretta Kavuchkis from 4 to **1**.

5. Switch to **PowerPoint**. Note that your linked chart object does not reflect Loretta's new Yin/Yang index. By specifying manual updating for the link, you prevented it from being automatically updated, thus preserving Loretta's pre-step 4 Yin/Yang status.

6. Select the **linked chart**. Choose **Edit, Links** to open the Links dialog box. Click on **Update Now** to update the linked chart. Click on **Close** to close the dialog box. Loretta's revised Yin/Yang index is shown.

PRACTICE YOUR SKILLS

1. In the Lithuania worksheet, make the following Yin/Yang index changes:

Adolphus Markeleonis	**3**
Jimmy Vidunis	**10**

70 • CHAPTER 5: P LINKING DATA TO OFFICE APPLICATIONS

2. Verify that these changes are reflected in the Lithuania worksheet chart, but not in the PowerPoint linked chart.

3. In PowerPoint, use the keyboard shortcut (*Ctrl+Shift+F7*) to update the linked chart. Your slide should match that shown in Figure 5.10.

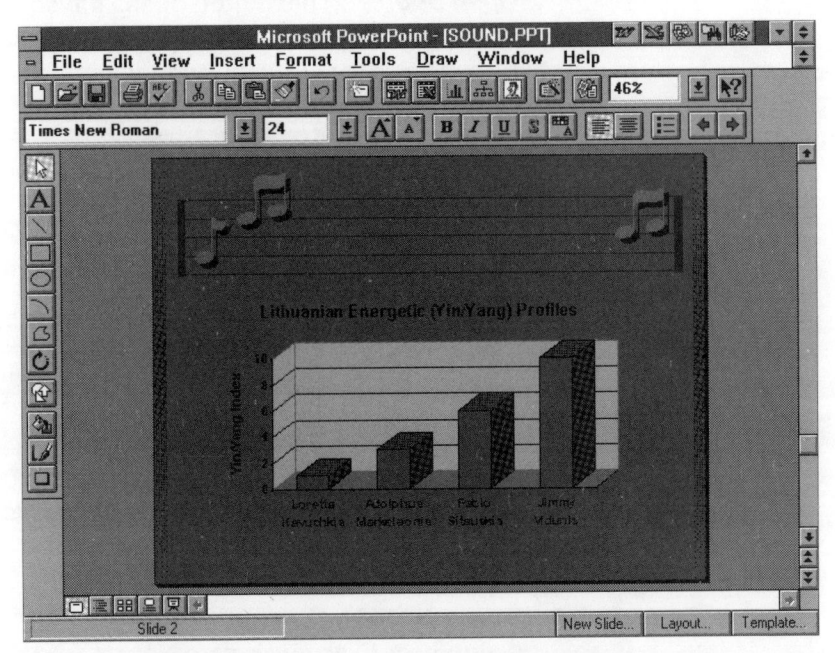

Figure 5.10   **Updating the linked chart manually**

4. Save the PowerPoint presentation to your OFFWORK directory as **mysound.ppt**.

LINKING A SOURCE OBJECT TO MULTIPLE DESTINATION FILES

As we explained earlier in this chapter, you can link a single source object to several different destination files (our company logo example, remember?). The great advantage of doing this is that it allows you to revise dozens (or even hundreds!) of linked objects simply by revising their one common source object.

LINKING A SOURCE OBJECT TO MULTIPLE DESTINATION FILES • 71

Our Excel source chart is already linked to a PowerPoint slide. Now let's link the same source chart to a Word document:

1. Start **Word**, and open the file **SOUND.DOC** from your OFF-WORK directory, as shown in Figure 5.11. Take a moment to browse through this four-page exegesis on S.O.U.N.D. (You'll soon fill pages 3 and 4 with linked objects.)

Figure 5.11 **Opening SOUND.DOC in Word**

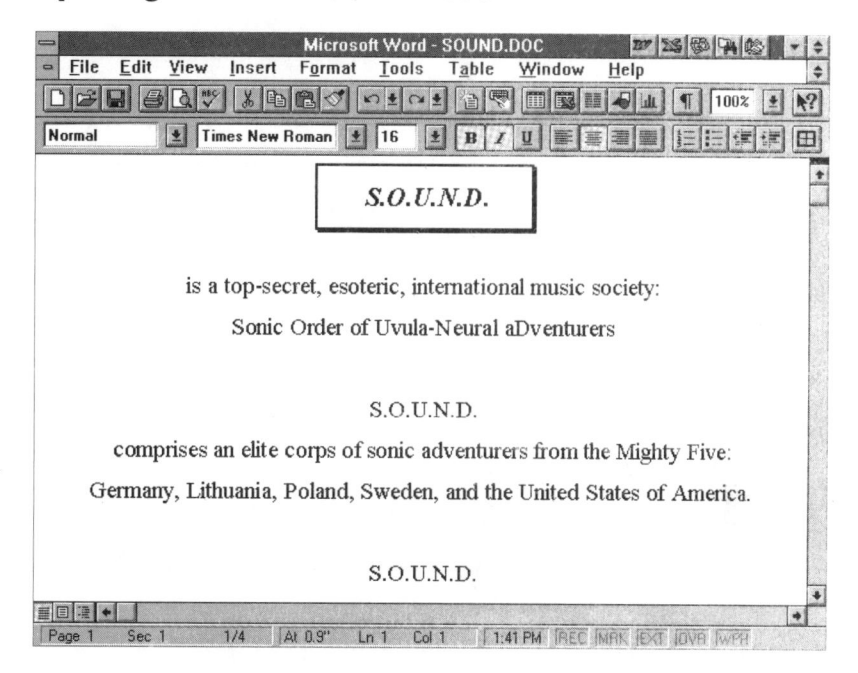

2. Switch to **Excel**, and copy the **Lithuania Energetic (Yin/Yang) Profiles chart** to the Clipboard.

3. Switch to **Word**, and place your insertion point at the bottom of page 3, just before the break to page 4. Here's where we'll create the link to the Excel chart.

4. Choose **Edit, Paste Special** to open the Paste Special dialog box. Select the **Paste Link** option. Verify that **Microsoft Excel 5.0 Chart Object** is selected in the As list box, and click on **OK** to create the link, as shown in Figure 5.12.

5. Save the Word document to your OFFWORK directory as **mysound.doc**.

Figure 5.12   **Creating a link in Word to the Excel chart**

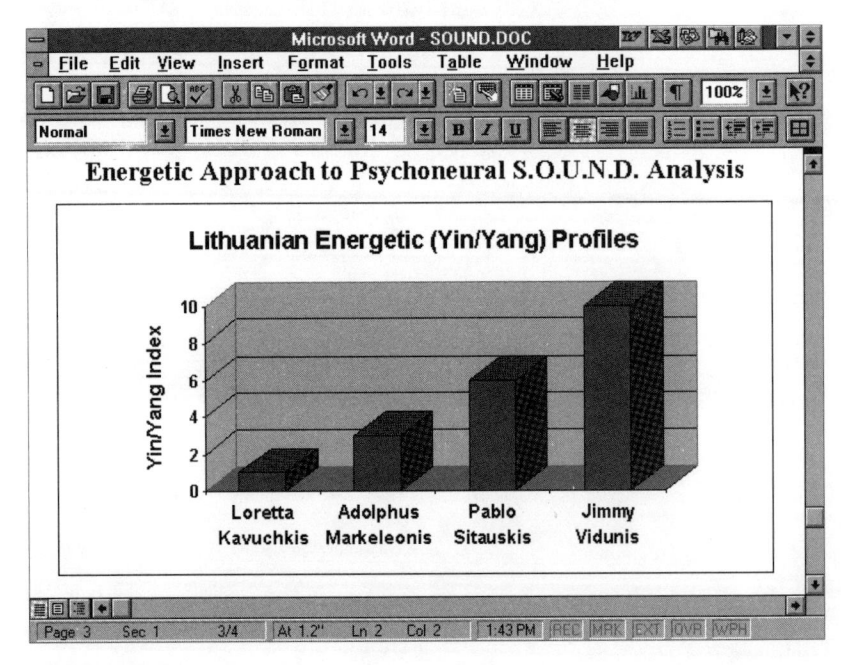

PRACTICE YOUR SKILLS

Let's see what happens when we modify the source object in Excel:

1. In the Lithuania worksheet, make the following Yin/Yang index changes:

Loretta Kavuchkis	**10**
Adolphus Markeleonis	**6**
Pablo Sitauskis	**3**
Jimmy Vidunis	**1**

2. Verify that these changes are reflected in the Excel source chart.

3. Verify that the changes are reflected in your newly created Word linked chart.

4. Verify that the changes are reflected in your PowerPoint linked chart. Hah, fooled you: They're not! The PowerPoint linked chart was not updated, because you specified manual updating for it. The Word linked chart was updated, because you specified automatic updating for it.

5. Update the PowerPoint linked chart. (**Hint:** Use the keyboard shortcut, instead of messing around with the Edit menu.)

BREAKING A LINK

Specifying manual updating for a linked object allows you to keep the linked object independent from its source object. There's another, more radical way to emancipate a linked object from its source: by *breaking* the link. When you break a link, you totally and permanently separate the linked object from its source object. The former linked object is converted to a format suitable to the program in which it resides (a PowerPoint picture, or a Word table, or picture, or Word text).

Note: Once you break a link, you cannot restore it (except by re-creating the link from scratch). So, rather than breaking the link, you might consider changing it to a manual link instead, which also keeps the linked object independent from the source object.

To break a link,

- Select the linked object.
- Choose *Edit, Links* to open the Links dialog box.
- Click on *Break Link*. A dialog box appears, warning you of the dire consequences of breaking the link.
- Think. If you're sure you can afford to permanently lose this link, click on *Yes*. If not, click on *No* or *Cancel*.

Note: You cannot break the link if the linked object you select resides in an Excel file.

Let's break the link between our Word linked chart object and Excel source chart object:

1. Switch to **Word**, and select the **linked chart object**.
2. Choose **Edit, Links** to open the Links dialog box.
3. Click on **Break Link**. A dialog box appears, warning you of the dire consequences of breaking the link.

4. Since we can afford to permanently lose this link, click on **Yes**. The link is broken, and the object is converted to a Microsoft Word 6.0 picture.

PRACTICE YOUR SKILLS

1. In the Lithuania worksheet, make the following Yin/Yang index changes:

Loretta Kavuchkis	2
Adolphus Markeleonis	4
Pablo Sitauskis	6
Jimmy Vidunis	8

2. Verify that these changes are *not* reflected in your Word chart. Select the Word **chart** and try to use the Edit, Links command to force it to update. Note that the Links command is dimmed (unavailable). Why? Because, you just broke the link from this chart to the Excel source chart.

3. Verify that the new Yin/Yang values are not reflected in your PowerPoint linked chart. Reset the PowerPoint linked chart to **automatic updating**. The chart should now reflect the changes you made to the Excel source chart.

4. In the Lithuania worksheet, make the following Yin/Yang index changes:

Loretta Kavuchkis	1
Adolphus Markeleonis	2
Pablo Sitauskis	5
Jimmy Vidunis	10

5. Verify that the PowerPoint linked chart was automatically updated to reflect these changes, as shown in Figure 5.13 in Slide Show view.

6. Switch to **Excel**, and save the workbook file as **mysound.xls** to your OFFWORK directory.

BREAKING A LINK • 75

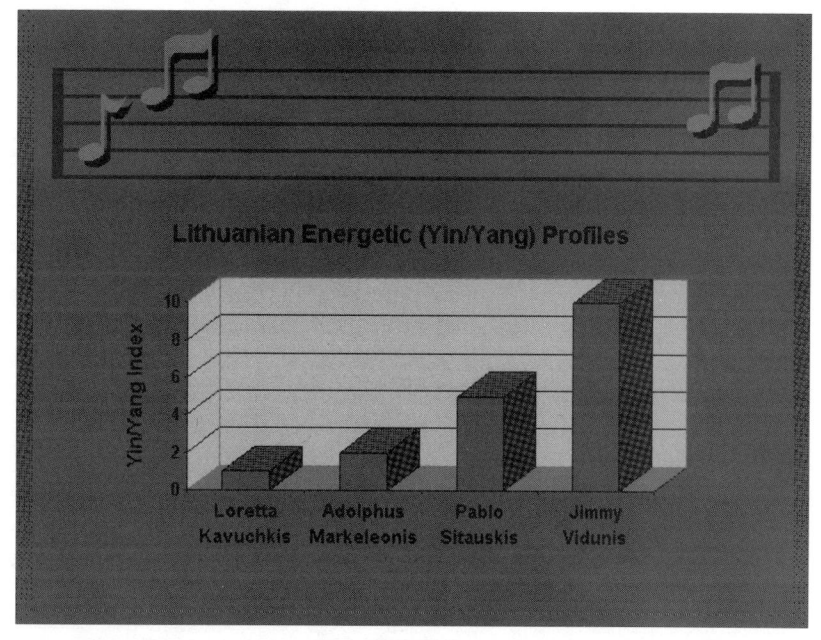

Figure 5.13   **The PowerPoint linked chart, automatically updated**

Uh-oh! You just renamed the source file, the site of the source object in our PowerPoint link. How is this going to affect the link? Let's see:

1. In PowerPoint, return to Slide view and select the linked chart.

2. Choose **Edit, Links** to open the Links dialog box. Note the path name of the source file, as shown in the Source line:

    ```
    c:\offwork\mysound.xls!Lithuania![MYSOUND.XLS]Lithuania Chart 1
    ```

    (If your Source line shows c:\..., do the following to view the full source-file path name: Click on **Change Source** to open the Change Source dialog box, and use your **Left Arrow** and **Right Arrow** keys to scroll through the contents of the Source text box. When you're done, click on **Cancel** to close the Change Source dialog box.)

3. PowerPoint was attentive enough to notice that you changed the name of this link's source file from SOUND.XLS to MY-SOUND.XLS. To keep the link active, it updated the source-file path name accordingly by changing all instances of SOUND.XLS to MYSOUND.XLS (as shown in step 2). Had your PowerPoint destination file been closed when you renamed the Excel source file, PowerPoint would *not* have updated the source-file pathname for this link. You would have had to use the Change Source feature (in the Links dialog box) to change the path name manually.

4. Close the **Links** dialog box.

LINKING OPTIONS

Thus far, you've worked with two kinds of links: one between an Excel source chart object and a PowerPoint destination file, and the other between the same Excel source chart object and a Word destination file. Many other kinds of links are possible among Excel, PowerPoint, and Word files. Table 5.1 lists them all. Proceeding from left to right across the table,

- The *Destination File* column shows the file (Excel workbook, PowerPoint presentation, or Word document) in which you create the link.

- The *Source File* column shows the file containing the source object.

- The *Linkable Objects* column lists the objects (text, table, cell(s), chart, drawing, clip art, slide) you can link from the source file to the destination file.

- The *Nonlinkable Objects* column lists the objects you cannot link from the source file to the destination file.

Note that you can link objects between files from different applications (an Excel worksheet and a PowerPoint slide, for example) or files from the same application (two Excel worksheets, for example). And—as you'll see in an upcoming activity—you can even create a link between two objects within the very same file (a single Word document, for example).

LINKING OPTIONS • 77

Table 5.1 **Linking Data among Excel, PowerPoint, and Word Files**

Destination File (site of linked object)	Source File (site of source object)	Linkable Objects	Nonlinkable Objects
Excel	PowerPoint	Entire slide	Individual text, graph, drawing, or clip-art object
	Word	Text, table	Drawing, clip art
	Excel	Cell(s)	Chart, drawing, clip art
PowerPoint	Excel	Cell(s), chart	Drawing, clip art
	Word	Text, table	Drawing, clip art
	PowerPoint	Entire slide[*]	Entire slide[**], individual text, graph, drawing, or clip-art object
Word	Excel	Cell(s), chart	Drawing, clip art
	PowerPoint	Entire slide	Individual text, graph, drawing, or clip-art object
	Word	Text, table	Drawing, clip art

[*] If the source file is different from the destination file.
[**] If the source file is the same as the destination file.

To get a feeling for how to use Table 5.1, let's go through its first entry. The destination file is an Excel workbook; this is the file in which you want to create a link to the desired source object. The source file is a PowerPoint presentation; this is the file in which the desired source object resides. The only linkable object, in this case, is an *entire* PowerPoint slide. All *individual* objects on a PowerPoint slide—text, graphs, drawings, and clip art—are unlinkable. In other words, if you wanted to create a link in an Excel worksheet to a source object in a PowerPoint presentation, your only choice would be to create a link to an entire PowerPoint slide.

PRACTICE YOUR SKILLS

We'll end this chapter with a dazzling series of Practice Your Skills activities in which you'll create, modify, update, and break several links among Excel, PowerPoint, and Word files. Let's get started by linking an Excel destination file to a Word source file:

1. Switch to **Word**. Copy the entire contents of page **2** (the heading and table) to the Clipboard. This is your source object.

2. Switch to **Excel**. Activate the **Events** worksheet (to the right of the U.S.A. worksheet), and select cell **A1**.

3. In Excel, create a link to the Word source object. Resize your **linked table object** to fit on one Excel screen, as shown in Figure 5.14.

Figure 5.14 **Creating a link in Excel to a Word source object**

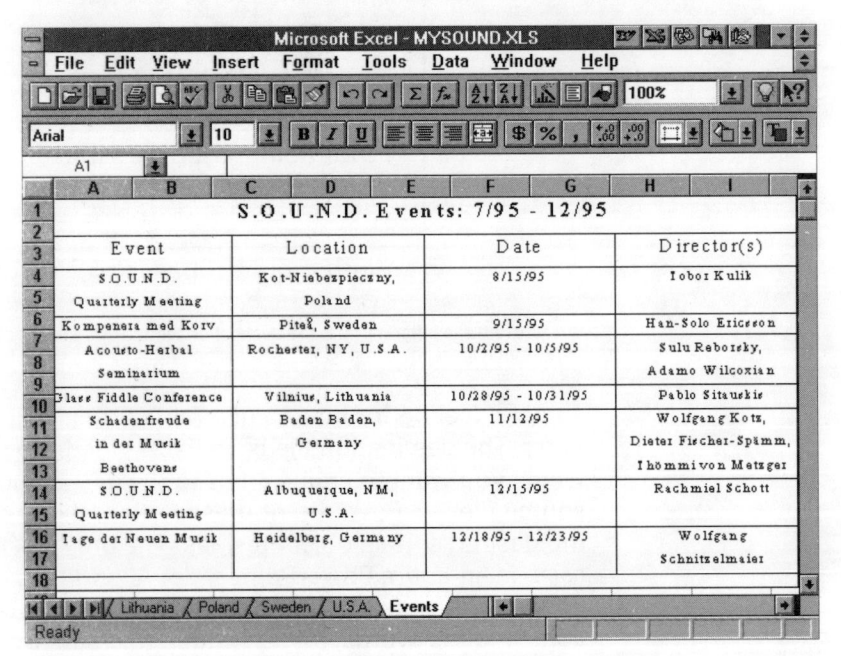

LINKING OPTIONS • 79

4. In the Word table, change the Director(s) column of the first event to

   Tobor Kulik,

   Lech Uwaga

5. Verify that your Excel linked table was updated automatically. (You may have to wait a few seconds for this to happen.)

Now let's create links between objects within the same Word file:

1. Switch to **Word**. Press **Ctrl+Home** to move the insertion point to the top of the MYSOUND.DOC document. Observe the S.O.U.N.D. header—it's boxed, bolded, and italicized. Scroll through the rest of page 1, and observe the four remaining S.O.U.N.D. headers—they're unboxed, unbolded, and unitalicized. Don't you wish all five headers looked as impressive as the top one?

2. Make your wish come true by deleting the four unboxed **S.O.U.N.D. headers** and replacing each with a link to the top, boxed header.

3. Add the following ornamental symbols to the beginning and end of your five S.O.U.N.D. headers:

   ≺S.O.U.N.D≻

   Hint: You need only modify the top, source-object header; the others will update automatically. To do this, place the **insertion point** at the beginning of the top header; choose **Insert, Symbol** to open the Symbol dialog box; select **Wingdings** in the Font drop-down list box; click on the ≺ symbol (as shown in Figure 5.15) to select it; then click on **Insert** to insert this symbol into your S.O.U.N.D. header. Use the same technique to add the ≻ symbol (also shown in Figure 5.15) to the end of the header.

4. Verify that the four linked S.O.U.N.D. headers were all automatically updated to match the modified top header. (Again, you may have to wait.)

Figure 5.15 **The ◁ and ▷ symbols**

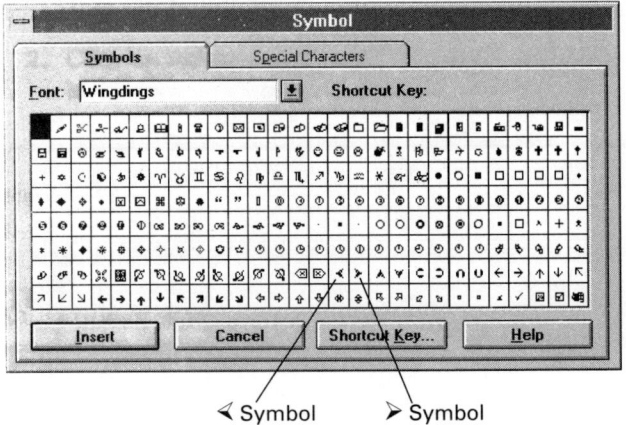

◁ Symbol   ▷ Symbol

Now you've experienced the dual thrills of linking to an Excel source object and linking to a Word source object. All that's left is linking to a PowerPoint source object. This means linking to an entire slide, as shown in Table 5.1:

1. In PowerPoint, change to **Slide Sorter** view, select slide **2** of the presentation MYSOUND.PPT, and copy it to the Clipboard. To select and copy a PowerPoint slide, you must be in Slide Sorter view.

2. Switch to **Word**. This is our first destination application. Press **Ctrl+End** to place the insertion point in page 4 (the last page). Create a link to the PowerPoint source slide. Resize your linked slide object to fit on one Word screen, as shown in Figure 5.16.

3. Switch to **Excel**, our second destination application. In the Events worksheet, under the S.O.U.N.D. Events table, create a link to the PowerPoint source slide. Resize your linked slide object to fit on one Excel screen, as shown in Figure 5.17.

4. Specify **Manual updating** for the Excel linked slide.

Ponder for a moment the full significance of what you just did. You created two links to a source object (a PowerPoint slide) which is, itself, linked to a different source object (an Excel chart).

LINKING OPTIONS • 81

Figure 5.16   **Creating a link in Word to a PowerPoint slide**

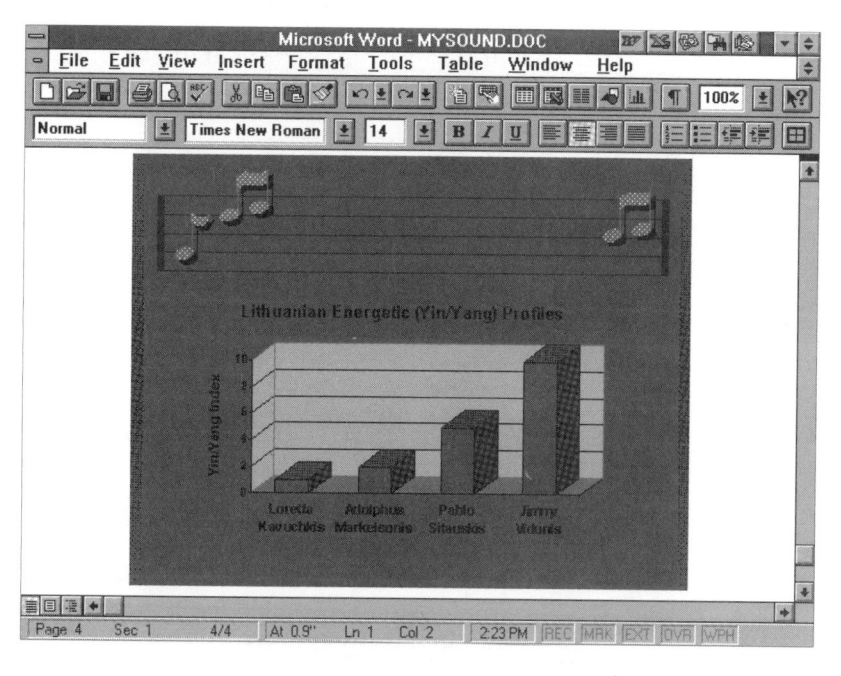

Figure 5.17   **Creating a link in Excel to a PowerPoint slide**

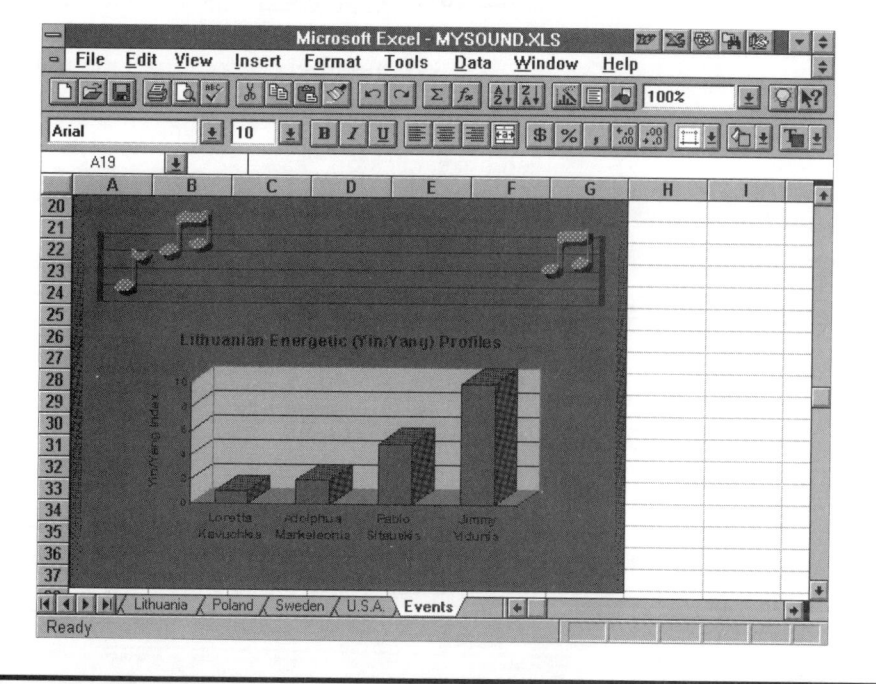

In effect, you've created links to a linked object! Can Office and Windows handle such a demanding situation? Let's check it out:

1. In the Lithuania worksheet, make the following Yin/Yang index changes:

Loretta Kavuchkis	5
Adolphus Markeleonis	5
Pablo Sitauskis	5
Jimmy Vidunis	5

2. Verify that the Lithuania worksheet chart reflects these new indexes.

3. Verify that the PowerPoint linked chart object was automatically updated to match the revised Lithuania worksheet chart. (Change to **Slide view**.)

4. Verify that the Word linked slide object was automatically updated to match the revised PowerPoint slide. If it wasn't, force-update it by selecting it and pressing **F9**, and see the Note following the next step.

5. Verify that the Excel linked slide object (in the Events worksheet) was *not* automatically updated to match the revised PowerPoint slide. (You specified manual updating for the Excel link, remember?) Force-update it by selecting it and pressing **Ctrl+Shift+F7**. If this doesn't work, save the Excel file, close it, then reopen it; when asked whether to reestablish links, click on **Yes**.

   Note: As mentioned earlier, some automatic and manual links will not update when you think they should. If all else fails, you can force a link to update by closing the destination file (the site of the link), and then reopening it.

6. In Excel, attempt to break the link between the linked slide object and its source object (the PowerPoint slide). Hah-hah, you can't! Don't act surprised: We told you so (in the section "Breaking a Link").

7. In Word, break the link between the linked slide object and its source object. Verify that the slide object was converted to a Word 6.0 picture (by selecting the object and observing the message in the Word status line).

8. In Word, save and close **mysound.doc.** In PowerPoint, save and close **mysound.ppt.** In Excel, save and close **mysound.xls.**

SUMMARY

In this chapter, you sampled the various and sundry joys of linking. Now you know how to create a link, to update a link automatically and manually, to link a source object to multiple destination files, and how to break a link.

Here's a quick reference for the techniques you learned in this chapter:

Desired Result	How to Do It
Create link	Copy source object to Clipboard; select desired link location; choose **Edit, Paste Special**; select **Paste Link**; select desired object format; click on **OK**
Specify automatic updating	Select linked object; choose **Edit, Links**; select **Automatic** (if Locked is checked, uncheck it); click on **OK** or **Close**
Specify manual updating	Select linked object; choose **Edit, Links**; select **Manual** (if Locked is checked, uncheck it); click on **Close** or **OK**
Manually update using menu	Select linked object; choose **Edit, Links**; click on **Update Now**; click on **OK** or **Close**
Manually update using keyboard	Select linked object; in Word, press **F9**; in PowerPoint, press **Ctrl+Shift+F7**
Manually update using shortcut menu	Select linked object; click **right mouse button** on linked object to open shortcut menu; choose **Update Links**
Force update	Close destination file, then reopen
Break link	Select linked object; choose **Edit, Links**; click on **Break Link**; click on **Yes**

In the next chapter, you'll tackle the second half of the OLE acronym by learning all about object embedding.

CHAPTER 6: EMBEDDING DATA IN OFFICE APPLICATIONS

Embedding Objects

Editing an Embedded Object

Using Drag-and-Drop to Embed an Object

Creating a New Embedded Object

In Chapter 5, we explored object linking, the first half of OLE (object linking and embedding). In this chapter, we'll take on OLE's second half, *object embedding*.

When you're done working through this chapter, you will know

- How to embed objects by using the Clipboard
- How to embed objects by using drag-and-drop
- How to edit an embedded object

EMBEDDING OBJECTS

When you *embed* a source object in a destination file, you create a dynamic connection between the embedded object and the source application (the application in which the source object was created). Double-clicking on the embedded object runs the source application and opens the embedded object, enabling you to easily revise it.

Note: You may encounter the terms *server application* and *client application* in reference to embedded objects. Don't let it faze you: Server application is simply a synonym for source application, and client application is a synonym for destination application.

Embedding is particularly useful when an object included in many files must be revised separately for each file. For example, let's say you wrote Word memos to your company's seven managers and needed to include in each memo the portion of the company's Excel profits chart that pertained to that manager's department. Rather than create seven partial Excel profits charts and then copy them, one by one, to your memos, you could create a single Excel chart for your entire company, embed this chart in each of your seven Word memos, and then edit the embedded chart from within each memo to delete the portions that did not pertain to the manager.

LINKING VERSUS EMBEDDING: A CLARIFICATION

Still unclear about the difference between linking and embedding?

- *Linking* connects an object to its *source object*. When you change the source object, the linked object is updated to match it.

- *Embedding* connects an object to its *source application*. When you double-click on the embedded object, it is opened in its source application, allowing you to edit it.

Study Table 6.1 to get a feeling for when to link an object and when to embed an object.

Table 6.1   **Linking versus Embedding**

Link an Object If:	Embed an Object If:
The linked object must match the most up-to-date information in the source object.	The embedded object is from another application, and you may need to edit it at a future date.
The source object will be modified regularly by you or others, and you want your linked object to reflect these changes.	You want to include objects from several applications in a single file, and these objects do not need to be used in other files.
Those who need to view the linked object have access to its source object. A linked object can be displayed only if its source object is accessible.	Those who need to view the embedded object do not have access to its source object. An embedded object can be displayed whether or not its source object is accessible.
You want to minimize the destination file size. Linking increases the destination file size only by the size of the image used to display the object (usually relatively small).	You don't care about the destination file size. Embedding increases the destination file size by the size of the object itself (may be very large).
	The embedded object will not be modified frequently and is unique to the destination file.

USING THE CLIPBOARD TO EMBED AN OBJECT

To use the Clipboard to embed an object in a file,

- Copy the source object to the Clipboard.
- In the destination file, select the place where you want to embed this object.

- Choose *Edit, Paste Special* to open the Paste Special dialog box.
- Select the *Paste* option.
- In the As list box, select the format you want to apply to your embedded object. The same formats are available for embedding as for linking: Object, Formatted Text (RTF), Unformatted Text, Picture, and Bitmap. For descriptions, please refer to Chapter 5.
- Click on *OK*.

You can also embed an object by using your mouse to drag-and-drop the object from the source file to the destination file. More on this toward the end of the chapter.

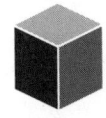

EMBEDDING EXCEL DATA IN A POWERPOINT SLIDE

Let's begin this chapter's hands-on journey by embedding a range of Excel cells in a PowerPoint slide:

1. Start **Windows**. If Office does *not* start automatically, start it manually.
2. Start **Excel** and **PowerPoint**. If any applications other than Office, Program Manager, Excel, and PowerPoint are running, please exit them.
3. In PowerPoint, open the file **SOUND2.PPT** from your OFFWORK directory. SOUND2.PPT—a close cousin of the SOUND.PPT presentation you worked with in the previous chapter—is the destination file in our embedding procedure; it's where you'll embed the Excel data.
4. Display slide **2** of the presentation. Here's where you'll embed.
5. In Excel, open the file **SOUND2.XLS** from your OFFWORK directory. SOUND2.XLS—again, an intimate relation of SOUND.XLS from the previous chapter—is the source file in our embedding procedure; it contains the source object (a range of worksheet cells) that you'll embed in the PowerPoint slide.
6. Activate the **U.S.A.** worksheet. Select cells **A1:E16**, and copy the selection to the Clipboard.
7. Switch to **PowerPoint**. Make sure slide 2 is displayed in Slide view.

8. Choose **Edit, Paste Special** to open the Paste Special dialog box. Verify that the **Paste** option is selected.

9. Observe the choices in the As list box. These are the various formats you can apply to the object you're about to embed (that is, the object that's currently on the Clipboard). Verify that **Microsoft Excel 5.0 Worksheet Object** is selected.

10. Click on **OK**. The cells you selected in the Excel U.S.A. worksheet are embedded in the slide. Change to **Slide Show** view to see the Excel data more clearly, as shown in Figure 6.1.

Figure 6.1 **Embedding an Excel worksheet object in a PowerPoint slide**

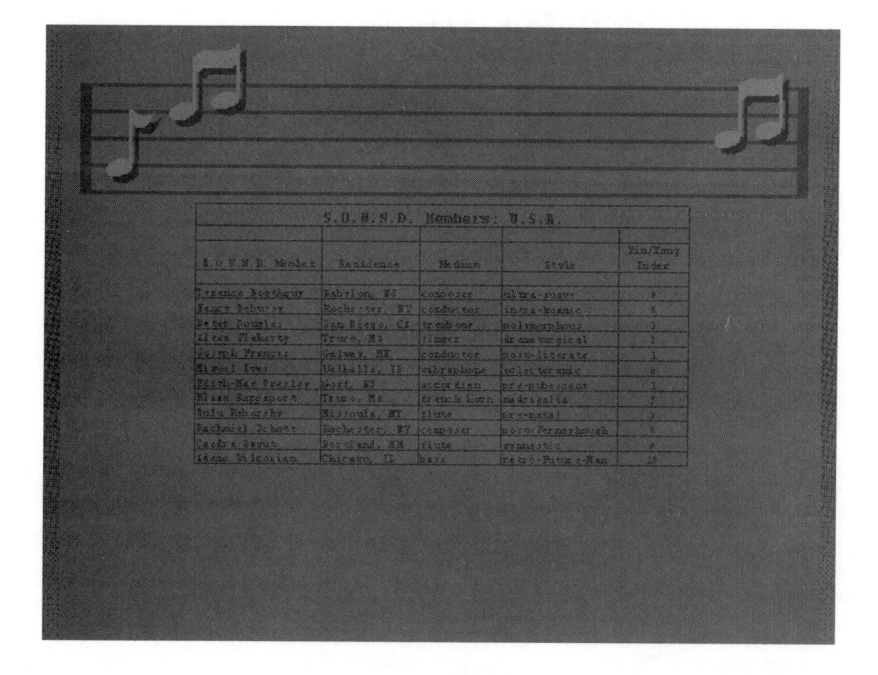

Now let's see what happens when we change the source object:

1. Switch to **Excel**. In the U.S.A. worksheet, change everyone's Yin/Yang index to **0** (a very Yin group).

2. Switch to **PowerPoint**, and verify that your Yin/Yang changes are *not* reflected in the embedded worksheet

object. Embedding connects the embedded object to the source *application*, not to the source *object*.

3. Change to **Slide** view, and select the **embedded worksheet object**.
4. Attempt to choose **Edit, Links**. You can't; the Links command is dimmed. You *embedded* the Excel cells in your PowerPoint slide; you did not *link* them.
5. Save the PowerPoint presentation as **mysound2.ppt** to your OFFWORK directory.
6. Save the Excel workbook as **mysound2.xls** to your OFFWORK directory.

EDITING AN EMBEDDED OBJECT

The main advantage of embedding an object over copying it is that you can easily edit an embedded object, even if its source application is different from its destination application. This is not necessarily true for a copied object. To edit an embedded object,

- Use one of the following techniques to open the embedded object:
  - Double-click on the embedded object. Depending on the situation, this either opens the embedded object in a small source-application window *within* the destination application, or in a full-sized source-application window *separate from* the destination application.
  - Or, select the embedded object, and choose *Edit, <Object>, Open*. This always opens the embedded object in a full-sized source-application window separate from the destination application. The name of *<Object>* depends on the type of object you're embedding. For example, when embedding a Word document object, you'd choose *Edit, Document Object, Open*.
- Edit the embedded object as desired, using standard editing techniques of the source application.
- Use one of the following methods to save your editing changes:
  - If you're editing the embedded object in a small window within the destination application, press *Esc*. (You may need to press Esc twice.)

- If you're editing the embedded object in a full-sized window separate from the destination application, choose *File, Update* (from the source application's menu). Then choose *File, Close* to close the embedded-object file and return to the destination program; or, choose *File, Exit & Return To <DestApp>* (where *<DestApp>* is the destination application).
- Exit the source application, if necessary.

The above editing procedure may look somewhat daunting, but it's really very simple. Let's try it on our embedded worksheet object:

1. Switch to **PowerPoint**. Double-click on your slide 2 **embedded worksheet object** to open it in its source application (Excel).

2. Observe the manifold results, as shown in Figure 6.2. On the left side of the screen, the PowerPoint Drawing toolbar disappears, and the slide layout adjusts accordingly. (Your PowerPoint toolbar layout may differ from ours.) On top of the screen, the PowerPoint menu bar and standard and formatting toolbars are replaced with the Excel menu bar and standard and formatting toolbars. The Excel formula bar appears beneath the formatting toolbar. And—most importantly—a small Excel window appears within the slide.

3. Things happened so fast you probably didn't get a chance to see the changes we described in step 2. Press **Esc** to return to normal PowerPoint view, then double-click on the **embedded worksheet object** again, observing the results. Repeat the process a few more times, if necessary. The changes are quick and quite subtle (particularly the shift from the PowerPoint to the Excel menu bar).

4. Use standard Excel editing techniques to change the Yin/Yang index of Terence Boothguy (the first S.O.U.N.D. member in the list) to **10**. Not so easy to edit such a tiny cell, eh? Try to use the Zoom control (in the standard toolbar) to increase the magnification. You can't. Fortunately, you *can* do something to save your eyes.

Figure 6.2 **Using double-clicking to edit the embedded worksheet object**

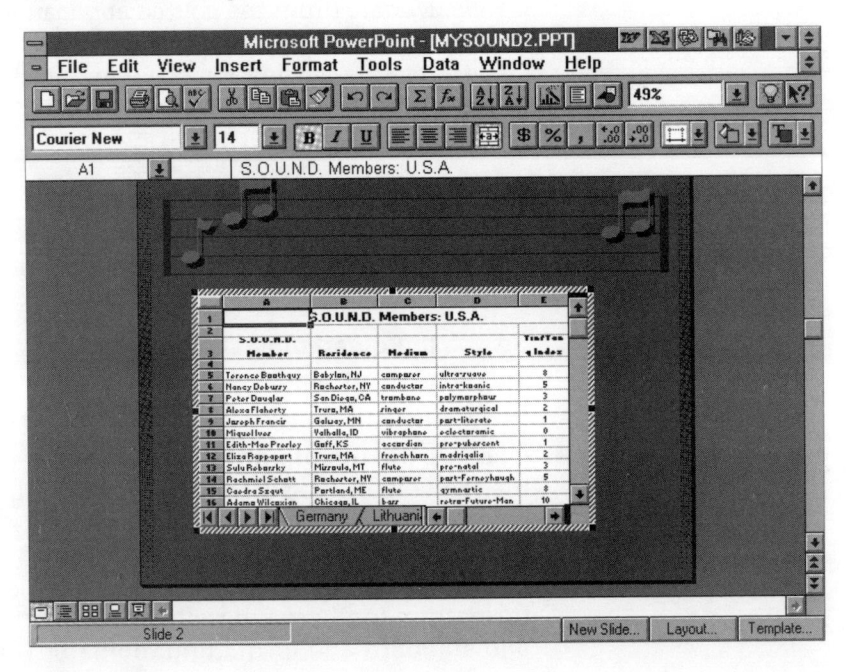

5. Press **Esc** to accept your Boothguy Yin/Yang change and return to normal PowerPoint view. Verify that the embedded worksheet object is still selected, and choose **Edit, Worksheet Object, Open** (or **Edit, Spreadsheet Object, Open**) to open the worksheet object in a separate Excel application window. Observe the title bar; it reads *Worksheet in MYSOUND2.PPT*. This lets you know that you're editing a worksheet object embedded in a PowerPoint file, rather than a standard Excel file.

6. Maximize the Excel application and worksheet windows, and then use the Zoom control (successfully, this time) to increase the magnification to **100%**, as shown in Figure 6.3. Much more ocular-friendly, yes?

7. Change all remaining U.S.A. S.O.U.N.D. members' Yin/Yang indexes to **10**.

8. Choose **File, Update** to accept your changes to the embedded worksheet object. Choose **File, Close** to close the *Worksheet in MYSOUND2.PPT* file and return to PowerPoint. Verify that the Yin/Yang indexes all read 10.

Figure 6.3 **Using Edit, Worksheet Object, Open to edit the worksheet object**

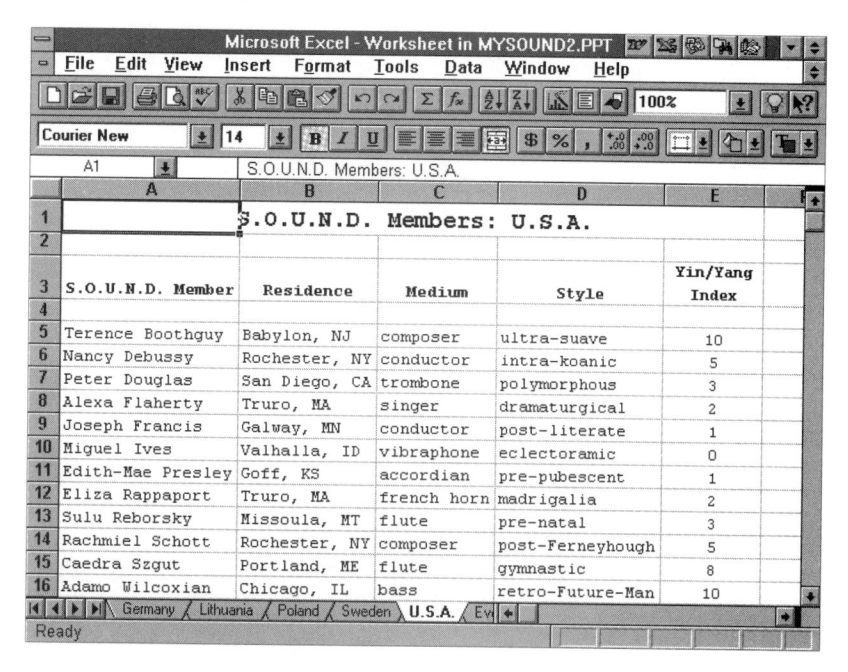

PRACTICE YOUR SKILLS

1. Change the embedded worksheet object's U.S.A. Yin/Yang indexes as follows. (**Hint:** Depending at which magnification you prefer working, use the double-clicking method or the Edit, Worksheet Object, Open method. Don't forget to use the appropriate method to save your changes!)

Terence Boothguy	0
Nancy Debussy	1
Peter Douglas	2
Alexa Flaherty	3
Joseph Francis	4
Miguel Ives	5
Edith-Mae Presley	6

94 • CHAPTER 6: EMBEDDING DATA IN OFFICE APPLICATIONS

    Eliza Rappaport   7

    Sulu Reborsky   8

    Rachmiel Schott   9

    Caedra Szgut   10

    Adamo Wilcoxian   11

(Note that Professor Wilcoxian is so Yang he's off the scale.)

2. Change to **Slide Show** view. Your screen should match that shown in Figure 6.4.

Figure 6.4   **Editing the embedded worksheet object**

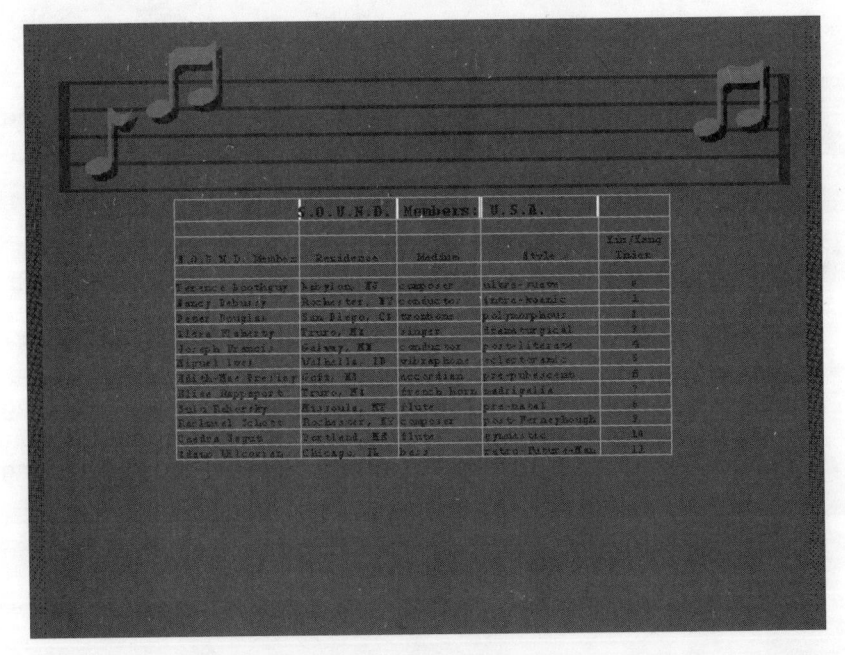

USING DRAG-AND-DROP TO EMBED AN OBJECT

As mentioned, you mousers out there can use drag-and-drop to embed objects. Here's how:

- In the source file, select the source object.

USING DRAG-AND-DROP TO EMBED AN OBJECT • 95

- In the destination file, display the place where you want to embed.
- Minimize all other open applications (except for the source and destination applications).
- Use the *Task List* to tile your screen so that the source file and destination file are displayed simultaneously.
- Press and hold *Ctrl*, drag the source object to the desired place in the destination file, release the *mouse button*, and then release *Ctrl*. (Make sure you release the mouse button *before* you release Ctrl, or you'll move the object rather than copy it, thereby deleting your source object.)
- Maximize the destination application, if desired.

Okay, let's use drag-and-drop to embed the same range of Excel cells that we embedded earlier using the Clipboard. This way, you can compare the relative ease of both methods:

1. Switch to **Excel**. In the U.S.A. worksheet, select cells **A1:E16**.

2. Switch to **PowerPoint**, and display slide **3**. This is where you'll embed the Excel worksheet object.

3. Minimize all your other open applications. (To minimize an application, activate it and click on the **Minimize button**, the boxed downward-pointing triangle on the right side of the application title bar.) Do *not* minimize Excel or PowerPoint!

4. Press **Ctrl+Esc** to open the Task List dialog box. Click on **Tile** to display your two maximized applications—Excel and Power-Point—on screen simultaneously, as shown in Figure 6.5. (Your windows may be positioned differently.)

Now we're all set to drag-and-drop:

1. Click on the **Excel title bar** to activate the Excel application window. (Don't click on a worksheet cell, or you'll deselect cells A1:E16.) This is your source file; the selected cells are your source object.

2. Click on the **right scroll arrow** to scroll the worksheet until the right edge of the selected cell range is visible. You drag a selected cell range by its *edge*, not by its center.

Figure 6.5 **Tiling Excel and PowerPoint**

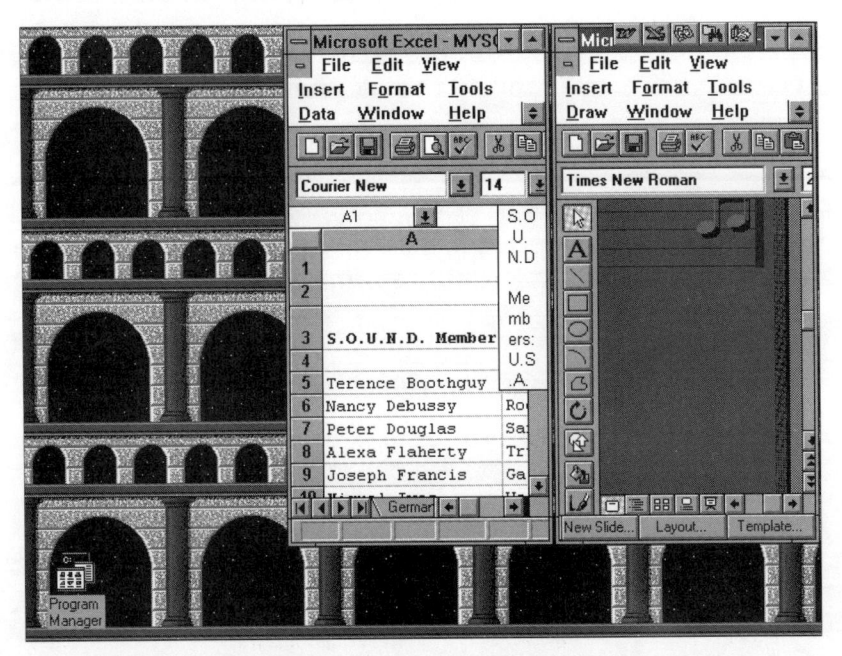

3. Press and hold **Ctrl**. Drag the **selected cell range** (by its edge) onto the PowerPoint slide. (Don't worry about the exact position of the embedded object now; we'll get to it in a moment.) Release the **mouse button**, and then release **Ctrl**. Once again, make sure you release the mouse button *before* you release Ctrl. If you release Ctrl first, you'll *move* the source object to the destination file.

4. Maximize the **PowerPoint application window**. In Slide view, use your mouse or arrow keys to center the **embedded worksheet object** within the slide, as shown in Figure 6.6 (in Slide Show view).

CREATING A NEW EMBEDDED OBJECT

Thus far, you've embedded *existing* objects. You can also create *new* embedded objects in your Office applications. Here's how:

- Open the file in which you want to create your new object, and select the location where you want to embed this object.

CREATING A NEW EMBEDDED OBJECT • 97

Figure 6.6 **Using drag-and-drop to embed a worksheet object in a slide**

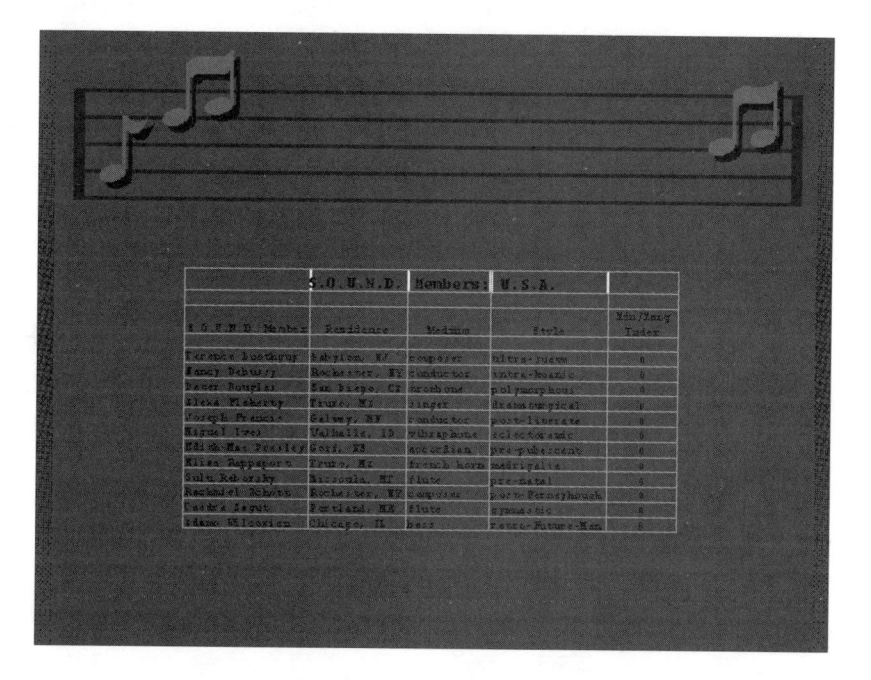

- Choose *Insert, Object* to open the Object dialog box.
- Click on the *Create New* tab to display the Create New options.
- Select the type of object you want to create, and click on *OK*.
- Create the embedded object.
- Use one of these methods to save your embedded object:
  - If you're creating the object in a small window within the destination application, press *Esc* once or twice.
  - If you're creating the object in a full-sized window separate from the destination application, choose *File, Update* (from the source application's menu). Then choose *File, Close* to close the embedded-object file and return to the destination program; or, choose *File, Exit & Return To* <DestApp> (where <DestApp> is the destination application).

You'll get a chance to use this procedure to create a new embedded object in just a few moments. Patience!

PRACTICE YOUR SKILLS

Let's finish up with a delightful series of Practice Your Skills embedding activities! We'll tell you what to do in broad terms, and leave you to the details. Feel free to use the Clipboard or drag-and-drop to embed, whichever feels better. If you need help, refer back to the appropriate section of this chapter.

1. Start **Word**. Open **sound2.doc** from your OFFWORK directory, and use Save As to rename the file **mysound2.doc**. Embed the header and table on page 2 of MYSOUND2.DOC in the Events worksheet of the Excel workbook MYSOUND2.XLS.

2. In Excel, resize the **embedded table object** to fit on one screen. Then edit the embedded object by deleting the entire entry **Tage der Neuen Musik**. (**Hint:** Don't forget to update and close when you're done.) Your worksheet should match that shown in Figure 6.7.

Figure 6.7 **Editing the embedded table object**

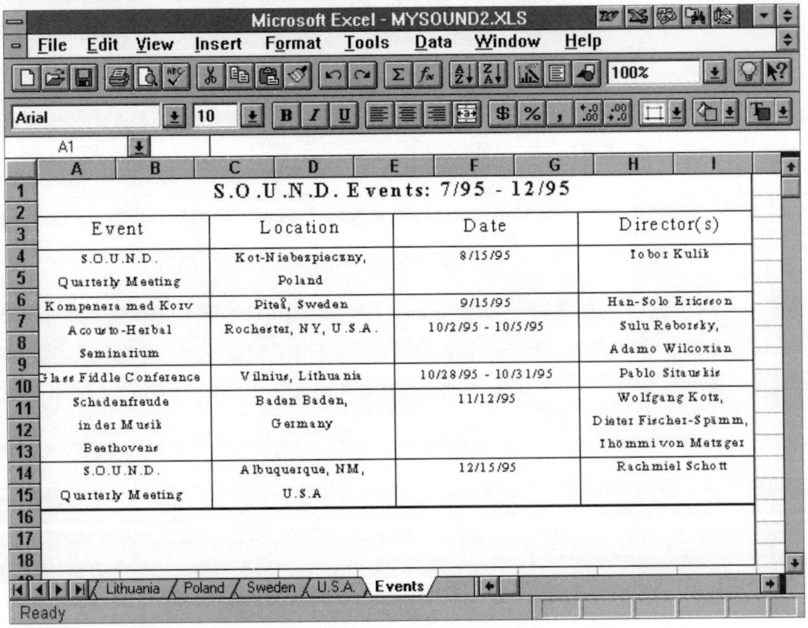

CREATING A NEW EMBEDDED OBJECT • 99

3. Embed the first entry on page 1 of the Word document MYSOUND2.DOC—from the top *S.O.U.N.D.* header through the paragraph that ends with *aDventurers*—in slide 4 of the PowerPoint presentation MYSOUND2.PPT.

4. In PowerPoint, center the **embedded document object** within the slide. Then edit the embedded object by changing the top header from S.O.U.N.D. to **s.O.u.N.d.** (a subtle, but important variation). Your slide should match that shown in Figure 6.8.

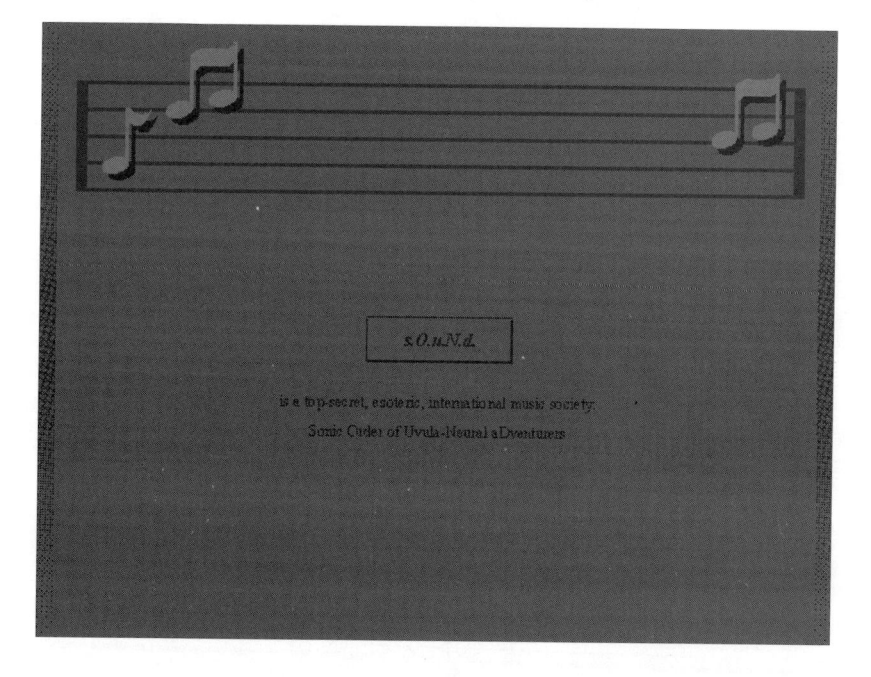

Figure 6.8   **Editing the embedded document object**

5. Embed slide 1 of the PowerPoint presentation MYSOUND2.XLS in a blank part of the Germany worksheet of the Excel workbook MYSOUND2.XLS.

6. In Excel, proportionally resize the **embedded slide object** to fit on one screen. Then edit the embedded object to match (or closely resemble) that shown in Figure 6.9.

7. For your finale, embed the graph on page 5 of the PowerPoint presentation in page 3 of the Word document.

Figure 6.9   **Editing the embedded slide object**

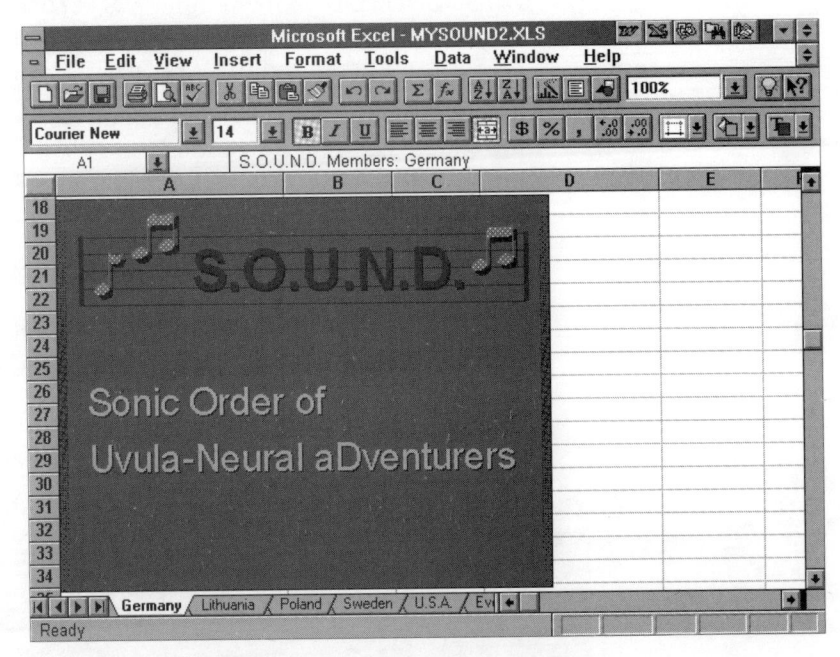

8. In Word, edit the **embedded graph object** to match that shown in Figure 6.10. (If you get a message stating that Word can't edit MS Graph, please skip this step.) Note that when you edit this object, it is opened in Microsoft Graph (its application-of-origin), not in PowerPoint. When you create a graph in PowerPoint, you are actually using Microsoft Graph to do it.

9. For your encore, we will—as promised—let you create a new embedded object. In a blank part of the Swedish worksheet of the Excel workbook MYSOUND2.XLS, create the embedded Word document object shown in Figure 6.11. (**Hint:** Use the method outlined above in "Creating A New Embedded Object.") If you have trouble creating a Word table, try searching for *tables* in on-line Word Help.

10. Save all your open files, then exit all Office applications.

Figure 6.10 **Editing the embedded graph object**

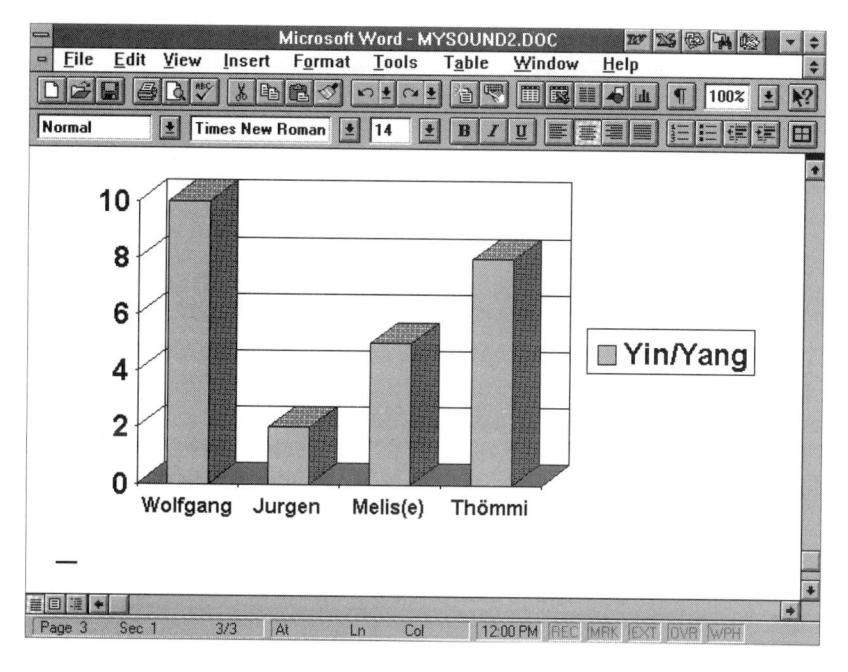

Figure 6.11 **Creating a new embedded object in Excel**

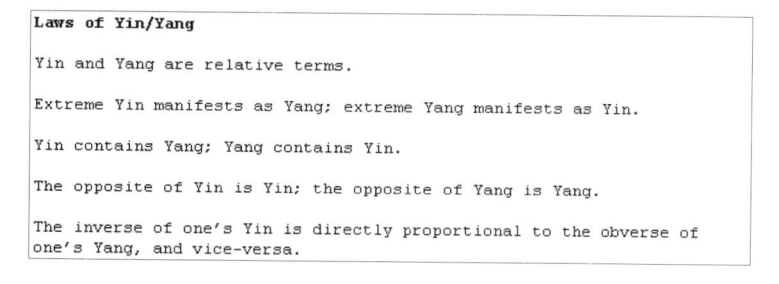

SUMMARY

In this chapter, you grappled with object embedding. You now know how to embed objects by using the Clipboard and drag-and-drop, and how to edit your embedded objects.

Here's a quick reference for the techniques you learned in this chapter:

Desired Result	How to Do It
Use Clipboard to embed object	Copy source object to Clipboard; in destination file, select place to embed; choose **Edit, Paste Special**; select **Paste**; in As list box, select format to apply to embedded object; click on **OK**
Use drag-and-drop to embed object	Select **source object**; in destination file, display place to embed; minimize all other open applications; use **Task List** to tile source file and destination file; press and hold **Ctrl**, drag **source object** to destination file, release **mouse button**, release **Ctrl**; maximize destination application, if desired
Edit embedded object	Open embedded object in source application either by double-clicking on **embedded object** or by selecting **embedded object** and choosing **Edit, *<Object>*, Open**; edit embedded object as desired; save your changes either by pressing **Esc** (if you're editing embedded object in small window within destination application) or by choosing **File, Update** then **File, Close** or **File, Exit & Return To** *DestApp* (if you're editing embedded object in full-sized window separate from destination application); exit source application, if necessary
Create new embedded object	Open destination file and select location for object; choose **Insert, Object**; click on **Create New** tab; select type of object to create and click on **OK**; create embedded object; save your changes by either pressing **Esc** (if you're editing embedded object in small window within destination application) or by choosing **File, Update** then **File, Close** or **File, Exit & Return To** *<DestApp>* (if you're editing embedded object in full-sized window separate from destination application)

In the next chapter, you'll learn how to use the Find File feature, how to move and size the Office toolbar, and how to minimize the toolbar. You'll also learn about adding Office toolbar buttons, removing an Office toolbar, and making the toolbar invisible.

CHAPTER 7: EXAMINING OFFICE IN GREATER DETAIL

The Find File Feature

Customizing Office

In Chapter 2, you learned the techniques that are basic to using Office. In this chapter, you'll learn about some of Office's advanced features, which allow you to do such things as find a file, and offer you many options for customizing the Office toolbar.

When you're done working through this chapter, you will know

- How to use the Find File feature
- How to move and size the Office toolbar
- How to minimize the toolbar
- How to add Office toolbar buttons
- How to remove an Office toolbar button
- How to make the toolbar invisible

THE FIND FILE FEATURE

Find File is a powerful tool for locating files. What makes Find File powerful is that it allows you to find a file even if you can't remember its name. You know that a file's Summary Info box contains text boxes that enable you to record a significant amount of information about the file: the Title, Subject, Author, Keywords, and Contents. Using Find File, you can search for a file by specifying only one such identifier. Of course, although the program you're working in automatically suggests an author in the Summary Info dialog box (when you're saving a file), the onus is on the user to supply any more information.

SEARCHING FOR A FILE WHEN YOU KNOW ITS NAME

To search for a file if you know its name,

- Click on the *Find File* button in the Office toolbar.
- In the View pop-up list, select the type of file information you wish to view:
  - *Preview* displays a portion of the file's contents.
  - *File Info* displays pertinent file statistics, such as file size, its title (if any), and the date it was last saved.
  - *Summary* displays all the information contained in the file's Summary Info box—and then some.
- Click on *Search* to open the Search dialog box.
- Under Search For, enter the file's name in the File Name box; if you know only the file's type—say, a Word file—select it from

the File Name drop-down list. If you know the file's location, type the disk directory in the Location box. If you know, for example, that the file is located somewhere on your hard disk, but do not know its directory location, make sure the root directory—for example, c:\—appears in the Location box, and check the *Include Subdirectories* option.

- Click on *OK* to begin the search.

At times, the information that might appear in the various text boxes of the Search dialog box can become confusing or distracting. To clear all the text boxes and uncheck all options in the Search dialog box, click on *Clear*.

To open a file from the Find File dialog box, select the file and click on *Open*, or double-click on the file's name. If the file requires that an application be running in order for it to be opened—for example, an Excel file, which requires that Excel be running—Find File runs that application, and then opens the file.

To close the Find File dialog box, click on *Cancel* or *Close*, depending on which button is available at the time.

Let's begin by taking a brief look at the Find File dialog box:

1. In the Office toolbar, click on the **Find File** button. The Find File dialog box is displayed (see Figure 7.1; this is how the dialog box appears the first time you open it).

2. If necessary, choose the **Preview** option from the View pop-up list (at the bottom-left corner of the dialog box). Notice that the dialog box is divided into three main areas:

    - At the left is the Listed Files box; this is where any found files are listed.

    - On the right is the "Preview of," or simply Preview, box. When you select a file in the Listed Files box, a preview of that file's contents is displayed here, provided that this information is available.

    - At the bottom is the View box and pop-up list, and various buttons that provide you with some important options. We'll examine some of these options as we begin our file searches. For now, notice that the Search, Cancel, and Help buttons are the only ones available (provided that your dialog box matches Figure 7.1).

Figure 7.1 **The Find File dialog box**

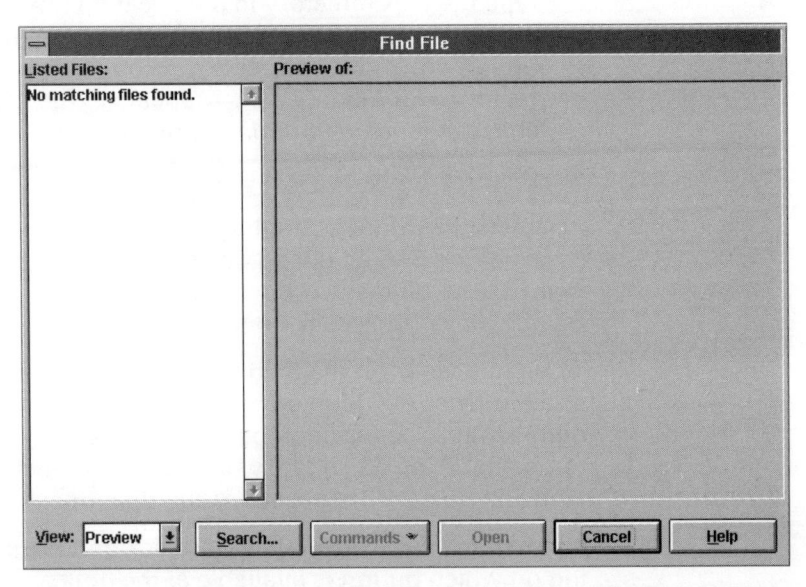

Let's perform our first file search. We'll begin with a file whose name we know:

1. In the Find File dialog box, click on **Search** to open the Search dialog box (see Figure 7.2). Take a moment to study its structure.

2. Under Search For, type **win.ini** in the File Name box. Case does not matter when you are typing file or directory names or drive letters. (WIN.INI is an important Windows file; we've chosen it because we know that it must be present on your computer in order for you to be running Office.) In the Location box, your hard disk's root directory is displayed.

3. If necessary, check the **Include Subdirectories** option. This option and the information in the Location box tell Find File to begin searching the root directory and, if necessary, to continue by searching all the subdirectories. It will do so until either it finds the file, or it has searched through every directory and subdirectory without success.

Figure 7.2   **The Search dialog box**

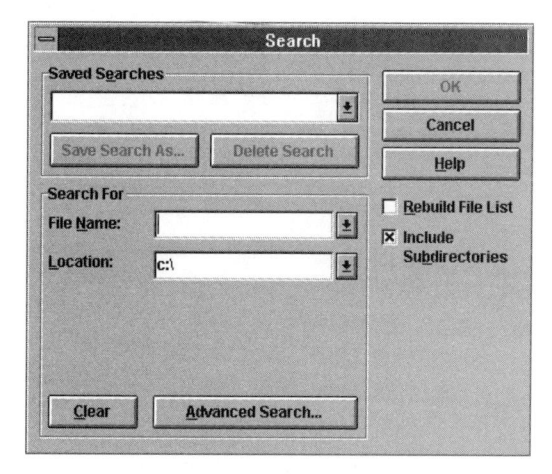

4. Click on **OK** to close the Search dialog box and begin the search. The Searching Directories box is displayed in the center of the Find File dialog box, informing you of the status of the search. Momentarily, it informs you that one file that matches our description has been found.

5. Now examine the Find File dialog box. Notice the following features (see Figure 7.3):

    - In the Listed Files box, a directory tree is displayed. Below it is our found file, which is highlighted. Working from bottom to top, the directory tree tells us that WIN.INI is located in the WINDOWS directory, which is a subdirectory of the root directory, C:. Notice the convenient file, directory, and drive icons: a sheet of paper, a folder, and a hard disk, respectively.

    - Above the Preview box, the drive, directory, and file name are again displayed. In the Preview box, the message

        ```
        No preview is available for this file.
        ```

        is displayed. Obviously, the Preview option in the View pop-up list didn't tell us anything about the file. We'll remedy this in a moment.

Figure 7.3 **The completed search for WIN.INI**

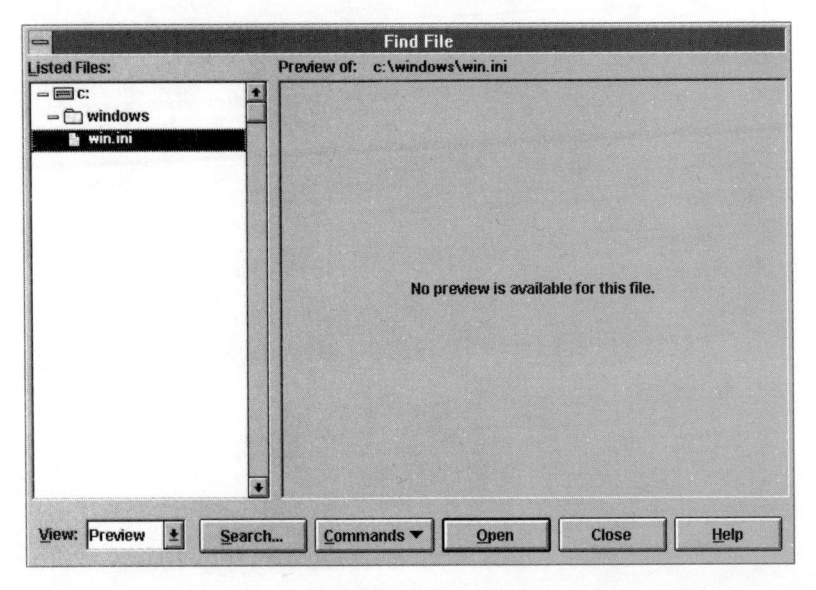

- At the bottom of the dialog box, notice that all buttons are now available. Notice also that the Cancel button has changed to *Close*.

6. Open the View pop-up list, and choose **File Info**. Pertinent file status information is displayed, where applicable, such as the file's size and the date it was last saved (see Figure 7.4; your file information will vary).

7. Now choose **Summary** in the View pop-up list. You can see that the information now displayed mirrors what would normally be displayed in a Summary Info box, plus some additional file information. Obviously, there isn't too much information to be gleaned about this file!

PRACTICE YOUR SKILLS

Return to the preview of WIN.INI. (**Hint:** In the View pop-up list, select **Preview**.)

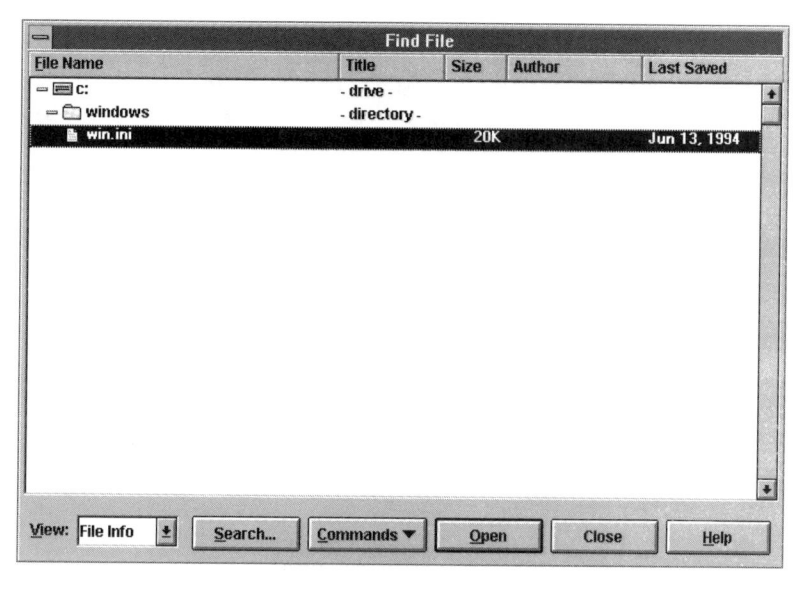

Figure 7.4 **File information displayed for WIN.INI**

![Find File dialog showing win.ini file entry with columns for File Name, Title, Size, Author, and Last Saved. The c: drive and windows directory are shown, with win.ini at 20K saved Jun 13, 1994. Buttons at bottom: View (File Info), Search..., Commands, Open, Close, Help.]

SEARCHING FOR A FILE WHEN YOU DON'T KNOW ITS NAME

If you do not know the name of the file you are looking for:

- In the Search dialog box, click on *Advanced Search* to open the Advanced Search dialog box.

- Display the desired tab—*Location, Summary,* or *Timestamp*—based on the information you wish to supply to begin your search. Location enables you to select, for example, a specific subdirectory to search; Summary enables you to specify any summary information you might be able to supply; and Timestamp enables you to specify time-related information pertaining to the file, such as a range of dates between which the file might have been last saved.

- Click on *OK* in the Advanced Search dialog box.

- Click on *OK* in the Search dialog box to begin the search.

Now, let's find some files whose names we can't remember. To find the files, we'll use only the author's name, the type of files they are, and their location:

1. From the Find File dialog box, open the Search dialog box (click on **Search**). Notice that the name of the file we previously

112 • CHAPTER 7: EXAMINING OFFICE IN GREATER DETAIL

searched for still appears in the File Name box. Notice also that this dialog box contains no provisions for specifying an author's name.

2. Click on **Advanced Search** to open the Advanced Search dialog box. Notice the three tabs contained in this dialog box: Location, Summary, and Timestamp. If necessary, click on the **Location** tab to display it (see Figure 7.5). Take a moment to look over the tab's contents.

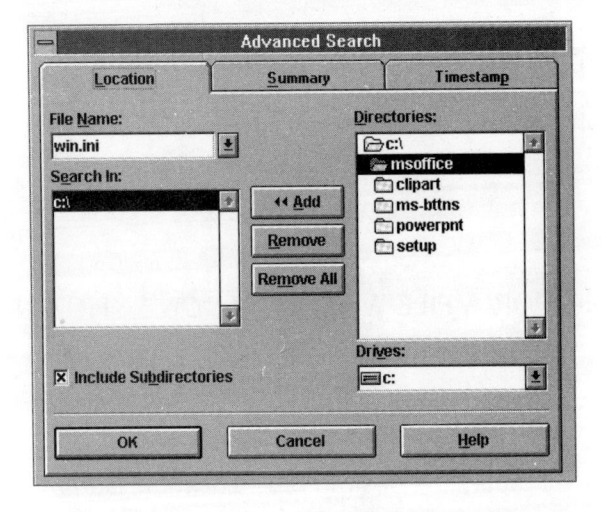

Figure 7.5   **The Location tab in the Advanced Search dialog box**

3. Open the File Name drop-down list, and select **Excel Files**. Even though we don't know the names of the files, we'll indicate that we know the files we are looking for are Excel files. The specification *.xl* appears in the File Name box.

4. Under Search In, select **c:** if necessary; then click on **Remove** to remove the root directory from the list of directories to be searched. We need to tell Find File that we want it to search in the OFFWORK directory.

5. On the right side of the Location tab, under Directories, double-click on the root directory to display the names of all directories that lie directly off the root. Scroll, if necessary, to view *offwork*.

THE FIND FILE FEATURE • 113

6. Click on **offwork** to select it. Then click on **Add** to place the directory name in the Search In box. Compare your screen to Figure 7.6.

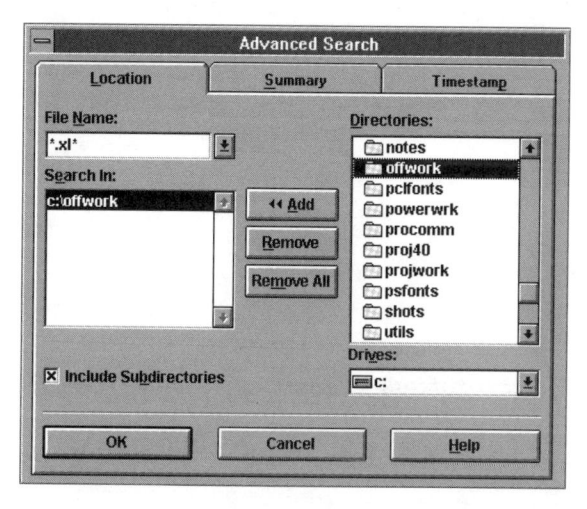

Figure 7.6   **The specified criteria in the Location tab**

7. Display the **Summary** tab (click on it). Take a moment to look over the tab's contents. We'll specify the author's name here.

8. Click in the Author box to place the insertion point, and type **Julie Nichols** to specify the author's name (see Figure 7.7).

9. Display the **Timestamp** tab (click on it), and take a moment to look over its contents. Here you can specify a range of dates between which the file was last saved, and/or between which the file was created. Under Created, notice that the author's name appears in the By box.

10. Click on **OK** to close the Advanced Search dialog box and return to the Search dialog box. Notice that all the information that we specified in the Advanced Search dialog box is contained here (see Figure 7.8). It doesn't matter that the Include Subdirectories option is checked. We've specified a single directory as one of our search criteria, and OFFWORK contains no subdirectories.

Figure 7.7 **Specifying an author in the Summary tab**

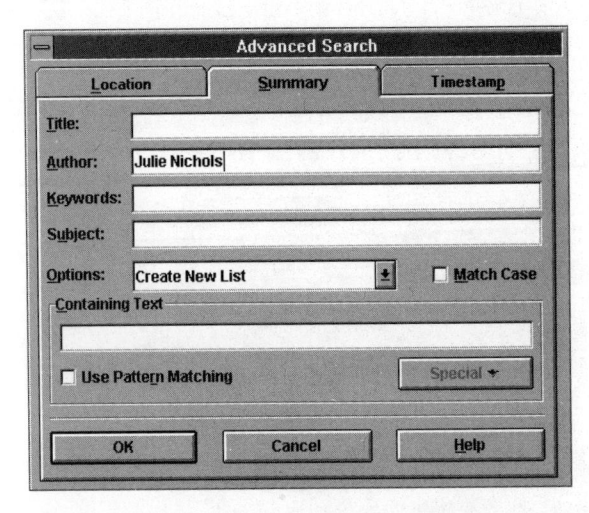

Figure 7.8 **The specified search criteria in the Search dialog box**

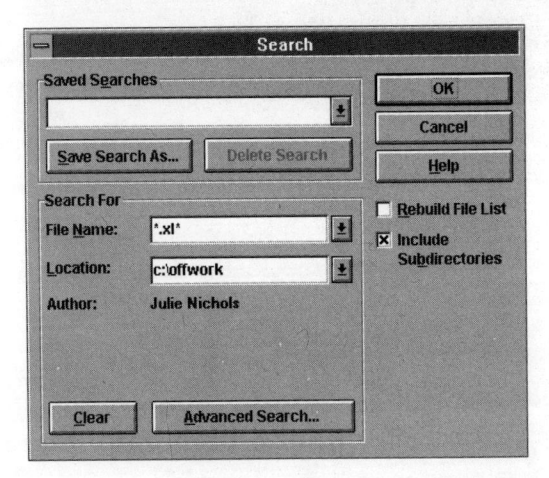

11. Click on **OK** to perform the search. Momentarily, two Excel files are listed. The file currently selected, herbcost.xls, is displayed in the Preview box. The first three columns and nine rows of its worksheet are shown (see Figure 7.9).

12. Select **xtrafile.xls** to preview its contents. Notice that its preview is the same as that of HERBCOST.XLS.

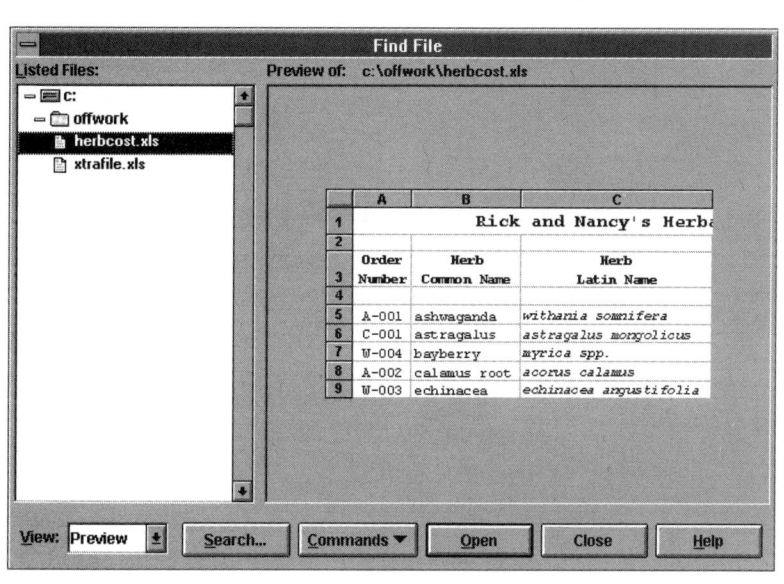

Figure 7.9   **The sought-for Excel files, found and previewed**

PRACTICE YOUR SKILLS

Compare HERBCOST.XLS and XTRAFILE.XLS by doing the following:

1. Display the **File Info** view. (**Hint:** Use the View pop-up list.)
2. Display the **Summary** view for both files. (**Hint:** After you display Summary view, select each file to switch between them.)

DELETING A FILE

The Commands button, at the bottom of the Find File dialog box, displays a menu, which allows you to further work with one or more selected files. The choices in the Commands menu allow you to perform actions such as copying, printing, deleting, or sorting selected files.

To delete a file in the Find File dialog box:

- Select the file(s) you wish to delete.
- Click on *Commands* to open the Commands menu.

- Choose *Delete*. A message is displayed asking you for confirmation.
- Click on *Yes*.

In the previous exercise, we found that, after displaying the Preview, File Info, and Summary views, our two Excel files are identical. Let's delete XTRAFILE.XLS:

1. In the Listed Files box, select **xtrafile.xls**.
2. Click on **Commands** to open the Commands menu, and choose **Delete**. A message is displayed, asking you to confirm the operation.
3. Click on **Yes**. The deleted file is removed from the Listed Files box.

PRACTICE YOUR SKILLS

Use the skills you learned thus far in this chapter to perform the following procedures:

1. Perform a search to find all the Word files in the OFFWORK directory written by Julie Nichols. (**Hint:** You'll need to perform an advanced search, using both the Location and the Summary tabs.)
2. After the files have been found, use all three views to compare the files' contents and statistics.
3. Delete the **xtrafile.doc** file. (**Hint:** Use the Command button.)
4. Close the Find File dialog box. (**Hint:** There's a button for this.)

CUSTOMIZING OFFICE

You have already seen some evidence of Office's power as a tool. Another wonderful feature of Office is how you can change its appearance to better serve you in the way you work at the computer. For example, if you'd like to include additional choices in the Office menu, you can do so. You can also change the size and position of the toolbar, add and remove buttons, and, if having the toolbar displayed at all times makes you feel as if Big Brother is watching, you can even remove it from view.

CUSTOMIZING OFFICE • 117

Except for moving and minimizing the toolbar, the remaining procedures that you'll learn in this chapter are all available through the Customize option in the Office menu—even the customization of that menu itself! You can also customize, size, and minimize by using the Office toolbar shortcut menu, which is available by clicking the right mouse button anywhere on the toolbar.

CUSTOMIZING THE OFFICE MENU

To add or remove choices from the Office menu:

- In the Office menu (or toolbar shortcut menu), choose *Customize* to open the Customize dialog box.
- Display the *Menu* tab.
- In the list of available menu choices, check the box next to a choice to add it to the menu; to remove a menu choice, uncheck the box next to that choice.
- Click on *OK*.

Let's add some choices to the Office menu:

1. Open the Office menu. Notice the current list of choices in the menu (see Figure 7.10).

2. Choose **Customize** to open the Customize dialog box, and display the **Menu** tab (see Figure 7.11).

Figure 7.10 **The default choices in the Office menu**

```
Microsoft Excel
Microsoft PowerPoint
Program Manager
File Manager
Find File
Microsoft Word
Customize...
Office Setup and Uninstall
Cue Cards
Help...
About Microsoft Office...
Exit
```

Figure 7.11   **The Menu tab in the Customize dialog box**

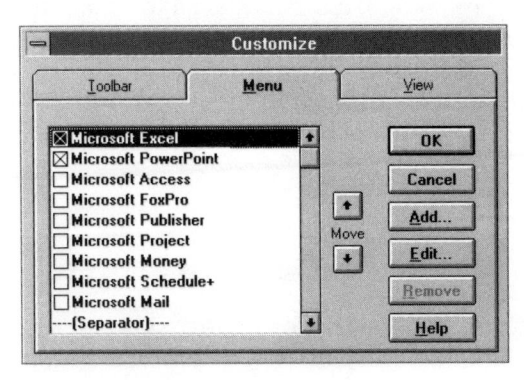

3. Scroll through the list of available menu choices. The menu options that are checked are those that are displayed when you open the Office menu.

4. Check (click on the box next to) the **Microsoft Mail** choice to include it in the Office menu; then click on **OK**.

5. Now open the Office menu. Notice the addition of the *Microsoft Mail* choice (see Figure 7.12). (Please do *not* choose this option at this time; we'll examine the Microsoft Mail application in Chapter 10.)

6. Close the Office menu.

Figure 7.12   **The Microsoft Mail option included in the Office menu**

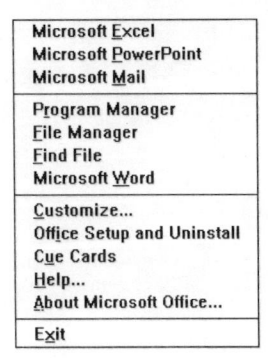

Now, let's remove the Microsoft Mail choice from the Office menu:

1. Open the Customize dialog box (choose **Customize** from the Office menu), and display the tab.
2. In the list of available menu choices, uncheck (click in the box next to) the **Microsoft Mail** option; then click on **OK**.
3. Open the Office menu, and observe the result: The Microsoft Mail choice has been removed from the menu.

PRACTICE YOUR SKILLS

1. Open the Customize dialog box, and display the **Menu** tab.
2. Add the **Microsoft Mail**, **Paintbrush**, and **Calculator** choices to the Office menu. (Paintbrush and Calculator are two of Windows's "accessory" applications.)
3. Open and observe the additions to the Office menu.
4. Remove the **Paintbrush** and **Calculator** choices from the Office menu.
5. Once again, open and observe the Office menu. The Paintbrush and Calculator choices have been removed; of the three choices added in step 2, only the Microsoft Mail choice still remains.
6. Close the Office menu.

SIZING THE TOOLBAR

You can change the size of the Office toolbar and its buttons. Office provides you with three sizes of buttons: *Small*, *Regular*, and *Large*. Small Buttons is the default setting; when this setting is chosen, the buttons are displayed near the upper-right corner of the Windows desktop. When an application is running, the small buttons are displayed near the right edge of the application's title bar.

When you change the toolbar's size to Regular or Large, a title bar is displayed for the toolbar, which includes a Control-menu box and a Minimize button, and the toolbar itself automatically appears close to the middle of the Windows desktop.

To change the size of the toolbar and its buttons:

- Open the Customize dialog box, and display the *View* tab.

- Under Toolbar Button Size, click on the desired button size to select it.
- Click on *OK*.

    (Remember, these size choices are also available in the Office shortcut menu.)

    Looking at the Office toolbar, you can see that its buttons are currently small. Let's change the size of the Office toolbar:

    1. Open the Customize dialog box, and display the **View** tab (see Figure 7.13). Take a moment to examine the contents of the View tab. Under Toolbar Button Size, notice that the *Small Buttons* option is currently selected.

Figure 7.13 **The View tab in the Customize dialog box**

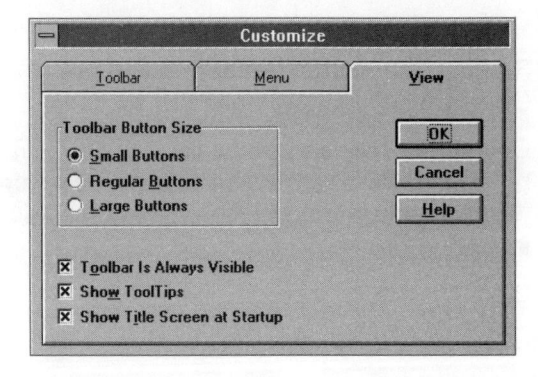

2. Click on the **Regular Buttons** option to select it, and click on **OK**. The toolbar is now considerably larger, it contains a title bar, and it has moved toward the middle of the desktop (see Figure 7.14).

Figure 7.14 **The Office toolbar with Regular Buttons**

3. Click the right mouse button on the toolbar to open the Office shortcut menu. You can see that the Regular Buttons option is currently checked.

4. Choose the **Large Buttons** option. Notice how much larger the toolbar and its buttons are now.

PRACTICE YOUR SKILLS

Practice changing the size of the toolbar to small, then to regular, and back to large. (**Hint:** Use either or both methods you just learned.)

MOVING THE TOOLBAR

Moving the Office toolbar is as simple as moving any window or dialog box that contains a title bar: Click on the toolbar's title bar and drag it to its new locations. Of course, the catch here is that the toolbar must be sized either Regular or Large in order to be moved; when Small, the toolbar has no title bar.

To change the orientation of the toolbar from horizontal to vertical and vice versa, double-click on the toolbar's title bar.

With the Office toolbar sized Large, let's try moving it around a bit:

1. Click on the Office toolbar's title bar, and drag it anywhere you like on your screen. Then release the mouse button. The toolbar appears in its new location.

2. Now double-click on the toolbar's title bar. The orientation of the toolbar is changed to vertical (see Figure 7.15).

PRACTICE YOUR SKILLS

1. Practice moving the vertically oriented Office toolbar around on your screen. You'll notice that when you try to drag the vertical toolbar away from the edge of the desktop, it returns to its horizontal orientation.

2. Drag the toolbar to the middle of the desktop, and release the mouse button. The toolbar is now horizontal.

3. Drag the toolbar to one edge of the desktop, and release the mouse button. The toolbar becomes vertical.

Figure 7.15   **The Office toolbar, displayed vertically**

   4. Without dragging, make the toolbar horizontal. (**Hint:** Double-click on its rather narrow title bar. Hope your aim is good!)

MINIMIZING THE TOOLBAR

You already know that when you minimize an object in any Windows application, it is reduced to an icon on your desktop while it runs in the background.

There are a few methods for minimizing the Office toolbar. Here are our two favorites:

- If the toolbar is sized either Regular or Large, click on the toolbar's *Minimize* button.

- Whatever the size of the toolbar, choose *Minimize* from the Office shortcut menu.

Let's minimize the Office toolbar:

   1. With the toolbar still sized Large, click on the **Minimize** button in its title bar. The toolbar becomes an icon at the bottom of the Windows desktop (see Figure 7.16).

   2. Double-click on the minimized **Office** icon to display the toolbar again.

Figure 7.16   **The minimized Office icon**

PRACTICE YOUR SKILLS

1. Use the Office shortcut menu to minimize the toolbar.
2. Redisplay the toolbar.
3. Change the size of the toolbar as many times as you like. Then, each time, use an appropriate method to minimize it.
4. Again, redisplay the toolbar.
5. If necessary, return the toolbar to its largest size.

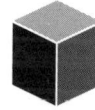

ADDING A BUTTON

Just as you can add a choice to the Office menu, so, too, can you add a button to the toolbar.

To add a button to the Office toolbar:

- Open the Customize dialog box, and display the *Toolbar* tab.
- In the list of available toolbar buttons, check the box next to the name of the button you wish to add.
- Click on *OK*.

Let's add some buttons to the Office toolbar:

1. Open the Customize dialog box, and display the **Toolbar** tab (see Figure 7.17). Take a moment to scroll through the list of available buttons. Notice that the ones checked are those that are currently displayed in the toolbar.
2. In the list of toolbar buttons, check the **Microsoft Mail** option. Since we have a choice for this application in the Office menu, we thought it would be nice to include its button on the toolbar.

Figure 7.17   **The Toolbar tab in the Customize dialog box**

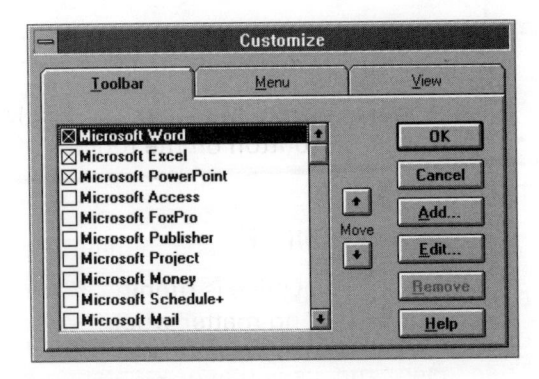

3. Click on **OK** to add the button, and observe the new addition to the toolbar (see Figure 7.18).

Figure 7.18   **The Office toolbar with the added Microsoft Mail button**

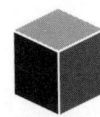

REMOVING A BUTTON

To remove a button from the toolbar:

- Open the Customize dialog box, and display the *Toolbar* tab.
- In the list of available toolbar buttons, uncheck the box next to the name of the button you wish to remove.
- Click on *OK*.

Let's remove the Mail button from the Office toolbar:

1. Open the Customize dialog box, and display the **Toolbar** tab.
2. In the list of toolbar buttons, uncheck **Microsoft Mail**.
3. Click on **OK**. The Mail button has been removed from the toolbar.

PRACTICE YOUR SKILLS

1. Add buttons for **Microsoft Mail**, **Program Manager**, and **File Manager** to the Office toolbar. Observe the new buttons.

2. Remove the **Program Manager** and **File Manager** buttons, leaving the Mail button on the toolbar.

MAKING THE TOOLBAR INVISIBLE

As you've seen, while Office is running, the toolbar is, by default, almost always visible, no matter what application you might be running along with it. You can, however, allow it to be "covered up" by any active window, rendering it temporarily invisible, or, more correctly, not always visible.

To make the toolbar not always visible:

- Open the Customize dialog box, and display the *View* tab.
- Uncheck the *Toolbar Is Always Visible* option.
- Click on *OK*.

To make the toolbar always visible, check the Toolbar Is Always Visible option.

Let's make the toolbar disappear:

1. Minimize the Windows Program Manager, if necessary.
2. Open the Customize dialog box, and display the **View** tab.
3. Uncheck the **Toolbar Is Always Visible** option.
4. Click on **OK**, and take a look at your screen. What happened? The toolbar is still visible! But only temporarily...
5. Now maximize the **Program Manager**. Notice that it has completely covered up the Office toolbar. With the Toolbar Is Always Visible option unchecked, any window that you activate will cover the Office toolbar.

PRACTICE YOUR SKILLS

1. Minimize the **Program Manager** window.
2. Return the Office toolbar to its always-visible status.

3. Try to cover up the Office toolbar with the Program Manager. What happens?

4. Change the size of the Office toolbar to its small (default) size. Where is the toolbar now?

SUMMARY

In this chapter, you learned how to use Find File to search for files whether or not you know their names. You also learned how to customize and change the position and orientation of the Office toolbar.

Here's a quick reference for the Office techniques you learned in this chapter:

Desired Result	How to Do It
Search for file if you know its name	Click on **Find File** button; in View pop-up list, select type of file information you wish to view; click on **Search**; enter file's name in File Name box; if you know file's type, select it from File Name drop-down list; if you know file's location, type disk directory in Location box; click on **OK**
Close Find File dialog box	Click on **Cancel** or **Close**, depending on which button is available
Search for a file when you don't know its name	Open Search dialog box, click on **Advanced Search**; display desired tab, based on information you wish to supply; enter any information; click on **OK**; click on **OK**
Delete file(s) in Find File dialog box	Select file(s) to be deleted; click on **Commands** to open Commands menu, choose **Delete**; click on **Yes**
Add or remove choices from Office menu	In Office menu (or toolbar shortcut menu), choose **Customize** to open Customize dialog box, display **Menu** tab; check menu choice you wish to add, or uncheck choice you wish to remove; click on **OK**

SUMMARY

Desired Result	How to Do It
Change size of toolbar	Open Office toolbar shortcut menu, choose desired button size
Move Office toolbar	With toolbar size set to Regular or Large buttons, drag title bar to desired location
Change horizontal/vertical orientation of toolbar	Double-click on title bar
Minimize Office toolbar	Choose **Minimize** from Office shortcut menu; or, if toolbar is sized either Regular or Large, click on its **Minimize** button
Add button to Office toolbar	Open Customize dialog box, display **Toolbar** tab; check name of button you wish to add; click on **OK**
Remove button from Office toolbar	Open Customize dialog box, display **Toolbar** tab; uncheck name of button you wish to remove; click on **OK**
Make Office toolbar invisible	Open Customize dialog box, display **View** tab; uncheck **Toolbar Is Always Visible** option; click on **OK**
Make Office toolbar always visible	Open Customize dialog box, display **View** tab; check **Toolbar Is Always Visible** option; click on **OK**

In the next chapter, you will learn how to use one Office application to gain access to others.

CHAPTER 8: USING ONE APPLICATION TO ACCESS OTHERS

Creating an Excel Worksheet in Word

Creating an Excel Worksheet in PowerPoint

Creating a Word Table in PowerPoint

Thus far, you've learned how to transfer information from one application to another using Cut, Copy, and Paste; linking; and embedding. However, between certain Office applications, there are also ways to use the tools and techniques normally available in only one application to create data within another application—without leaving the other application! For example, you can create an Excel worksheet in Word without leaving Word or—technically speaking—even running Excel.

When you're done working through this chapter, you will know

- How to create an Excel worksheet in Word
- How to create an Excel worksheet in PowerPoint
- How to create a Word table in PowerPoint

CREATING AN EXCEL WORKSHEET IN WORD

To create a table of numerical information in a Word document, you can, as you know, simply use Word's Insert Table command. However, you also know that when it comes to performing complex calculations and using formulas, you can accomplish much more using an Excel worksheet.

Well, you can have the best of both worlds by creating an Excel worksheet in the Word document.

To create an Excel worksheet in a Word document:

- Place the insertion point where you want to create the worksheet.
- Click on the *Insert Microsoft Excel Worksheet* button in Word's standard toolbar.
- Drag down in the grid to select the desired number of rows, and to the right to select the desired number of columns in your worksheet. Then release the mouse button.

After you've performed this procedure, a selected, blank worksheet is displayed with the number of rows and columns you've specified. In addition, the Word menu bar and the standard and formatting toolbars are replaced with those of Excel. So, in effect, you have all of Excel's features and commands at your disposal, yet you haven't left your Word document.

To turn the "master control" of your document back over to Word and redisplay the Word menu and toolbars, simply click anywhere in the document other than the worksheet.

Let's run Word and open a document; then we'll create an Excel worksheet in it:

1. Start **Word**. Then open the **intermem.doc** document.
2. Scroll down in the memo until the heading *Quarterly Report* is near the top of the document window (see Figure 8.1). This is where we'll create our worksheet.

Figure 8.1 **The Quarterly Report heading visible near the top of the window**

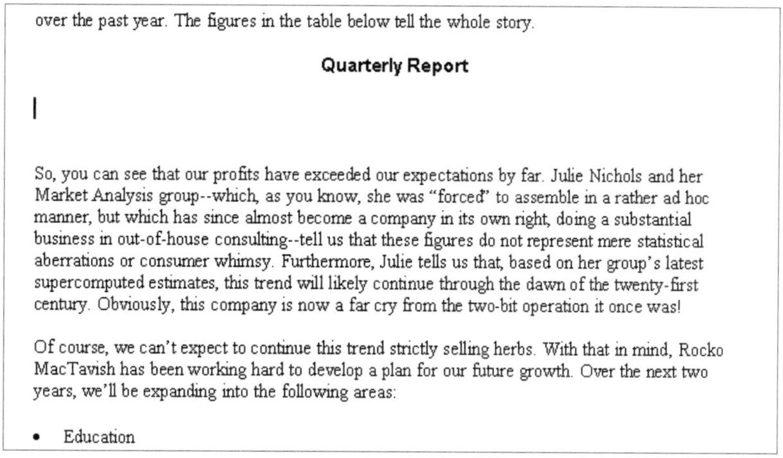

> over the past year. The figures in the table below tell the whole story.
>
> **Quarterly Report**
>
> So, you can see that our profits have exceeded our expectations by far. Julie Nichols and her Market Analysis group--which, as you know, she was "forced" to assemble in a rather ad hoc manner, but which has since almost become a company in its own right, doing a substantial business in out-of-house consulting--tell us that these figures do not represent mere statistical aberrations or consumer whimsy. Furthermore, Julie tells us that, based on her group's latest supercomputed estimates, this trend will likely continue through the dawn of the twenty-first century. Obviously, this company is now a far cry from the two-bit operation it once was!
>
> Of course, we can't expect to continue this trend strictly selling herbs. With that in mind, Rocko MacTavish has been working hard to develop a plan for our future growth. Over the next two years, we'll be expanding into the following areas:
>
> - Education

3. Place the insertion point two lines below the Quarterly Report heading.

4. Click on the **Insert Microsoft Excel Worksheet** button in the standard toolbar (see the following icon). A blank grid opens below the button.

5. Beginning at the upper-left corner of the grid, drag down to select six squares, and then right to select four (see Figure 8.2). Notice that the message at the bottom of the grid box tells you the dimensions you've specified. Release the mouse button. Momentarily, a miniature worksheet window appears in the document, enclosed by selection handles, and the Word menu and toolbars have been replaced with the Excel menu and toolbars (see Figure 8.3). The title bar, status bar, and view buttons remind you that you're still in Word.

6. Click in another area of the document to deselect the worksheet. Momentarily, the Excel row numbers and column letters disappear, and the Word menu and toolbars have returned. Where we created the worksheet, the mere skeleton of a table was displayed, and the table was selected.

7. Save the document as **mymemo**, and compare your screen to Figure 8.4.

132 • CHAPTER 8: USING ONE APPLICATION TO ACCESS OTHERS

Figure 8.2   **Specifying a six-row by four-column worksheet**

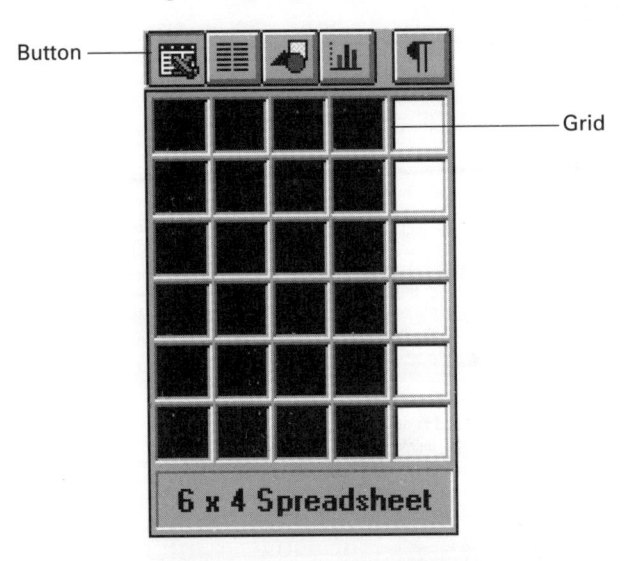

Figure 8.3   **The created worksheet**

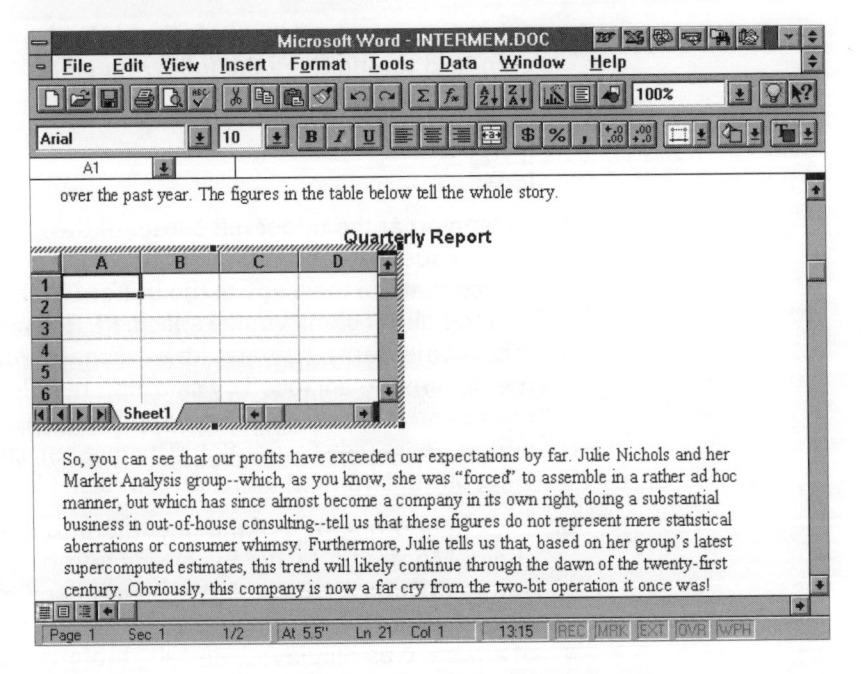

CREATING AN EXCEL WORKSHEET IN WORD • 133

Figure 8.4   **The selected table skeleton**

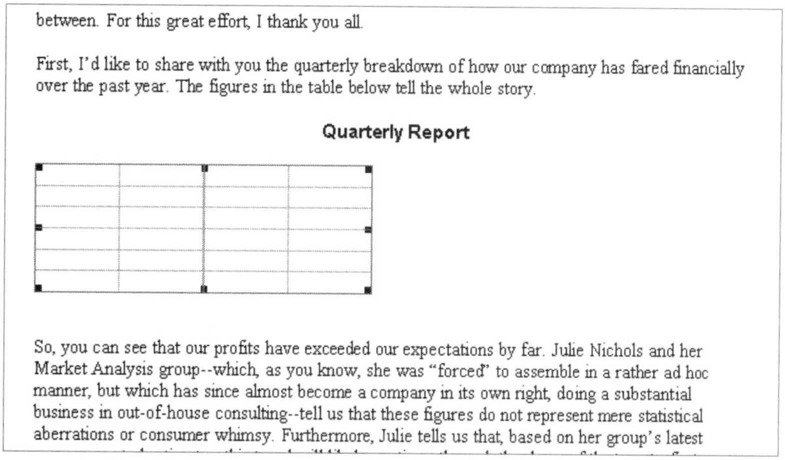

> between. For this great effort, I thank you all.
>
> First, I'd like to share with you the quarterly breakdown of how our company has fared financially over the past year. The figures in the table below tell the whole story.
>
> **Quarterly Report**
>
> [table skeleton]
>
> So, you can see that our profits have exceeded our expectations by far. Julie Nichols and her Market Analysis group--which, as you know, she was "forced" to assemble in a rather ad hoc manner, but which has since almost become a company in its own right, doing a substantial business in out-of-house consulting--tell us that these figures do not represent mere statistical aberrations or consumer whimsy. Furthermore, Julie tells us that, based on her group's latest

8. Now, attempt to click (once) in the worksheet to place the insertion point. Notice that the message

   ```
   Double-click to Edit Microsoft Excel 5.0
   Worksheet
   ```

   is displayed in the status bar. The only way to enter information in the worksheet is to enter edit mode. We'll do this in the next section.

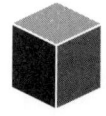

EDITING THE WORKSHEET

To edit an Excel worksheet created from a Word document, double-click on it. This allows you to edit the worksheet by using Excel's features. You no doubt have recognized this technique from the chapter on embedding. In fact, that's exactly what happens when you create a worksheet using the Insert Microsoft Excel Worksheet button; the worksheet is automatically embedded in the Word document.

Here are a couple of important additional notes:

- Though you specified the exact number of rows and columns when you created the worksheet, these values determine only the number of rows and columns that are *visible* when the worksheet is created. However, you can still access the myriad cells normally available in a standard Excel worksheet, by using Excel navigation techniques. You can also change the size of the visible worksheet by dragging the selection handles outside the worksheet in the desired direction.

- While you are working in an embedded worksheet, the Save button in the (Excel) toolbar is disabled. This is because the file you are working on is a Word document; the Word Save button does become available once you click on another part of the document. (The File, Save command remains functional in the Excel context; however, using it can result in data formats being changed. For this reason, we recommend that you wait to save the file until you return to the Word context.)

Let's access our embedded worksheet, so that we can enter data:

1. Double-click on the table skeleton, which is functioning as our worksheet placeholder. Momentarily, the Excel menu and toolbars once again replace those of Word, and the worksheet is displayed in the document.

2. Now try clicking on various cells in the worksheet to select them. You now have access to the worksheet.

PRACTICE YOUR SKILLS

1. Enter the following data in the worksheet, beginning with cell A1:

Quarter	Gross Revenues	Expenses	Profits
1st	$75,250	$52,375	$22,875
2nd	$86,825	$53,450	$33,375
3rd	$83,461	$55,675	$27,786
4th	$97,358	$55,450	$41,908
Totals	$342,894	$216,950	$125,944

2. Get the best fit for each column. (**Hint:** Double-click on the right border of each column's heading. For example, to widen column B, click on the border between column headings B and C.)

3. Make **Quarter**, **Gross Revenues**, **Expenses**, and **Profits** bold; then center them.

CREATING AN EXCEL WORKSHEET IN WORD • 135

4. Make the contents of cell A6, *Totals*, bold. Then center *Totals*.

5. In the Quarter column, change *1st, 2nd, 3rd,* and *4th* to **1, 2, 3,** and **4**, respectively. Then center these numbers in their cells.

6. Add a thin bottom border to the cell range A5:D5. (**Hint**: Use the **Borders** button in the formatting toolbar.)

7. Select cell A1, and compare your screen to Figure 8.5.

Figure 8.5   **The completed worksheet**

	A	B	C	D
1	Quarter	Gross Revenues	Expenses	Profits
2	1	$75,250	$52,375	$22,875
3	2	$86,825	$53,450	$33,375
4	3	$83,461	$55,675	$27,786
5	4	$97,358	$55,450	$41,908
6	Totals	$342,894	$216,950	$125,944

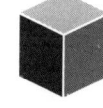

MOVING THE WORKSHEET

To change the position of the worksheet in the Word document, use the appropriate standard Word techniques. For example, to move the worksheet to another line, select it, then drag it to its new location. It's important to view moving the worksheet within a Word document as a Word function. Therefore, you must be in the Word context to do so.

Our worksheet is currently aligned with the left margin of our document. However, we'd like it centered under the heading Quarterly Report. To do so, we'll need to return to the Word context:

1. Click somewhere outside the worksheet to return to the Word context. Notice that, while all of our Word features are once again available, the data we entered in our worksheet remains in the document in the form of a Word table (our skeleton comes to life!). The table remains selected; notice the selection handles.

2. Click again outside the table. Now the table is deselected.

3. Click once in the table to select it. The selection handles return. As was true when our table was visible in the form of a worksheet, you can change the size of the table by dragging

the appropriate selection handle in the desired direction. Please do *not* do so now.

4. With the table selected, center it under the Quarterly Report heading (click on the **Center** button). Our table is now centered.

5. Deselect the table, and compare your screen to Figure 8.6.

Figure 8.6 **The centered table**

over·the·past·year.·The·figures·in·the·table·below·tell·the·whole·story.¶

Quarterly·Report¶

Quarter	Gross Revenues	Expenses	Profits
1	$75,250	$52,375	$22,875
2	$86,825	$53,450	$33,375
3	$83,461	$55,675	$27,786
4	$97,358	$55,450	$41,908
Totals	$342,894	$216,950	$125,944

So,·you·can·see·that·our·profits·have·exceeded·our·expectations·by·far.·Julie·Nichols·and·her·Market·Analysis·group--which,·as·you·know,·she·was·"forced"·to·assemble·in·a·rather·ad·hoc·manner,·but·which·has·since·almost·become·a·company·in·its·own·right,·doing·a·substantial·business·in·out-of-house·consulting--tell·us·that·these·figures·do·not·represent·mere·statistical·aberrations·or·consumer·whimsy.·Furthermore,·Julie·tells·us·that,·based·on·her·group's·latest·supercomputed·estimates,·this·trend·will·likely·continue·through·the·dawn·of·the·twenty-first·century.·Obviously,·this·company·is·now·a·far·cry·from·the·two-hit·operation·it·once·was!¶

6. Save and close the file.

7. Exit Word.

CREATING AN EXCEL WORKSHEET IN POWERPOINT

You can also create an Excel worksheet in PowerPoint, using all the same techniques that you used in Word (see the previous section). Of course, when you're using PowerPoint, everything happens inside a PowerPoint presentation, and while you're working with the worksheet, the Excel menu and toolbars take the place of those of PowerPoint.

Let's create an Excel worksheet in a PowerPoint presentation:

1. Run **PowerPoint**, and open the presentation file **addsheet.ppt**, located in the OFFWORK directory.

2. Display slide 10. This slide has the title *Annual Financial Statement*.

CREATING AN EXCEL WORKSHEET IN POWERPOINT • 137

3. Click on the **Insert Microsoft Excel Workshee**t button in the standard toolbar. (It looks exactly the same as its counterpart in Word. Be careful not to click on the Insert Microsoft Word Table button; we'll do that later.)

4. Drag to select a two-by-three grid, and release the mouse button. Momentarily, a tiny Excel worksheet, containing two rows and three columns is displayed. We'll have to make it larger in order to work with it more easily. We'll do this in the next section.

MOVING AND SIZING THE WORKSHEET

To move and size a worksheet created in PowerPoint, you must return to the PowerPoint context. (You'll remember that, to change the position of the worksheet we created in Word, we first had to return to the Word context.) You can then freely move and size the worksheet object using PowerPoint techniques.

Let's move and size the worksheet object:

1. Click in another part of the slide to return to the PowerPoint context.

2. Move (drag it) and size (using the selection handles) the worksheet object so that it more or less matches Figure 8.7.

EDITING THE WORKSHEET

As you did with the Excel worksheet that was embedded in our Word document, you double-click on the worksheet object to access the worksheet cells, as well as Excel's commands and features. You can then enter, edit, and otherwise enhance cell data using Excel techniques. Of course, you can then return to the PowerPoint context to add features to the worksheet object, such as a fill or a drop shadow, or to change the color of the text.

PRACTICE YOUR SKILLS

Let's enter our worksheet data:

1. Display the worksheet in the Excel context. (**Hint:** Double-click on the worksheet object.)

138 • CHAPTER 8: USING ONE APPLICATION TO ACCESS OTHERS

Figure 8.7 **The moved and sized worksheet object**

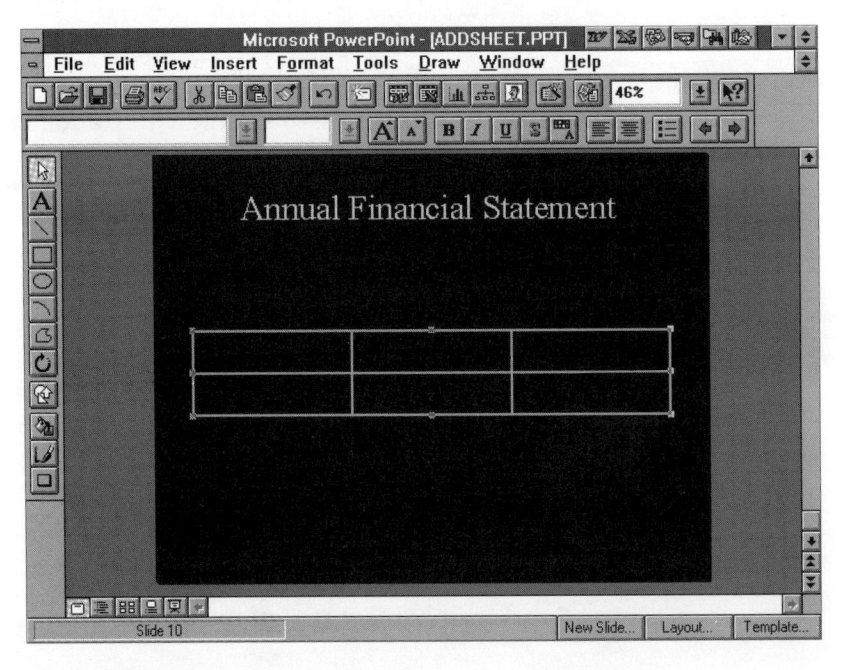

2. Starting at cell A1, enter the following data in your worksheet:

Gross Revenues	Expenses	Profits
$342,894	$216,950	$125,944

3. Adjust the width of each column for the best fit. (**Hint**: Double-click on the right column border of each column heading.)

4. Center the data in each cell of the worksheet.

5. Return to the PowerPoint context. The worksheet object now contains the entered data.

6. Resize and reposition the worksheet object to place it at or near the center of the slide.

7. Use the Shadow tool to add a drop shadow to the object.

8. Change the color of the data to yellow, so that it will show up better against the blue background. (**Hint**: Use the **Tools,**

Recolor command; then use the **New** drop-down list to change the original color of the data (black) to **yellow**.)

9. Deselect the worksheet object, and compare your screen to Figure 8.8.

10. Save the presentation as **mysheet**; then close it.

Figure 8.8   **The completed worksheet**

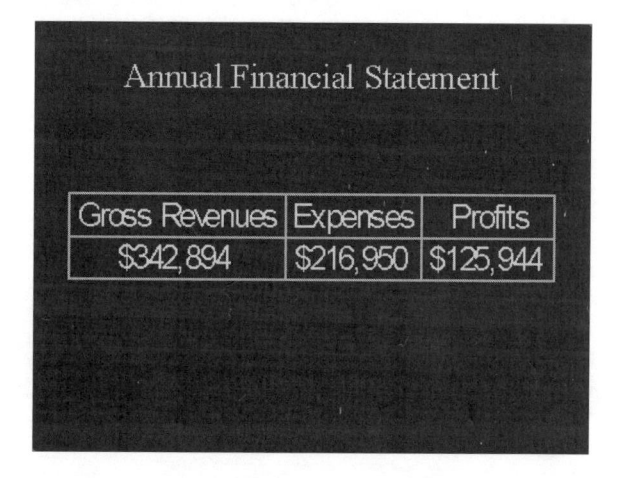

Annual Financial Statement

Gross Revenues	Expenses	Profits
$342,894	$216,950	$125,944

CREATING A WORD TABLE IN POWERPOINT

PowerPoint is unique in that it also enables you to create a Word table without leaving PowerPoint. To create a Word table in PowerPoint:

- Click on the *Insert Microsoft Word Table* button (with the little *w*) in the standard toolbar.

- Drag over the grid to select the number of rows and columns you wish to include in the table.

Let's open a new presentation; then we'll create our Word table:

1. In the OFFWORK directory, open **addtable.ppt**.

2. Display slide 4. This slide contains the title *Comparing Strengths of Approaches*.

3. Click on the **Insert Microsoft Word Table** button in the standard toolbar (see the following icon). A grid opens below the button, similar to the worksheet you used earlier in this chapter.

4. Drag to select a five-by-two grid; then release the mouse button. Momentarily, the PowerPoint menu and toolbars change to those of Word, and a blank table with rulers appears on the slide. Notice that the table consists of five rows and two columns (see Figure 8.9).

Figure 8.9   **The blank Word table added to the slide**

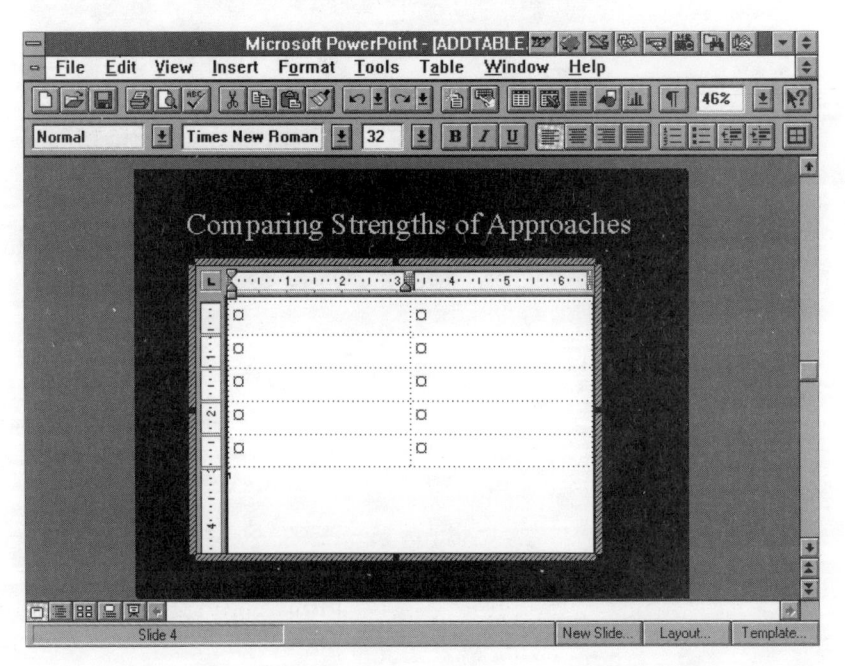

5. Click on a blank area of the slide to return to the PowerPoint environment. Notice that an object has been created for the Word table.

CREATING A WORD TABLE IN POWERPOINT • 141

EDITING THE TABLE

As you did in the case of the Excel worksheet, you must be in the Word environment in order to enter and edit your table data. To do so, double-click on the Word table object.

Another similarity to working with an Excel worksheet in PowerPoint is that to move or size the Word table in relation to the slide, you must be in the PowerPoint environment. To return the controls to PowerPoint, click on a blank area of the slide.

PRACTICE YOUR SKILLS

Enter table information and modify it, using Figure 8.10 as a guide:

Figure 8.10 **The Word table, with entered and modified data**

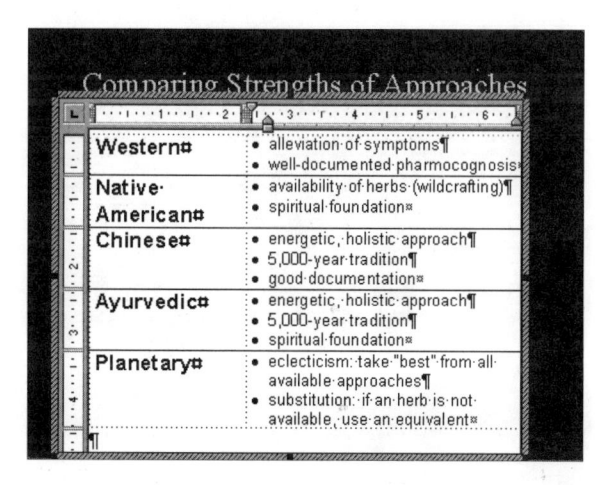

Western	• alleviation of symptoms¶ • well-documented pharmocognosis
Native American	• availability of herbs (wildcrafting)¶ • spiritual foundation
Chinese	• energetic, holistic approach¶ • 5,000-year tradition¶ • good documentation
Ayurvedic	• energetic, holistic approach¶ • 5,000-year tradition¶ • spiritual foundation
Planetary	• eclecticism: take "best" from all available approaches¶ • substitution: if an herb is not available, use an equivalent

Comparing Strengths of Approaches

1. Enter the table information shown in Figure 8.10. (**Hint:** In each right-column cell, remember to press **Enter** where indicated by the paragraph marks in Figure 8.10. Bear in mind that initially your table will not resemble the figure.)

2. Change the font of the left column to **Arial** (or some other sans serif font, such as Helvetica), and change its size to **24** points. (**Hint:** Use the formatting toolbar.)

3. Make the five row headings in the left column bold.

4. Change the font of the right column to **Arial** (or some other sans serif font), and change its size to **18** points.

5. Change the information in the right column to bulleted lists. (**Hint**: Use the **Bullets** button in the formatting toolbar.)

6. Adjust the width of the left column to match Figure 8.10.

7. Add a thin bottom border to each row of the table. (**Hint**: Display the **Borders** toolbar; select the entire table; if necessary, select the **3/4-pt** line; and click on the **Bottom Border** button.)

8. Return to the PowerPoint environment.

9. If necessary, move and size the table so that it matches Figure 8.11 as closely as possible.

Figure 8.11 **The completed Word table**

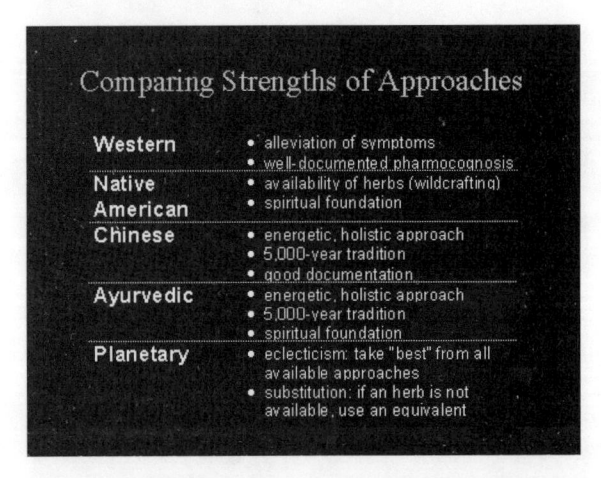

Comparing Strengths of Approaches

Western	• alleviation of symptoms • well-documented pharmacognosis
Native American	• availability of herbs (wildcrafting) • spiritual foundation
Chinese	• energetic, holistic approach • 5,000-year tradition • good documentation
Ayurvedic	• energetic, holistic approach • 5,000-year tradition • spiritual foundation
Planetary	• eclecticism: take "best" from all available approaches • substitution: if an herb is not available, use an equivalent

10. Deselect the table, and compare it to Figure 8.11.

11. On slide 5, create another five-by-two table.

12. Enter the information shown in Figure 8.12 in the table. Then use the same character and paragraph formatting and bottom borders you used for the table on slide 4. (**Hint**: As a shortcut, feel free to copy and paste any information that is the same from one table to the other. Also, you can copy formats by using the **Format Painter** button in the standard toolbar.)

Figure 8.12   **The completed Word table on slide 5**

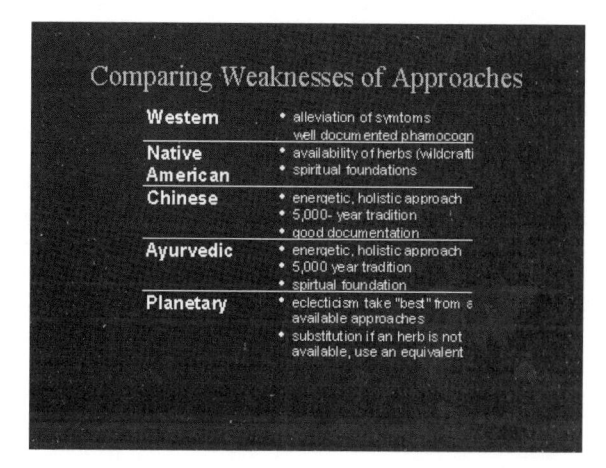

![Comparing Weaknesses of Approaches table]

13. Move and size the table to roughly match Figure 8.12.
14. Save the file as **mytables**. Then close the file.

SUMMARY

In this chapter, you learned how to create an Excel worksheet in both Word and PowerPoint. You also learned how to create a Word table in PowerPoint.

Here's a quick reference for the Office techniques you learned in this chapter:

Desired Result	How to Do It
Create Excel worksheet in Word	Place insertion point where you want to create worksheet; click on **Insert Microsoft Excel Worksheet** button; drag down in grid to select desired number of rows, and right to select desired number of columns in worksheet; release mouse button
Create Excel worksheet in PowerPoint	Display desired slide; click on **Insert Microsoft Excel Worksheet** button; drag down in grid to select desired number of rows, and right to select desired number of columns in worksheet; release mouse button

Desired Result	**How to Do It**
Create Word table in PowerPoint	Display desired slide; click on **Insert Microsoft Word Table** button; drag down in grid to select desired number of rows, and right to select desired number of columns in table; release mouse button
Return control to host application	Click in area outside table or worksheet
Enter data in or edit table or worksheet	Double-click on table or worksheet, and use commands and features of guest application
Size or move table or worksheet	Use techniques of host application

In the next chapter, you will learn how to make PowerPoint slides from a Word outline, and how to import a PowerPoint outline into Word.

CHAPTER 9: ADDITIONAL OFFICE TECHNIQUES

Making a PowerPoint Presentation from a Word Outline

Making a Word Document from PowerPoint Text

Changing the Default Position of the Office Toolbar

Throughout this book, you've learned many basic and advanced techniques for getting the most out of Office. In this chapter, we will add to this list two very powerful features that are available in Word and PowerPoint: *Present It* and *Report It*.

Word's Present It feature enables you to create an entire PowerPoint presentation from an existing Word outline. PowerPoint's Report It allows you to create a Word document from the text in a PowerPoint presentation. You could, of course, use many of the techniques you've already learned, such as copying and pasting, linking, or embedding, to use data from one application in another, depending on your needs. However, what gives Present It and Report It their power is the speed at which they can take an entire file's worth of information and then use it to create a file in the other application, potentially saving you much time.

When you're done working through this chapter, you will know

- How to make a PowerPoint presentation from a Word outline
- How to import the text from a PowerPoint presentation into Word
- How to change the default position of the Office toolbar

MAKING A POWERPOINT PRESENTATION FROM A WORD OUTLINE

You can use Word's Present It feature to convert—within seconds—just about any Word document that even vaguely resembles an outline into a PowerPoint presentation. It doesn't matter whether the outline levels in the Word document are numbered and/or bulleted, or are simply indented, with no numbers or bullets. To create the presentation, PowerPoint makes a copy of the Word document, thereby leaving the original document intact.

To create a PowerPoint presentation from a Word outline:

- Open the Word document that you wish to use to create your presentation.
- Display the Microsoft toolbar, and click on the *Present It* button.

When the conversion is completed, the new presentation is displayed in Outline view. During conversion, PowerPoint attempts to recognize outline text that it can use. Running text or text that it doesn't recognize as level-heading text will not be converted. Any desired text that PowerPoint failed to convert can, of course, be added afterward using, for example, standard PowerPoint techniques—or you can copy the missing text from the Word document and paste it onto the destination slide.

Let's examine a Word document that contains an outline:

1. Start **Word**.

2. In the OFFWORK directory, open **wordout.doc** (see Figure 9.1; slightly less of the document will be visible in your document window if the ruler is displayed).

3. Scroll through the document, and compare it to the printout shown in Figure 9.2. Observe the following features:

    - Most of the document is in standard outline form.

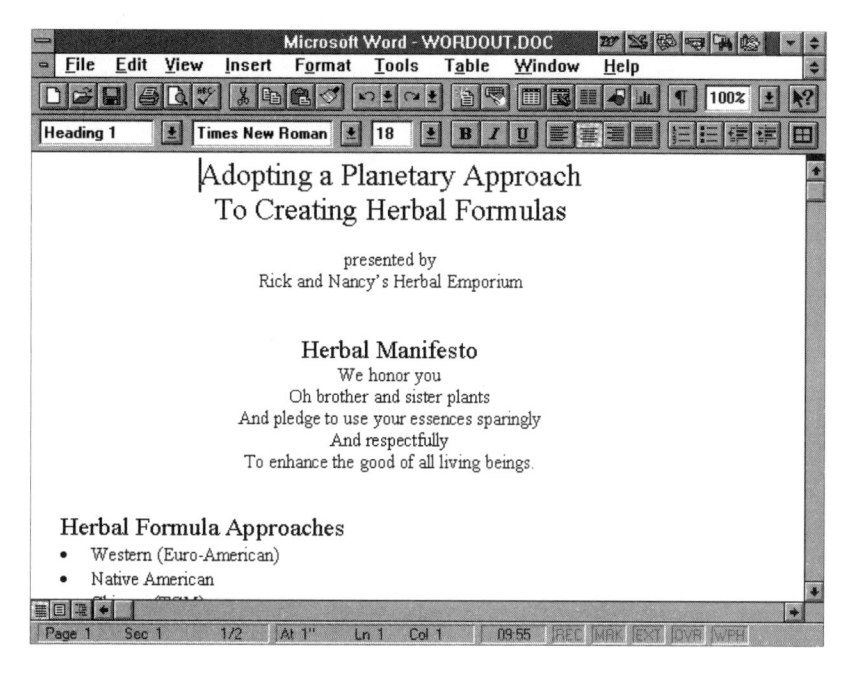

MAKING A POWERPOINT PRESENTATION FROM A WORD OUTLINE • 149

Figure 9.1   **The WORDOUT.DOC outline**

```
                    Microsoft Word - WORDOUT.DOC
  File  Edit  View  Insert  Format  Tools  Table  Window  Help

          Adopting a Planetary Approach
           To Creating Herbal Formulas

                      presented by
               Rick and Nancy's Herbal Emporium


                    Herbal Manifesto
                      We honor you
                 Oh brother and sister plants
             And pledge to use your essences sparingly
                     And respectfully
               To enhance the good of all living beings.


     Herbal Formula Approaches
       •  Western (Euro-American)
       •  Native American
```

- The first- (and second-) level headings are aligned with the left margin.

- The third-level headings are once-indented and are denoted by asterisk bullets.

- The lower the heading level, the smaller the type size.

- The first two bold titles in the document, and the text directly below them, are centered, and do not appear in outline form.

Let's create a PowerPoint presentation from our Word outline:

1. Display the Microsoft toolbar (choose **Microsoft** from the toolbar shortcut menu). The small Microsoft toolbar appears near the top of the document window (see Figure 9.3). You'll recognize a few of the application buttons from the Office toolbar.

Figure 9.2   **Printout of WORDOUT.DOC**

Adopting a Planetary Approach
To Creating Herbal Formulas

presented by
Rick and Nancy's Herbal Emporium

Herbal Manifesto
We honor you
Oh brother and sister plants
And pledge to use your essences sparingly
And respectfully
To enhance the good of all living beings.

Herbal Formula Approaches
- Western (Euro-American)
- Native American
- Chinese (TCM)
- Ayurvedic
- Planetary

Western (Euro-American)
- Strengths
  * alleviation of symptoms
  * well-documented pharmocognosis
- Weaknesses
  * nonenergetic, nonholistic approach
  * nontreatment of underlying cause

Native American
- Strengths
  * availability of herbs (wildcrafting)
  * spiritual foundation
- Weaknesses
  * lack of documentation
  * loses efficacy when separated from spiritual context

Chinese (TCM)
- Strengths
  * energetic, holistic approach
  * 5,000-year tradition
  * good documentation
- Weaknesses

Figure 9.2   **Printout of WORDOUT.DOC (Continued)**

* nonavailability of certain herbs
* complexity of therapeutic approach

Ayurvedic
- Strengths
  * energetic, holistic approach
  * 5,000-year tradition
  * spiritual foundation
- Weaknesses
  * documentation not so good
  * too exotic for Westerners ?

Planetary
- Strengths
  * eclecticism: take "best" from all available herbal approaches
  * substitution: if an herb is not available, use an equivalent herb
- Weaknesses
  * confusion resulting from eclectic approach
  * intercultural clash

Figure 9.3 **The Microsoft toolbar**

— Present It

2. Click on the **Present It** button in the Microsoft toolbar (see Figure 9.3). Notice that the button's icon depicts an arrow pointing away from a document and toward slides. The Present It feature automatically starts PowerPoint; therefore, you need not run it beforehand. Momentarily, our outline is displayed as a PowerPoint presentation, in Outline view. Maximize the presentation window, scroll to the top of the outline, and compare your screen to Figure 9.4. The temporary name *Presentation* appears in the title bar.

Figure 9.4 **The new presentation in Outline view**

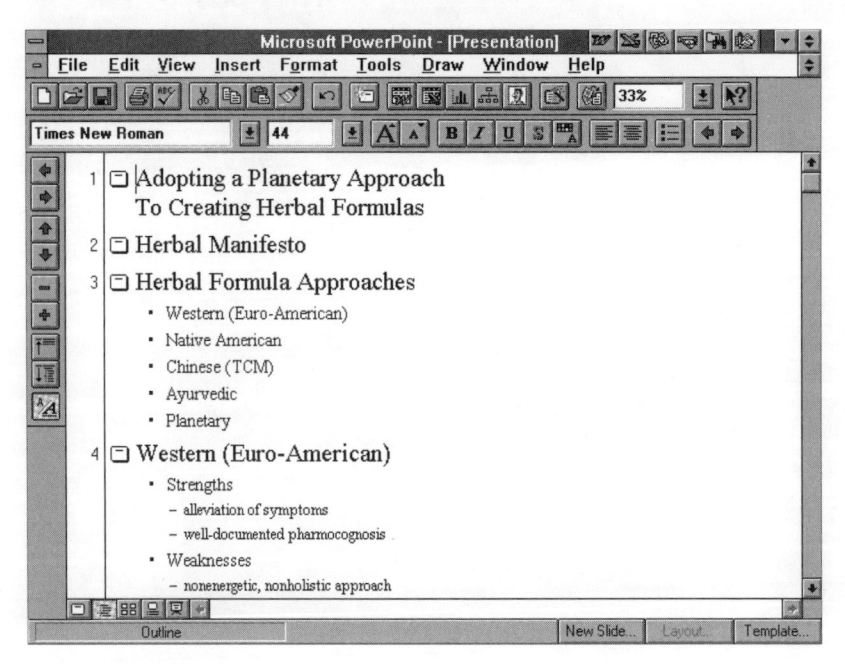

MAKING A POWERPOINT PRESENTATION FROM A WORD OUTLINE • 153

PRACTICE YOUR SKILLS

1. Save the presentation as **mywrdout** as a reminder that you created this file from a Word outline.
2. Scroll through the outline, and observe its contents.
3. Switch between **Word** and **PowerPoint**, and observe how PowerPoint decided to handle the data it received from the Word document. Are the bullets the same or different? What about the type size? Notice that the Word outline's two centered headings have each been assigned a slide. What happened to the text directly below them?
4. Display the presentation in **Slide view**, and display slides 1 and 2. You can see that, although the Word outline's centered headings were converted appropriately, the centered text directly below them was not converted (see Figures 9.5 and 9.6).

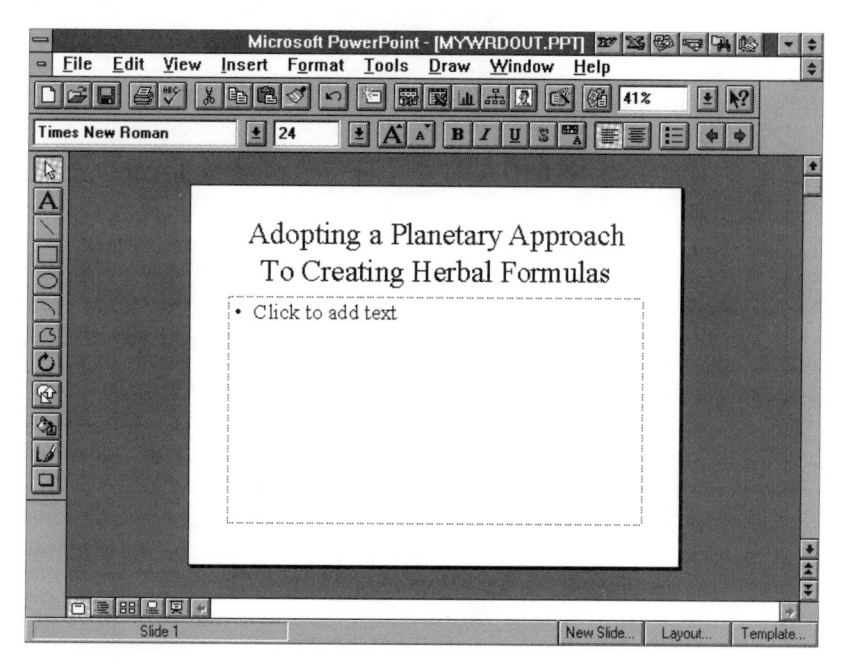

Figure 9.5 **Slide 1 of MYWRDOUT.PPT**

154 • CHAPTER 9: ADDITIONAL OFFICE TECHNIQUES

Figure 9.6   **Slide 2 of MYWRDOUT.PPT**

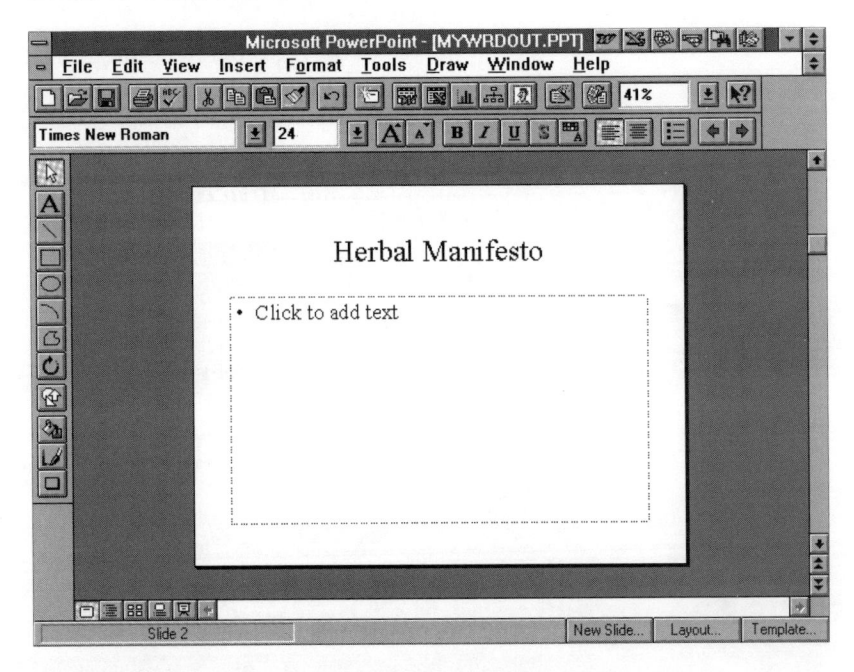

5. Examine the rest of the slides in the presentation.

6. Switch to **Word**, and remove the **Microsoft** toolbar. (**Hint:** Use the toolbar shortcut menu.)

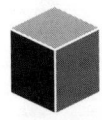

EDITING THE CONVERTED OUTLINE IN POWERPOINT

As you might have already guessed, once you've used Present It to create the PowerPoint presentation from your Word outline, you can use standard PowerPoint editing procedures to change or enhance the slides and their text in any way you wish.

PRACTICE YOUR SKILLS

Let's edit slides 1 and 2, and then we'll experiment with enhancing the slides:

1. Add the missing text to slides 1 and 2. (**Hint:** One easy method is to copy and paste it. Paste the text directly to the bulleted list object on each slide.)

2. Remove the bullets from the bulleted text on slides 1 and 2. (**Hint:** Use the **Bullets On/Off** button.)

3. Center the new text on slide 1, and then size and position the text object until the text roughly matches Figure 9.7.

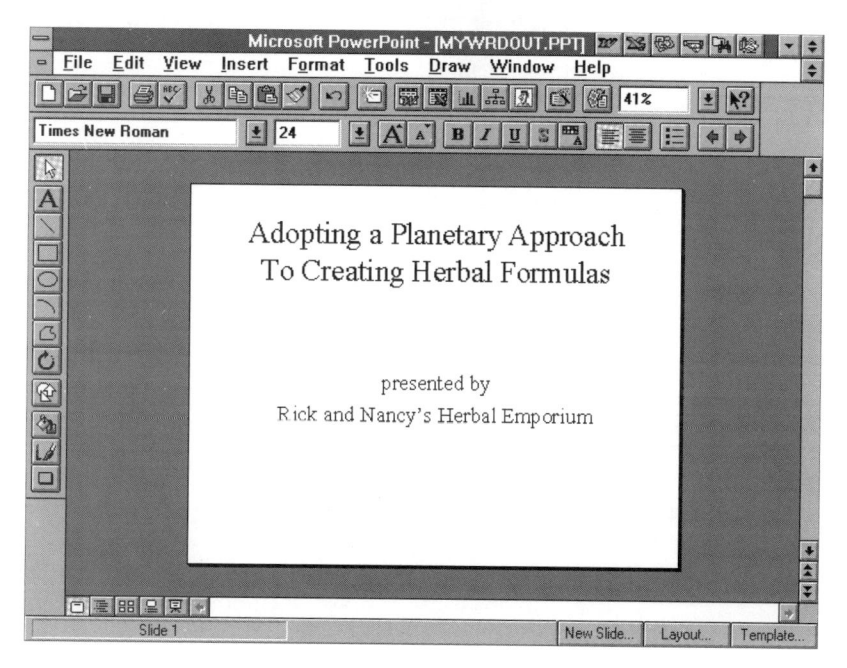

Figure 9.7   **The sized and moved text on slide 1**

4. Repeat step 3 for slide 2, and compare your screen to Figure 9.8.

5. Use your PowerPoint skills to enhance the presentation in any way you wish. For example, you might change the color and size of slide text; or you might add some fill, or change the color of the slides themselves.

6. When you've completed your enhancements, save and close the file.

7. Exit Word.

Figure 9.8   **The sized and moved text on slide 2**

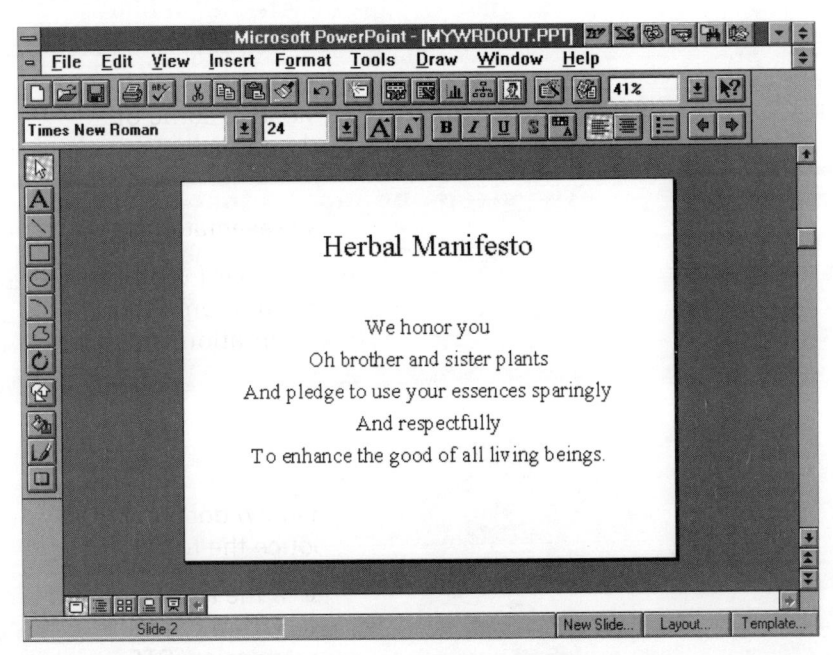

MAKING A WORD DOCUMENT FROM POWERPOINT TEXT

PowerPoint's Report It feature allows you to convert all the text in a presentation to a Word document. Report It converts a copy of the text, leaving the original PowerPoint presentation intact. Though the font of the text remains the same after conversion, its size is adjusted to one more appropriate to a Word document. (You've no doubt noticed that the default size of, say, title text on a PowerPoint slide is 44 points, which is quite large.) Text alignment is retained in the conversion, as well as any bullets and/or numbers.

Note: It's important to bear in mind that Report It converts only the text of a presentation; graphic objects are completely ignored in the conversion.

To create a Word document from a PowerPoint presentation, click on the Report It button in PowerPoint's standard toolbar.

MAKING A WORD DOCUMENT FROM POWERPOINT TEXT • 157

Let's open and take a look at a new presentation:

1. In the OFFWORK directory, open **pppres.ppt**.

2. Display each slide in the presentation. Notice that its text is quite similar to those of some of the other presentation files we've looked at. In particular, notice the alignment of text on each slide.

Now, let's convert this presentation's text to a Word document:

1. In PowerPoint's standard toolbar, click on the **Report It** button (shown here). Momentarily, Word is run, and the text from our presentation is displayed in a new Word document.

2. Scroll through the new document, shown in the printout in Figure 9.9, and notice the following features:

   - The file's name in the title bar is PPPRES.RTF. Report It has used the *PPPRES* from the name of the presentation file, and added the extension *RTF*, which stands for Rich Text Format. PowerPoint uses this file format so that the text formatting in a presentation can be retained.

   - Text alignment has been retained. Text that was centered on the slide remains centered in the Word document; text that was left-aligned remains left-aligned.

   - The bullets have been carried over to the Word document.

   - All the slide titles are displayed bold in the Word document.

   - All the slide titles are the same size, except for the first one, which is somewhat smaller.

3. Return to the PowerPoint presentation, and examine the difference in point size between the title of slide 1 and the title of slide 2. Notice that slide 1's title is 40 points, while that of slide 2 is 44 points. You can see that PowerPoint converted the text relative to its original size.

Figure 9.9   **Printout of PPPRES.RTF**

Adopting a Planetary Approach
To Creating Herbal Formulas
                          presented by

                Rick and Nancy's Herbal Emporium

Herbal Manifesto
We honor you
Oh brother and sister plants
And pledge to use your essences sparingly
And respectfully
To enhance the good of all living beings.

Herbal Formula Approaches
- Western (Euro-American)
- Native American
- Chinese (TCM)
- Ayurvedic
- Planetary

Western (Euro-American)
- Strengths
  - alleviation of symptoms
  - well-documented pharmocognosis
- Weaknesses
  - nonenergetic, nonholistic approach
  - nontreatment of underlying cause

Native American
- Strengths
  - availability of herbs (wildcrafting)
  - spiritual foundation
- Weaknesses
  - lack of documentation
  - loses efficacy when separated from spiritual context

Chinese (TCM)
- Strengths
  - energetic, holistic approach
  - 5,000-year tradition
  - good documentation
- Weaknesses
  - nonavailability of certain herbs
  - complexity of therapeutic approach

Ayurvedic
- Strengths
  - energetic, holistic approach
  - 5,000-year tradition
  - spiritual foundation
- Weaknesses
  - documentation not so good
  - too exotic for Westerners ?

Planetary

Figure 9.9   Printout of PPPRES.RTF (Continued)

- Strengths
  - eclecticism: take "best" from all available herbal approaches
  - substitution: if an herb is not available, use an equivalent herb
- Weaknesses
  - confusion resulting from eclectic approach
  - intercultural clash

EDITING THE CONVERTED TEXT IN WORD

Of course, once you've converted the text of the PowerPoint presentation into a Word document, you can use standard Word editing and other techniques to manipulate the document as you see fit. If you intend to use the converted text strictly within the context of Word, it's probably a good idea to save the file with the .DOC (standard Word document) extension. If you intend to use the document in another application that does not handle .DOC files, and wish to retain the document's text formatting, you can retain (or resave it in) the .RTF format.

If you intend to eventually reconvert the Word document to a PowerPoint presentation, you have the option of either retaining the .RTF format or saving the file in .DOC format; either format will convert accurately.

Note: Keep in mind that, upon conversion, the document has not yet been saved. To retain the converted version, you must save the file using Save (to save it with the .RTF extension) or Save As.

PRACTICE YOUR SKILLS

Edit the Word document using the guidelines that follow:

1. Change the font, style, and alignment of text (where appropriate). For the sake of clarity, use the same text enhancements for each heading level.
2. Save the file as **mypppres.doc**.
3. Create a PowerPoint presentation from MYPPPRES.DOC. (**Hint:** Use Word's Present It feature.)
4. Save the new presentation as **mypppres.ppt**.
5. Compare your new presentation to PPPRES.PPT. Which do you like better?
6. Close both presentations; then exit PowerPoint.
7. Close MYPPPRES.DOC.

CHANGING THE DEFAULT POSITION OF THE OFFICE TOOLBAR

In Chapter 7, you learned how to change the position of the Office toolbar by dragging. However, using the dragging technique does

CHANGING THE DEFAULT POSITION OF THE OFFICE TOOLBAR • 161

not change its *default* position, which is the position at which it is located every time Office is started. Furthermore, you could not use that technique to change the position of the toolbar when it was at its smallest size.

You can, however, change the left/right default position of the toolbar. The instruction that tells Windows where to place the Office toolbar is located in the WINDOWS directory, in a file named MSOFFICE.INI. This file contains the instructions that tell Windows how to deal with the Office program.

To change the default position of the toolbar:

- Exit Office and Word, if necessary.
- In the Windows Program Manager, open the group *Microsoft Office*, if necessary.
- Double-click on the *Microsoft Word* program icon to start Word.
- In Word, open the file *MSOFFICE.INI*, located in the WINDOWS directory.
- Under [Options], change the *RightPos* value as desired. This value gives the distance of the toolbar from the right edge of the Windows desktop; the greater the number, the greater the distance, and the lesser the number, the lesser the distance.
- Save and close the file.
- Start *Office* to view the result.

Let's change the default position of the Office toolbar:

1. Take a look at the current location of the Office toolbar. (It's a bit easier to judge the position of the toolbar in relation to an application window.)
2. Exit Word. Again, notice the position of the Office toolbar in relation to the Windows desktop.
3. Exit Office.
4. In the Program Manager, double-click on the **Microsoft Office** program group to open its window, if necessary.

162 • CHAPTER 9: ADDITIONAL OFFICE TECHNIQUES

5. Double-click on the **Microsoft Word** program icon (shown selected in Figure 9.10) to start Word.

6. Open the **msoffice.ini** file, located in your WINDOWS directory.

Figure 9.10 **The selected Microsoft Word program icon**

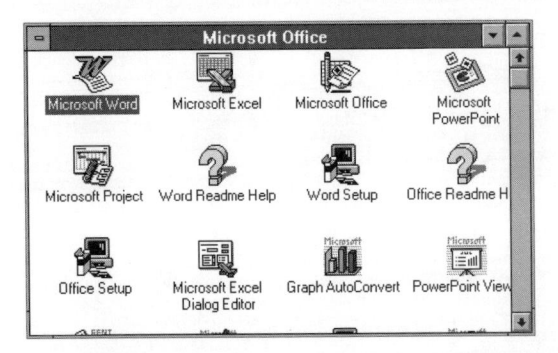

7. Scroll through the file. Notice that the lines of instruction are separated into five groups. You can see that the RightPos instruction line is the last line in the [Options] group. The current, default, value is *48* pixels (see Figure 9.11). A *pixel* is a unit used to measure screen position.

Figure 9.11 **The [Options] section of the MSOFFICE.INI file**

```
[Options]
ShowCueCard=2
UseLargeBtn=2
AlwaysOnTop=1
ShowToolTip=1
ShowTitle=0
RightPos=48
```

8. Change the RightPos value to **96**.

9. Save and close the file.

10. Minimize the Word window.

11. Start **Office** (in the Microsoft Office program group, double-click on the **Microsoft Office** program icon). Notice the current position of the Office toolbar. It is now much farther—

twice the distance, to be precise—from the right edge of the desktop.

12. Maximize the Word window. Here you can better judge the change in the Office toolbar's location. Compare the position of your Office toolbar to that in Figure 9.12.

Figure 9.12   **The Office toolbar, 96 pixels from the right edge of the screen**

PRACTICE YOUR SKILLS

1. Change the location of the Office toolbar to **384** pixels from the right edge of the screen. (**Hint:** Don't forget to exit Word *and* Office before you do anything else!)
2. Close the MSOFFICE.INI file, and compare the position of your Office toolbar to that in Figure 9.13.

Figure 9.13   **The Office toolbar, 384 pixels from the right edge of the screen**

3. Return the Office toolbar to its original location (**48** pixels from the right edge of the screen).
4. Exit Word.

SUMMARY

In this chapter, you learned how to make PowerPoint slides from a Word outline, and how to import a PowerPoint outline into Word. You also learned how to change the default position of the Office toolbar.

Here's a quick reference for the Office techniques you learned in this chapter:

Desired Result	How to Do It
Create PowerPoint presentation from Word outline	Open Word document that you wish to use to create your presentation; display Microsoft toolbar; click on **Present It** button
Create Word document from PowerPoint presentation text	Click on **Report It** button in PowerPoint standard toolbar
Change default position of Office toolbar	Exit Office and Word, if necessary; in Windows Program Manager, open **Microsoft Office** group; double-click on **Microsoft Word** program icon; open MSOFFICE.INI, located in WINDOWS directory; under [Options], change RightPos value as desired; save and close file; start **Office**

In the next chapter, you will learn how to use Office's electronic-mail application, Microsoft Mail.

CHAPTER 10: WORKING WITH MICROSOFT MAIL

An Important Note on Installing Microsoft Mail

Starting Microsoft Mail

Reading an Inbox Message

Deleting an Inbox Message

Creating and Sending a Message

Working with Folders

Forwarding a Message

Replying to a Message

Using Mail to Share Files

In this chapter, we'll present you with a miniprimer on Microsoft Mail. You'll learn how to send and receive Mail messages and how to share your files with other Mail (or compatible mail-program) users.

When you're done working through this chapter, you will know

- How to start Mail manually and automatically
- How to create, send, read, delete, forward, and reply to Mail messages
- How to work with Mail folders
- How to use Mail to share files

Note: Unlike the preceding nine, this chapter does not contain any hands-on activities. It does, however, contain several general procedures with instructions for performing standard Microsoft Mail tasks.

AN IMPORTANT NOTE ON INSTALLING MICROSOFT MAIL

If Microsoft Mail is not already installed on your computer, please have your system administrator install it. **Do not attempt to install Mail yourself!** There are just too many potential pitfalls in the installation procedure. You wouldn't want to get started on the wrong foot, now, would you?

Note: You must install Microsoft Mail using the *server version* of *Microsoft Mail for PC Networks* to use Mail with your other Office applications. This installation does not come with Office; you can order it from Microsoft customer service or your Microsoft Office retailer.

STARTING MICROSOFT MAIL

You can start Mail manually or automatically. When you start Mail *manually*, you must enter your mailbox name and your password; when you start Mail *automatically*, Mail enters your name and password for you.

Note: To start mail, you must know your mailbox name and password. For help, ask your system administrator.

STARTING MAIL MANUALLY

To start Mail manually,

- Use any of the following methods to launch Mail:
    - Click on the *Microsoft Mail* button in the Office toolbar (as shown in Figure 10.1).

Figure 10.1   The Microsoft Mail button

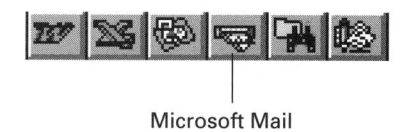

Microsoft Mail

- Or click on the *Microsoft Office* button in the Office toolbar to open the Office menu, and then choose *Microsoft Mail* from this menu.
- Or double-click on the *Microsoft Mail* icon in Program Manager.
- The Sign In dialog box appears. In the Name text box, type your mailbox name.
- In the Password text box, type your password.
- Press *Enter*.

If your Office toolbar does not include a Microsoft Mail button, you can use the Customize command to add it to the toolbar (for help, see Chapter 7). Likewise, if your Office menu does not include a Microsoft Mail command, you can use Customize to add it to the menu (for help, see Chapter 7).

STARTING MAIL AUTOMATICALLY

To configure Mail to start automatically, you must edit the *Command Line property* of your Microsoft Mail icon as follows:

- Select the *Microsoft Mail* icon (in Program Manager).
- Choose *File, Properties* to open the Program Item Properties dialog box.
- Press *Tab*, and then press *End* to move the insertion point to the end of the Command Line text box.
- Type a space, and then type your mailbox name.
- Type another space, and then type your password.
- Your Command Line text should now be of the form

```
drive:\path\msmail.exe mailboxname password
```

where *drive:\path\msmail.exe* is the path name of your executable Mail program file, *mailboxname* is your mailbox name, and *password* is your password. For example, if the path name of your Mail executable program file were *c:\msmail\msmail.exe*, your mailbox name were *rickscott*, and your password were *astragalus*, your Command Line text would be

```
c:\msmail\msmail.exe rickscott astragalus
```

- Click on *OK*.

Once you've modified your Microsoft Mail icon Command Line property as described earlier, you can use any of the following methods to start Mail automatically (without having to enter your mailbox name or password):

- Click on the *Microsoft Mail* button in the Office toolbar.

- Or click on the *Microsoft Office* button to open the Office menu, and then choose *Microsoft Mail* from this menu.

- Or double-click on the *Microsoft Mail* icon in Program Manager.

READING AN INBOX MESSAGE

When you start Mail, it opens your *Inbox*, a folder that contains the Mail messages you've received. Observe our sample Inbox in Figure 10.2. Note that its *message headers* show salient information for each message: whom it's *from*, its *subject*, and the date and time it was *received*. Each message's *priority* is also shown: *high* (preceded by an *!*, see *Administrator* and *Nancy Double...* in Figure 10.2); *normal* (preceded by a blank, see the remaining four messages in Figure 10.2); or *low* (not shown in Figure 10.2). A message's priority conveys its relative urgency to the recipient.

To read an Inbox message by using the mouse,

- Double-click on the message.

To read an Inbox message by using the keyboard,

- Select the message (by using *Tab* to activate the message headers, then using the *Up Arrow* and *Down Arrow* keys to select the message), and press *Enter*.

Figure 10.2   **Our sample Inbox**

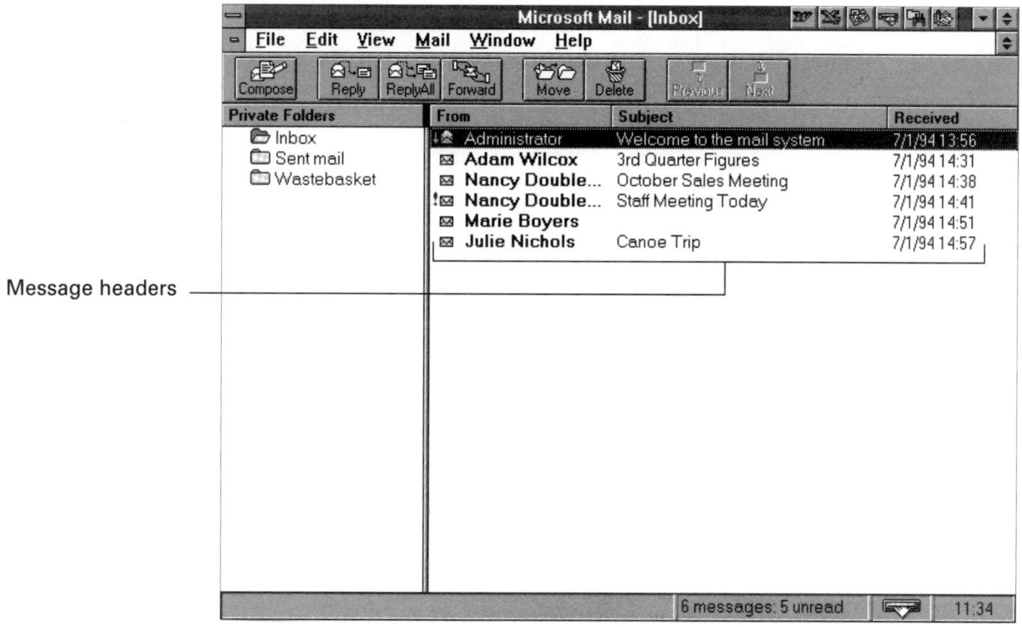

Message headers

Both methods display the selected message in a *Read Note form*, as shown in Figure 10.3. The *message heading* (the gray area at the top of the Read Note form) shows the following information for the message: *from* whom it was sent, the *date* it was sent, *to* whom it was sent, to whom it was *Cc*ed (carbon-copied), and its *subject*.

DELETING AN INBOX MESSAGE

To keep your Inbox streamlined and up to date, you should make it a habit to delete messages you've read and no longer need. To delete an Inbox message,

- If the Inbox is displayed—rather than a Read Note form—select the message with your mouse or keyboard, and then click on the *Delete* button (as shown in Figure 10.2) or choose *File, Delete*. Or, drag the message over to the Wastebasket folder.

- If a Read Note form is displayed, click on the *Delete* button or choose *File, Delete*. After deleting the message, Mail automatically displays your next unread Inbox message, as shown in Figure 10.4.

172 • CHAPTER 10: WORKING WITH MICROSOFT MAIL

Figure 10.3   **Reading an Inbox message**

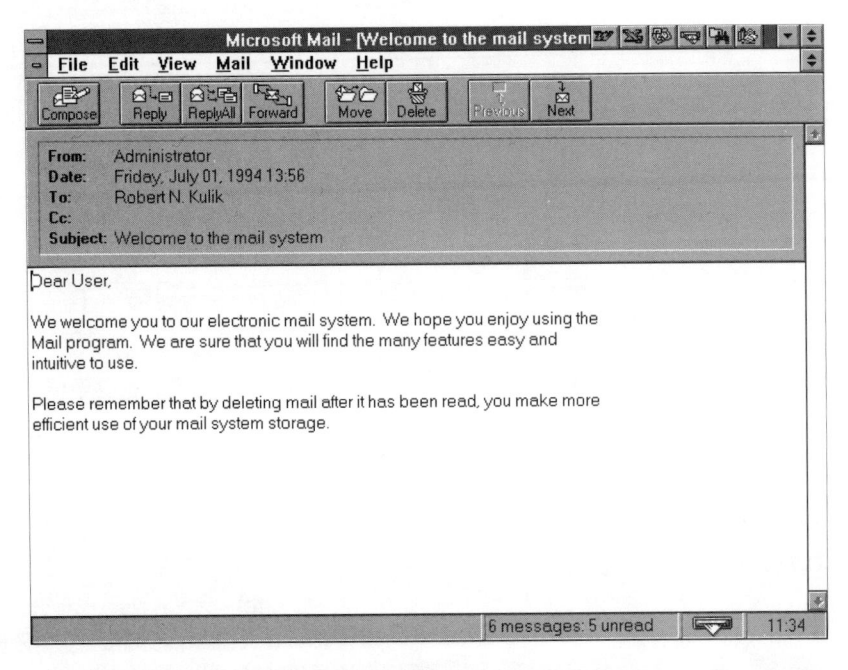

Figure 10.4   **Next unread Inbox message**

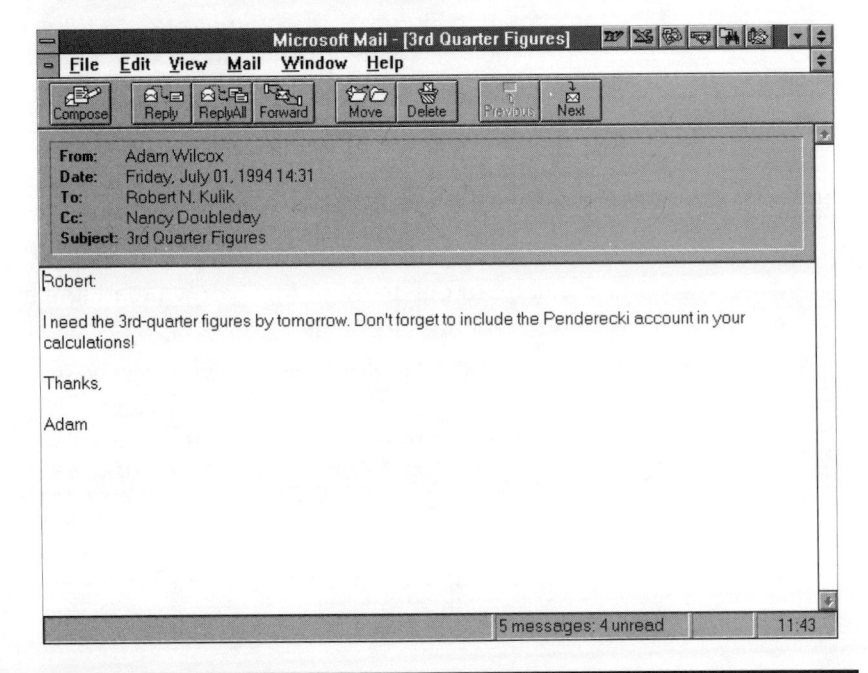

THE METAPHYSICS OF DELETION

When you delete a message, it's not actually deleted from your mailbox—at least not right away. Instead, the deleted message is moved to the *Wastebasket*, a special folder that serves as a "way station" to actual deletion, a "Twilight Zone" between digital being and nothingness. You can retrieve messages that you've banished to the Wastebasket at your leisure, provided that the Wastebasket has not yet been "emptied." Normally, your Wastebasket is emptied every time you exit Mail; your Mail program may, however, be set up to do otherwise.

CREATING AND SENDING A MESSAGE

Here are the general steps for creating and sending a message,

- Open a Send Note form.
- Address the message.
- Specify the message subject.
- Write the message.
- Set the send options, if desired.
- Send the message.

Let's tackle these steps one by one.

OPENING A SEND NOTE FORM

To open a Send Note form, as shown in Figure 10.5,

- Click on the *Compose* button, or choose *Mail, Compose Note*.

ADDRESSING THE MESSAGE

To address a message,

- In the Send Note form, click on the *Address* button to open the Address dialog box, as shown in Figure 10.6. Note that individual user names (Adam Wilcox, Administrator, and so on) are displayed in regular letters, while group names (*Consulting* and *Everyone*) are bolded.

Figure 10.5   **The Send Note form**

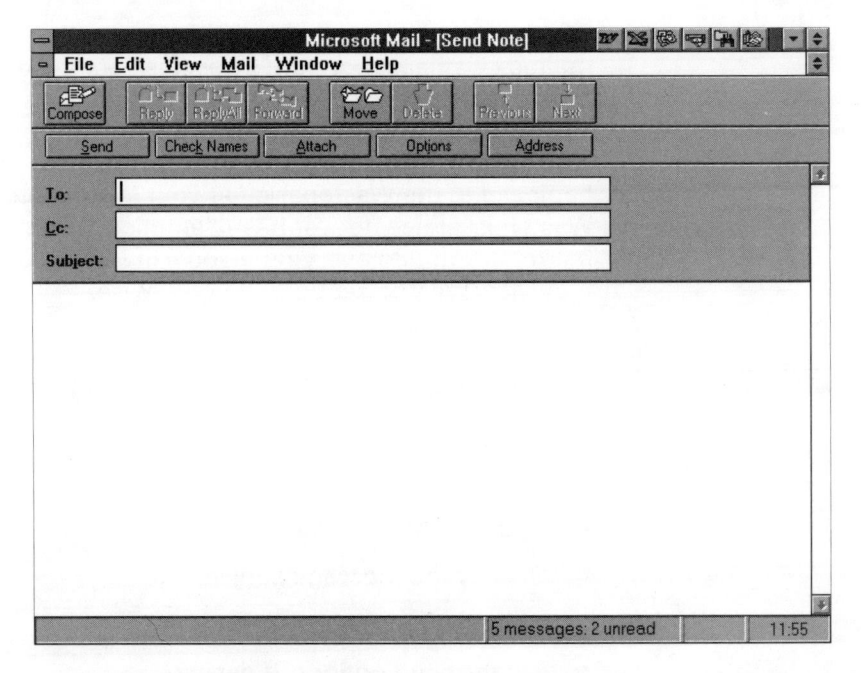

Figure 10.6   **The Address dialog box**

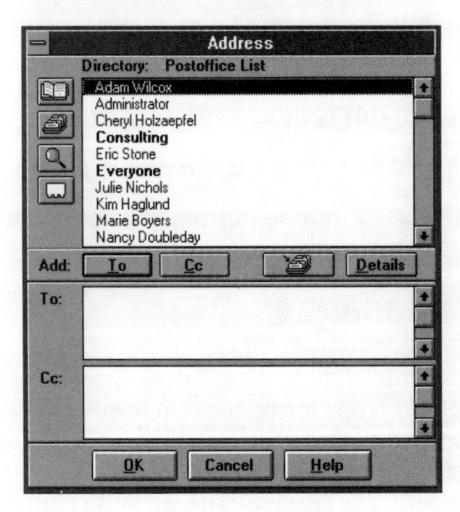

CREATING AND SENDING A MESSAGE • 175

- Use either of the following methods to select your desired recipient (the individual or group to whom you want to send the message):

    - Use your mouse or arrow keys to scroll to the recipient's name.

    - Or, type the first few characters of the recipient's name to jump directly to that name.

- Click on the *To* button to add your selected recipient to the To box. Or, click on the *Cc* button to add your selected recipient to the Cc box.

- To specify additional recipients, repeat the preceding two steps. Figure 10.7 shows two To recipients and three Cc recipients.

- Click on *OK*. The Send Note form reappears with your recipient name(s) displayed in the To and Cc boxes.

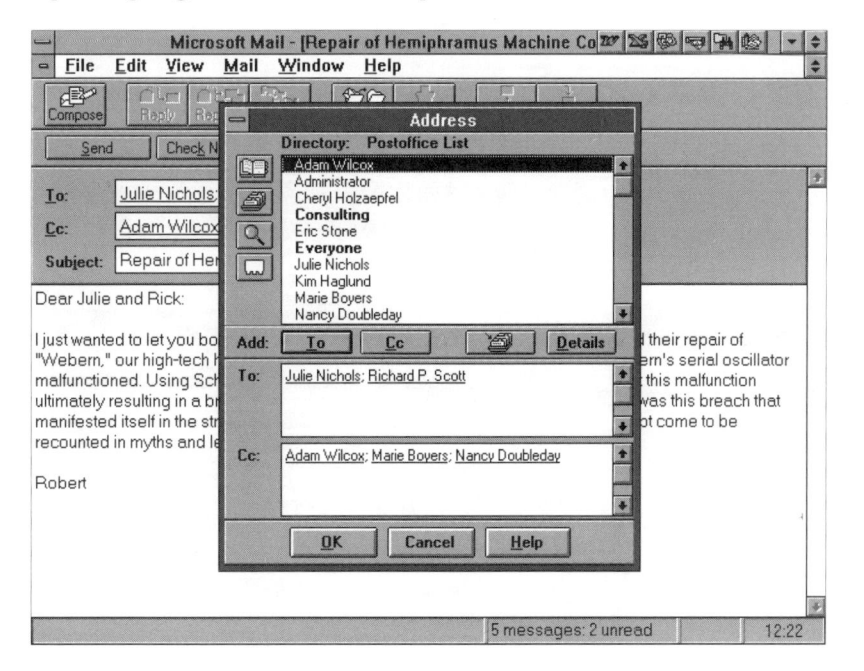

Figure 10.7 **Specifying To and Cc recipients**

SPECIFYING THE MESSAGE SUBJECT

To specify the message subject,

- In the Send Note form, activate the Subject box.
- Type the desired message subject.

WRITING THE MESSAGE

To write the message,

- Place the insertion point in the *message body* of the Send Note form (as shown in Figure 10.8) by pressing *Tab* or by clicking anywhere within the message body.
- Type your message. Should you need to edit, Mail provides the standard text-editing features.

Figure 10.8 shows a completed message, with To, Cc, and Subject information and the message itself. Please take this opportunity to study it carefully.

Figure 10.8 **The completed message**

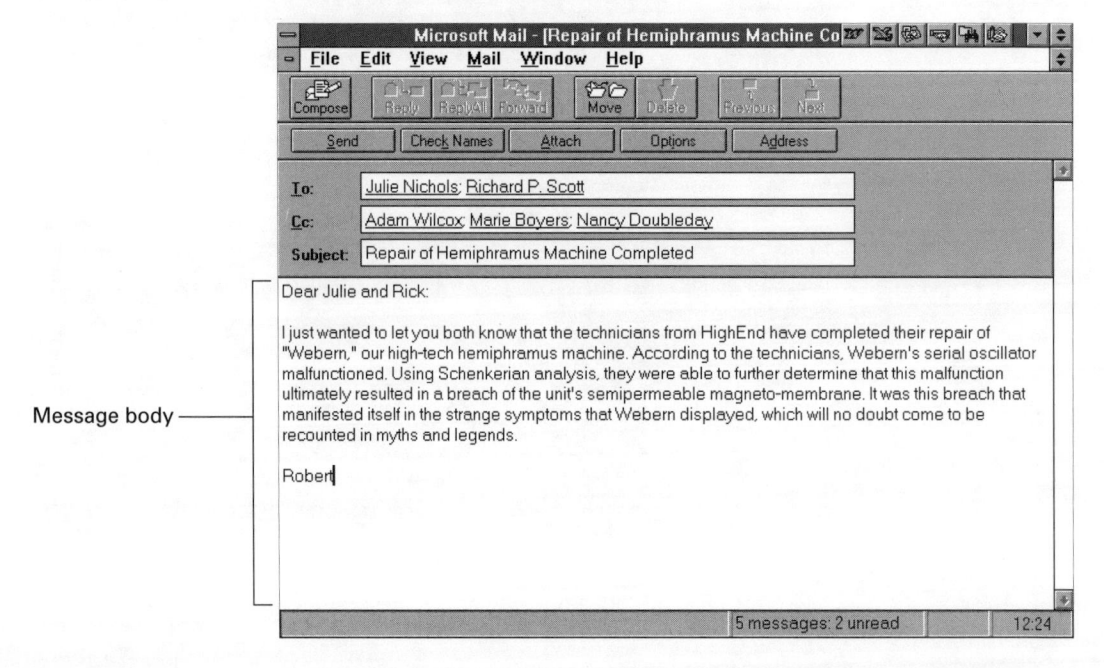

SETTING THE SEND OPTIONS

Mail provides three send options:

- *Return Receipt* deposits a receipt in your mailbox informing you that a recipient has received your message. You use Return Receipt to verify the delivery of important messages.
- *Save Sent Messages* saves a copy of your sent message in a special folder called *Sent Mail*.
- *Priority* determines if the message is sent with *high*, *normal*, or *low* priority. These are subjective indicators used to alert recipients to the relative urgency of the message.

To set the send options,

- In the Send Note form, click on the *Options* button to open the Options dialog box, shown in Figure 10.9.

Figure 10.9 **The Options dialog box**

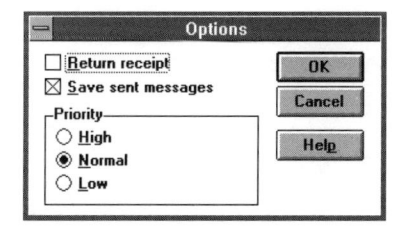

- Set your desired options.
- Click on *OK*.

Note: You do not *need* to set the send options. You can, instead, skip this procedure and leave your send options in their current settings.

SENDING THE MESSAGE

Your final step in the message-creation-and-sending process is to send the completed message. To do this,

- Click on the *Send* button.

WORKING WITH FOLDERS

Folders are containers in which messages are stored, such as the Inbox or Wastebasket. Mail provides two types of folders:

- *Private* folders, which are usually stored on your hard disk, but may also be stored on your postoffice, are for your use only.

- *Shared* folders, which are always stored in your postoffice, and—depending on which access permissions they are assigned—can be shared either by all members of a selected postoffice group or by anyone on the network.

PERMANENT FOLDERS

Mail provides several *permanent* folders that you cannot delete from your mailbox. These include Inbox, Sent Mail, and Wastebasket, as shown in the Private Folders pane on the left side of the screen in Figure 10.10. Note that the Sent Mail folder is selected—as indicated by its open folder icon and the *[Sent mail]* appended to *Microsoft Mail* in the application title bar—and that its contents are displayed (in this case, just one message to Julie Nicho…).

OPENING AN EXISTING FOLDER

To open an existing folder,

- Double-click on the folder. Its contents are displayed in the Message Headers pane.

CREATING A NEW FOLDER

To create a new folder,

- Choose *File, New Folder* to open the New Folder dialog box, as shown in Figure 10.11.

- In the Name box, type your desired folder name.

- Under Type, select *Private* or *Shared*.

- To assign access permissions to a shared folder, click on the *Options* button, and then select your desired permissions in the Other Users Can box.

Figure 10.10 **The Sent Mail folder**

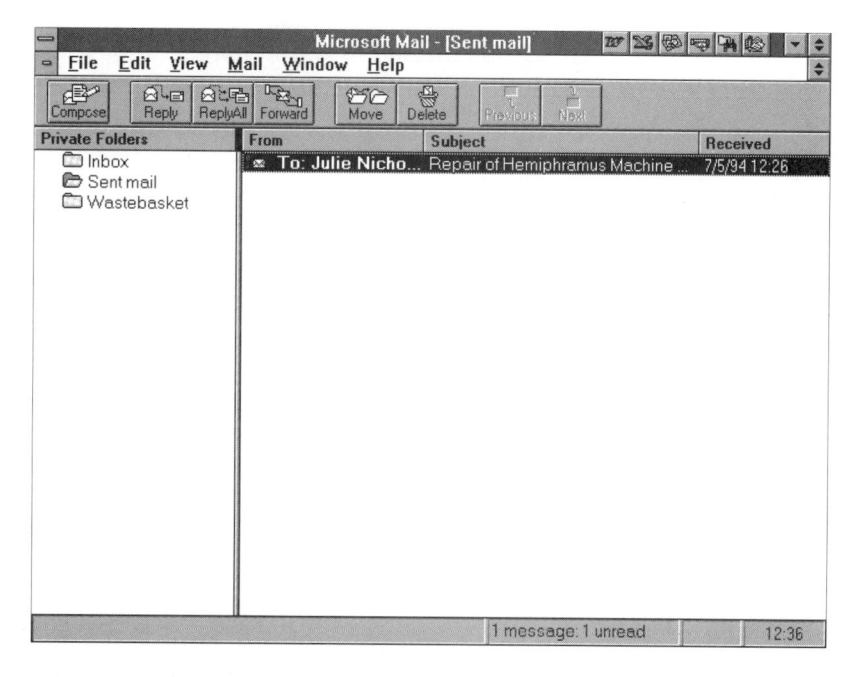

Figure 10.11 **The New Folder dialog box**

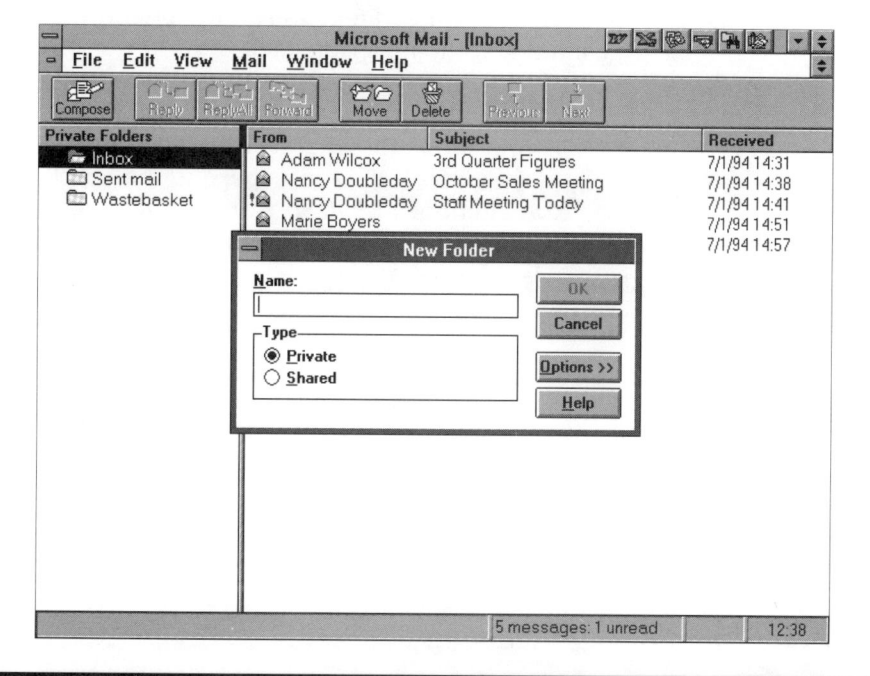

- Click on *OK*.

Note: Just as you can create subdirectories within directories, you can create subfolders within folders. Interested readers should refer to their Mail documentation or on-line Help.

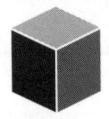

DELETING A FOLDER

To delete a folder,

- Select the folder.
- Click on the *Delete* button, or choose *File, Delete*.

You cannot delete a folder that contains one or more subfolders; you must delete all the subfolders first. You can, however, delete a (sub)folder that contains messages; before doing so, make sure the (sub)folder doesn't contain any messages you want to save.

FORWARDING A MESSAGE

When you *forward* a message, you send a copy of the message to another user. The forwarded message is identified by its message header, which reads FORWARDED FROM followed by your user name. You can add text above the forwarded message, but you cannot edit the message itself.

To forward a message,

- If your Inbox (or whatever folder contains the message) is displayed, select the message, and then click on the *Forward* button or choose *Mail, Forward*. If the message itself is displayed (in a Read Note form), click on the *Forward* button or choose *Mail, Forward*.
- In the To box, specify your desired recipient(s) of the forwarded message (Cheryl Holzaepfel in Figure 10.12).
- Type any desired text before the forwarded message in the message body (as shown in Figure 10.12).
- Click on the *Send* button.

Figure 10.12 **Forwarding a message**

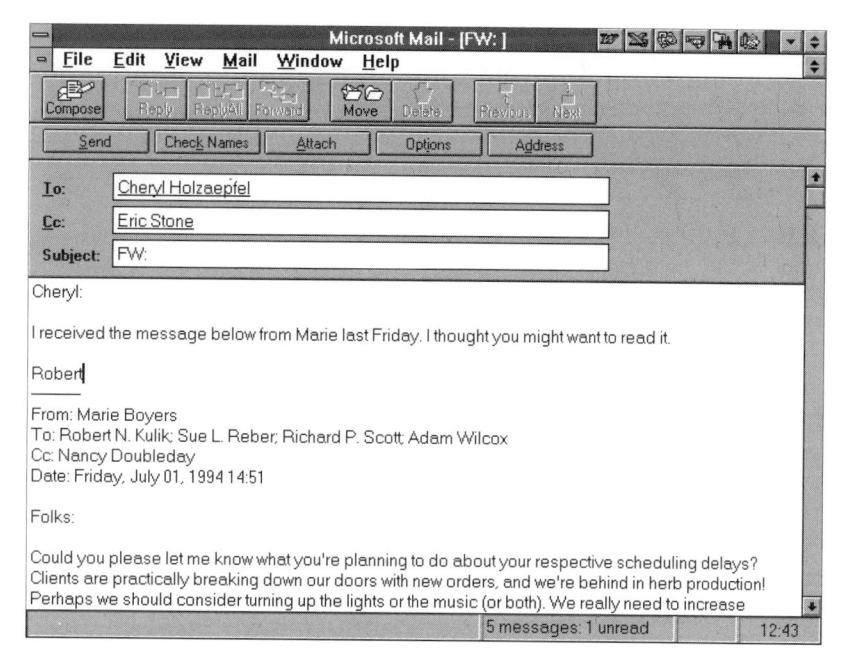

REPLYING TO A MESSAGE

To send a reply to the person who sent you a message,

- Click on the *Reply* button, or choose *Mail, Reply*. A Send Note form appears, as shown in Figure 10.13. The name of the original sender is in the To box, and the title of the original message is in the Subject box (preceded by *RE:*, which stands for *Reply* or *with Regard to*). The original message appears below a solid line (see Figure 10.13); you cannot edit this message.

- Type your reply above the original message, as shown in Figure 10.13.

- Click on the *Send* button.

Figure 10.13   **Replying to a message**

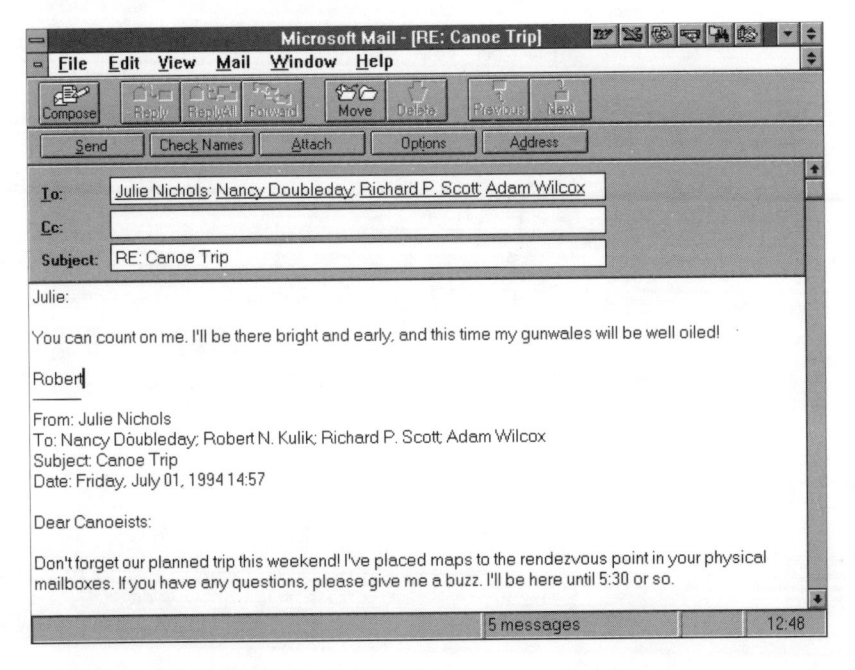

![Microsoft Mail - RE: Canoe Trip window showing reply composition with To: Julie Nichols; Nancy Doubleday; Richard P. Scott; Adam Wilcox, Subject: RE: Canoe Trip, and message text beginning "Julie: You can count on me. I'll be there bright and early, and this time my gunwales will be well oiled! Robert" followed by the original message from Julie Nichols.]

USING MAIL TO SHARE FILES

Up to now, we've shown you how to use Mail to send and receive messages created within Mail. You can also use Mail to share files created outside of Mail. Here's how:

- You can send a file to another Mail (or compatible-program) user by *attaching* the file to a message, and then sending the message. You can use this technique to send *any* accessible file on your hard disk or network.

- You can send a file to another Mail (or compatible-program) user by sending the file from its source application. You can use this technique to send *only* those files whose source applications contain a File, Send command.

SENDING A FILE BY ATTACHING IT TO A MESSAGE

To attach a file to a message,

- Click on the *Compose* button, or choose *Mail, Compose*.

USING MAIL TO SHARE FILES • 183

- Place the insertion point in the body of the message at the point where you want the attached file icon to appear.
- Click on the *Attach* button to open the Attach dialog box.
- In the File Name box, type the path name of the file you want to attach. Or, select the file by using the Drives and Directories boxes.
- Click on the *Attach* button.
- To attach additional files, repeat the above steps.

To send the message and attached file(s),

- Simply send the message as usual.

Figure 10.14 shows a Word file, WORDOUT.DOC, attached to a message. Note the WORDOUT.DOC attached file icon. Note also that the message's To, Cc, and Subject fields are not filled in yet.

Figure 10.14   Attaching a Word file to a message

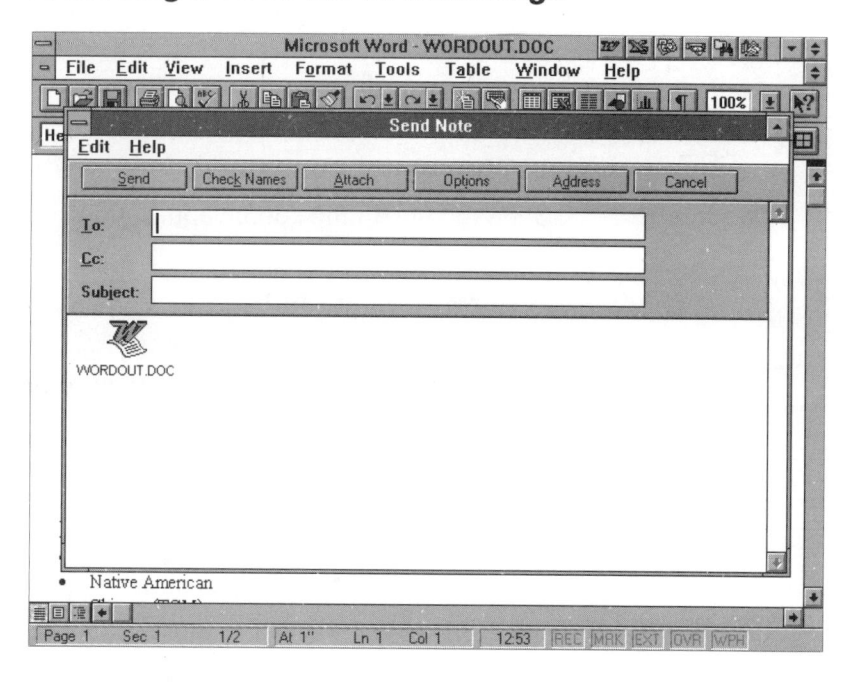

SENDING A FILE FROM ITS SOURCE APPLICATION

As mentioned, you can send a file to another Mail (or compatible-program) user from within the file's source application, only if the source application contains a File, Send command. (When you install Mail, your trio of Office programs—Excel, PowerPoint, and Word—should all contain File, Send commands.) You use a different method to send a file to a single recipient or to several recipients, as explained in the following sections.

Sending a File to a Single Recipient

To send a file from its source application to a single recipient,

- Open the file (in the source application).

- Choose *File, Send*.

- In the To box, specify the recipient name.

- In the Message Text box, type any text you want to accompany the file.

- Send the message.

Routing a File to Several Recipients

To send—or *route*—a file from its source application to several recipients,

- Open the file (in the source application).

- Choose *File, Routing Slip* to open the Routing Slip dialog box, as shown in Figure 10.15.

- In the To box, specify the recipients' names. In the Message Text box, type any text you want to accompany the file.

- Click on *Add Slip*.

- Send the message.

Figure 10.15 **The Routing Slip dialog box**

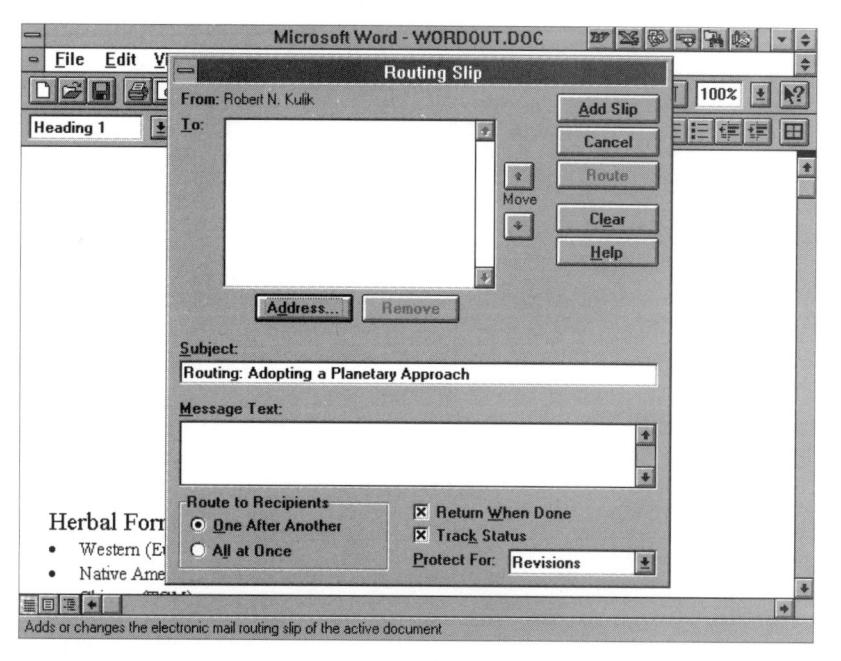

Here's a quick reference for the techniques you learned in this chapter:

Desired Result	How to Do It
Start Mail	In Office toolbar, click on **Microsoft Mail** button or choose **Microsoft Mail** from Office menu, or double-click on **Microsoft Mail** icon in Program Manager; if prompted, type mailbox name and password
Configure Mail to start automatically	Edit Command Line property of Microsoft Mail icon (in Program Manager) to form **drive:\path\msmail.exe mailboxname password**

Desired Result	How to Do It
Read Inbox message	Double-click on message, or select message with keyboard and press **Enter**
Delete Inbox message	If Inbox is displayed, select message and click on **Delete** button, or choose **File, Delete**, or drag message to **Wastebasket**; if Read Note form is displayed, click on **Delete** button or choose **File, Delete**
Create and send message	Open **Send Note** form; address message; specify message subject; write message; set desired send options; send message
Open Send Note form	Click on **Compose** button, or choose **Mail, Compose Note**
Address message	Click on **Address** button; select desired recipient (using mouse or arrow keys, or typing first few characters); click on **To** button or **Cc** button; repeat to specify additional recipients; click on **OK**
Specify message subject	Activate **Subject** box and type subject
Write message	Place insertion point in message body of Send Note form; type message
Set send options	Click on **Options** button; set desired options; click on **OK**
Send message	Click on **Send** button
Open existing folder	Double-click on folder
Create new folder	Choose **File, New Folder**; type desired folder name; select **Private** or **Shared**; to assign access permissions, click on **Options** button, then select desired permissions; click on **OK**
Delete folder	Select folder; click on **Delete** button or choose **File, Delete**

Desired Result	**How to Do It**
Forward message	If folder is displayed, select message, click on **Forward** button, or choose **Mail, Forward**; if Read Note form is displayed, click on **Forward** button, or choose **Mail, Forward**; specify desired recipient(s); type desired text; click on **Send** button
Send reply	Click on **Reply** button, or choose **Mail, Reply**; type reply; click on **Send** button
Attach file to message	Click on **Compose** button, or choose **Mail, Compose**; place insertion point where attached file icon is to appear; click on **Attach** button; type path name of file to attach, or select file using Drives and Directories boxes; click on **Attach** button; repeat preceding to attach additional files
Send message and attached file(s)	Send message as usual
Send file from source application to single recipient	Open file; choose **File, Send**; specify recipient name; type desired text; send message
Route file from source application to several recipients	Open file; choose **File, Routing Slip**; specify recipients' names; type desired text; click on **Add Slip**; send message

SUMMARY

In this chapter, we bestowed upon you a Mail miniprimer. You now know how to start Mail manually and automatically; how to create, send, read, delete, forward, and reply to messages; how to work with folders; and how to use Mail to share files.

Congratulations on completing this book and attaining Microsoft Office proficiency! It's been a long and sometimes arduous journey (remember linking?). But now you've arrived. May your Office toolbar and menu never fail you!

APPENDIX A: INSTALLING MICROSOFT OFFICE 4.2

Who This Appendix Is For

Installation Prerequisites

Installation Options

Installing Office 4.2 on Your Computer

Modifying Your Office Setup

In this appendix, we'll guide you through the process of installing Microsoft Office 4.2 on your computer.

WHO THIS APPENDIX IS FOR

If you intend to run Office from your personal computer's hard disk, this appendix is for you. Keep reading!

If, instead, you intend to run Office from your network, this appendix is *not* what you need. What you *do* need is to have your friendly network administrator set up your workstation to run Office. **Do not try to do this by yourself!**

INSTALLATION PREREQUISITES

Before you install Office 4.2, your system must have the following:

- MS-DOS 3.1 (or later)
- Any one of these Windows platforms:
    - Windows 3.1 (or later)
    - Windows for Workgroups 3.1 (or later)
    - Windows NT or Windows NT Advanced Server 3.1 (or later)
- A 386 (or higher) microprocessor
- 4 megabytes of RAM (to run one Office program at a time); 8 megabytes (to run two or more Office programs simultaneously)
- Microsoft Office Standard: approximately 21 megabytes of free hard-disk space (minimum installation); 49 megabytes (typical installation); 68 megabytes (maximum installation)
- Microsoft Office Professional: approximately 29 megabytes of free hard-disk space (minimum installation); 58 megabytes (typical installation); 82 megabytes (maximum installation)
- A 3½-inch high-density floppy disk drive or a 5¼-inch high-density drive
- A VGA (or higher resolution) video card and monitor
- A mouse or compatible tracking device

Note: To use Microsoft Mail with your other Office applications, you must install Mail using the *server version* of *Microsoft Mail for PC Networks*. This software does not come with Office; you can order it from Microsoft customer service or your Microsoft Office retailer.

INSTALLATION OPTIONS

Microsoft provides four options for installing Office 4.2:

- *Typical* installs the most often-used features of Office. It takes up less hard-disk space than the Complete installation.

- *Complete/Custom* allows you to install all the Office features (Complete), or to install only those features you desire (Custom). It's the most flexible installation option.

- *Laptop (Minimum)* installs the minimum features you need to run Office. It's ideal for laptop users with limited hard-disk space.

- *Workstation* installs the files you need on your workstation to be able to run Office from your network. It's only available if you're connected to a network on which Office is installed; ask your network administrator for help.

We chose the Typical option when installing Office 4.2 for this book.

INSTALLING OFFICE 4.2 ON YOUR COMPUTER

Okay, here we go:

1. If you are using a virus-detection utility, disable it before proceeding. You can reenable it when you're done installing Office.

2. Start **Windows**. Close all applications except Program Manager.

3. Procure your massive stack of Office Setup floppy disks, and insert **Office Setup Disk 1** in the appropriate floppy drive. If you are attempting to install Office from a network, **STOP NOW! Get your network administrator to perform the installation.**

4. In Program Manager, choose **File, Run** to open the Run dialog box. In the Command Line text box, type a command of the form

    drive:setup

    where *drive* is the drive in which you just inserted Office Setup Disk 1. For example, if you inserted your disk in drive A, you'd type

    a:setup

5. Click on the **OK** button to start the Setup program. Setup prompts you for some introductory information (your name, your Office ID number, and so on). Follow the on-screen instructions to give Setup what it needs. If you need help at any time during the installation process, click on the **Help** button.

6. Setup then prompts you for the installation option. Based on the descriptions in the previous section, "Installation Options," select your desired option.

7. If you select *Complete/Custom*, Setup prompts you for the Office components you want to install. Check/uncheck the check boxes of the components you want to install/not to install. To install part of a component, select it, click on the **Change Option** button, check/uncheck the subcomponents you want to install/not to install, and then click on **OK**. When you're done, click on **Continue**.

8. Respond to any additional Setup prompts.

MODIFYING YOUR OFFICE SETUP

You can modify your Office setup by rerunning the Setup program directly from your hard disk. The following options are available:

- *Add/Remove* allows you to add new components or remove existing components from your Office setup. For example, you could add or remove clip-art files or the entire PowerPoint application.

- *Reinstall* repeats your last installation and, in doing so, restores all missing files and settings. For example, if an Excel program file were damaged, you could use the Add/Remove option to remove Excel, and then use Reinstall to reinstall it.

- *Remove All* uninstalls all of Office. For example, if your Office applications were behaving bizarrely, you could use Remove All to uninstall all of Office, and then use Reinstall to reinstall Office.

Before you attempt to modify your Office setup, ponder these tips:

- Use the same Setup program to modify a component that you originally used to install that component. For example, if you installed Word by using the Office Setup program, use the Office Setup program to modify it. If, however, you installed Word by using its own Setup program, use this Setup program to modify it.

- If you are upgrading from a previous version of Office, you do not need to uninstall the existing version before installing the new one.

Follow these steps to modify your Office setup—that is, to add/remove Office components, reinstall Office components or all of Office, or uninstall all of Office:

1. If you are using a virus-detection utility, disable it. You can reenable it when you're done with this procedure.

2. If Office is installed on your computer's hard disk, click on the **Microsoft Office** button in the Office toolbar to open the Office menu, and then click on **Office Setup And Uninstall** in this menu. If you are running Office from a network, **STOP NOW! Get your network administrator to modify your Office setup.**

3. If one of your Office applications was set up separately from your other Office applications, Setup displays a dialog box to this effect. Select the Office application you want to change, and then click on **OK**.

4. In the Microsoft Office 4.2 Setup dialog box, click on your desired option: **Add/Remove**, **Reinstall**, or **Remove All**. (For information on these options, see the beginning of this section.)

5. If you clicked on Add/Remove, Setup prompts you for information on the component you want to add or remove.

    - To remove an *entire* component, uncheck its check box, make sure it's selected (highlighted), and then click on *OK*.

    - To add an *entire* component, check its check box, make sure it's selected, and then click on *OK*.

    - To add or remove *part of* a component, select it, click on the *Change Option* button, check or uncheck the option you want to change, and then click on *OK*.

6. Click on **Continue** and follow the Setup prompts.

APPENDIX B: SHARING INFORMATION ON A NETWORK

Overview

Network-Navigating Prerequisites

Sharing Office Files on a Network

In this appendix, we'll show you network users out there how you can share information with your network colleagues.

OVERVIEW

If you are on a network, you can share files with other network users by using these methods:

- Copying the files to a network directory that both you and your recipients can access.
- Sending the files to your recipients through electronic mail.

We discussed the electronic-mail approach in Chapter 10's "Using Mail to Share Files." Rather than repeat ourselves, we'll devote this appendix to the copying-to-a-network-directory approach.

NETWORK-NAVIGATING PREREQUISITES

To perform many of the networking tasks described in this appendix—for example, connecting to a file server or to a shared directory—you'll need to know how to navigate your network. For help, turn to your network administrator.

SHARING OFFICE FILES ON A NETWORK

To share Office files with other network users,

- Connect to a network file server. If you have Windows for Workgroups, you can create a *shared directory* on your local hard disk, and other Office users can connect to this directory as if it were a file server.
- Copy the files to a directory on the network file server that both you and your recipients can access.

OPENING A SHARED FILE

To open a file stored in a shared network directory,

- Connect to the shared directory.
- Start the source Office application (the application in which the file was created).
- Choose *File, Open* to display the Open dialog box.
- Select the file's drive, directory, and name.
- Click on *OK*.

Depending on a shared file's *protections*, your ability to open and modify it may be limited, as follows:

- If the file is protected by a password, you can open it only if you know this password.

- If the file is *read-only*, you can open it, but you can only modify it by saving it to a different file name, drive, or directory.

- If the file is *read-write*, you can open it and modify it—unless it is already opened by another user, in which case you can only modify it by saving it to a different file name, drive, or directory.

PROTECTING SHARED INFORMATION

When information is shared on a network, a potential problem arises: Several users may be working with the same information at the same time. The solution: To protect important information from unauthorized access and modification.

Here are some things you can do to protect information you share with other network users:

- You can require that a password be entered before a file can be opened or saved.

- You can save a file as a read-only file, in which case others cannot modify the file under the same file name and location.

- In Word, you can use a password to prevent others from filling in specified parts of a Word form. You can also *lock* a Word file, so that others can comment on it but not modify it.

- In Excel, you can use a password or *information-locking* to prevent others from modifying a worksheet, formula, or range of cells.

- You can create *master documents* composed of *subdocuments*. The authors of the subdocuments have read-write privileges to their own subdocuments, while all others have read-only privileges.

Word and Excel offer additional protection for shared information. To find out what, search for *protecting* in Word and Excel on-line Help.

SHARING FILES WITH DIFFERENT FORMATS

You can share files with different formats by using the appropriate conversion utility. For example, if your friend Wolfgang had QuattroPro for DOS, but did not have Excel, you could convert your Excel workbook file to QuattroPro's *WQ1* format, and then copy it to the network server or e-mail it directly to Wolfi.

To convert a file you're sending to another user to a format compatible with that user's application,

- Open the file.
- Choose *File, Save As* to open the Save As dialog box.
- Under Save File As Type, select the format to which you want to convert.
- Specify the file's name, drive, and directory.
- Click on *OK*.

To convert a file you receive from another user to a format compatible with your application,

- Run your application.
- Choose *File, Open* to display the Open dialog box.
- Under List Files Of Type, select the format of the file to convert.
- Specify the file's name, drive, and directory.
- Click on *OK*.

Word and PowerPoint use external converters and filters to convert file formats, while Excel performs most conversions internally. If the format you want to convert to/from is not listed in your Save As or Open dialog box, you may be able to add this format to your list by running Setup. For help, see Appendix A's "Modifying Your Office Setup."

INDEX

Note: Page numbers in italic denote figures, illustrations, or tables.

Symbols

! (exclamation mark), 170–171
◄ or ►, 79, *80*
+ (plus sign), 2

A

Address dialog box, Microsoft Mail, 173–175, *174*
Advanced Search dialog box
    Location tab in, *112*, 112–113
    searching for files whose names you can't remember, 111–115
    Summary tab in, 113–114, *114*
    Timestamp tab in, 113–114
Alt+click, exiting an application with, 18
Alt+F4, exiting a running application with, 18
Alt+Tab
    restoring toolbar from icon with, 13
    switching between applications with, 14–17
applications, starting from Office menu, 9, 12

B

Bitmap format, for linked objects, 59
bulleted steps, 2
Bullets On/Off button, 155

C

C:\..., in Links list box, 68
client application, 86. *See also* destination application
Commands button, in Find File dialog box, 115–116
Copy and Paste commands, 47–50
copying
    data among applications, 51–53
    Excel data to a PowerPoint slide, 48–50
    and pasting data between applications, 41–53
creating
    Excel worksheets in PowerPoint, 136–137
    Excel worksheets in Word, 130–133
    PowerPoint presentations from Word outlines, 147–154
    Word documents from PowerPoint presentations, 156–159
    Word tables in PowerPoint, 139–140
Ctrl+Esc
    displaying Task List with, 14
    opening Task List dialog box with, 95
Ctrl+Shift+F7, updating linked objects in PowerPoint with, 67
Cue Cards
    dialog box, 35
    exiting (closing), 36
    getting step-by-step Help with, 34–36
Customize dialog box, *118*
    customizing Office menu with, 117–118
    customizing toolbar buttons with, 11
Cut and Paste commands, 43–44
cutting data from an application file, 51–53

D

data
    copying, 51–53
    cutting from application file, 51–53
    linked. *See* linked data; linking
    transferring between applications, 41–53
Data Disk, installing, 3
deleting, a file in Find File dialog box, 115–116

destination application, 57
destination file, 57, 76, 77. *See also* linked data; links
dialog-box help, 32–34
    exiting, 32
disk. *See* Data Disk
drag-and-drop, embedding objects with, 94–96
dynamic reference, creating, 57–58

E

editing
    converted PowerPoint text in Word, 160
    copied data, 50–51
    embedded objects, 90–93, 98–101
    Excel worksheets created in PowerPoint, 137
    Excel worksheets created in Word, 133–135
    moved text, 46–47
    and saving edited changes, 90–91
    Word tables in PowerPoint, 141–143
Edit menu, Word, *42*
embedded objects
    creating new, 96–97
    editing, 90–93, 98–101
embedding
    Excel data in a PowerPoint slide, 88–90
    formats for, 88
embedding objects, 56, 85–101
    advantage over copying, 90
    with the Clipboard, 87–88
    with drag-and-drop, 94–96
    editing after, 90–93
    versus linking, 86–87
    with Paste Special dialog box, 88
Excel data. *See also* Excel worksheets
    embedding in a PowerPoint slide, 88–90
    linking to a PowerPoint slide, 59–64, *63*, 88–90
Excel worksheets
    creating in PowerPoint, 136–137
    creating in Word, 130–133
    editing, 133–135, 137
    moving one created in Word, 135–136
    moving and sizing one created in PowerPoint, 137

F

F1, getting dialog-box Help with, 33
F9, updating linked objects in Word with, 67
filename extensions, 160
files, deleting in Find File dialog box, 115–116
Find File
    button on Office toolbar, 106–107
    exiting, 18
    Help, 26, *27*
    searching for files with, 106–115
Find File dialog box, 33, *108*
    Commands button in, 115–116
    deleting a file in, 115–116
    examining, 109–110, *109*
    opening a file from, 107
folders, Microsoft Mail
    creating new, 178–180
    deleting, 180
    opening existing, 178
    types of, 178
formats, for linked objects, 58–59
Formatted Text (RTF), for linked objects, 58

G

general Help, 25–32
    exiting, 32
    searching for topics in, 25
Go To button, in Search dialog box, 30

H

Help, 24–34
    exiting, 32
    for individual applications, 34
    searching for a topic in, 25
Help Contents window, *26*
    opening, 25

I

Insert, Object command, opening Object dialog box with, 97

installing
  Data Disk, 3
  Microsoft Mail, 168
  Microsoft Office, 42, 189–193

L

Linkable Objects, 76, *77*
linked data
  effect of renaming source files for, 75
  updating automatically, 64–66
  updating manually, 64, 66–69
linked objects, formats for, 58–59
linking
  data among Office applications, 76–78, *77*
  data to Office applications, 59–64
  Excel data to a PowerPoint slide, 59–64, *63*, 88–90
  formats for, 58–59
  objects, 56–83
  options, 76–78
  source objects to multiple destination files, 70–73
  versus embedding, 86–87
links
  breaking, 73–76
  creating, 58
  effect of renaming source files for, 75
  updating, 64–69
Links dialog box, 73–76
  opening, 73

M

Mail. *See* Microsoft Mail
memory requirements, Office, 17–18
Menu options, Customize dialog box, 11
Microsoft Mail
  Address dialog box, 173–175, *174*
  including in Office menu, 117–118
  installing, 168
  message priority, 170–171
  New Folder dialog box, 178–180, *179*
  opening a Send Note form, 173
  Options dialog box, 177
  removing from Office menu, 119
  Routing Slip dialog box, 184, *185*
  sending files from source applications, 184–185
  Send Note form, 173–177, *174*
  server version for PC networks, 190
  sharing files with, 182
  Sign In dialog box, 169
  starting, 168–170
  starting automatically, 169–170
  toolbar button, *169*
  wastebasket for deleted mail, 173
  working with, 168–187
Microsoft Mail folders
  types of, 178
  working with, 178–180
Microsoft Mail messages
  addressing, 173–175
  attaching files to, 182–183
  creating, 173–176
  deleting, 170–171
  forwarding, 180–181
  priority, 170–171
  reading, 170–171
  replying to, 181, *182*
  sending, 177
Microsoft Office 4.2. *See also* Office
  converting files with different formats, 198
  creating work directory in, 3–4
  getting started in, 1–5
  installing, 190–192
  modifying your Setup file, 192–193
  sharing files on a network, 196–198
Microsoft Office Cue Cards. *See also* Cue Cards
  dialog box, 35
Microsoft Office Manager. *See* Office; Office Manager
Microsoft toolbar, 152. *See also* Office toolbar
  displaying, 149
modifying. *See also* editing
  copied data, 50–51
  moved text, 46–47

moving
    Excel worksheet created in Word, 135–136
    and sizing Excel worksheet created in PowerPoint, 137
    Word text to a PowerPoint slide, 44–46
MSOFFICE.INI file, changing position of Office toolbar with, 161–163

N

network
    opening a shared file on, 196–197
    protecting shared information on, 197
    sharing files with different formats, 198
    sharing Office files on, 196–198
New Folder dialog box, Microsoft Mail, 178–180, *179*
nonlinkable objects, 76, 77
numbered steps, 2

O

Object dialog box, creating new embedded objects with, 97
object embedding, 56, 85–101. *See also* embedding
    versus linking, 86–87
object format, for linked objects, 58
object linking, 56–83. *See also* linking
    versus embedding, 86–87
object linking and embedding (OLE)
    linking objects, 56–83
    embedding objects, 85–101
Office
    converting files with different formats in, 198
    Customize dialog box, 11, 117–118, *118*
    customizing, 116–117
    dialog box Help, 32–34
    drop-down menu, 12
    exiting, 19
    general help, 25–32
    Help system, 24–34
    installing, 190–192
    issuing commands in, 8–10
    memory requirements for, 17–18
    modifying your Setup file, 192–193
    sharing files on a network in, 196–198
    starting, 10–13
    starting manually, 19
Office applications
    exiting, 18
    starting, 13–14
    switching between, 14–17
Office Help, 24–34
Office Help Contents window. *See* Help Contents window
Office Manager, getting help from, 23–38
Office menu
    adding Microsoft Mail to, 117–118
    customizing, 117–118
    starting applications with, 9, 13
Office shortcut menu, *10*
    customizing Office with, 9–10
Office toolbar
    adding buttons to, 123–124
    changing default position of, 160–163
    changing horizontal/vertical orientation of, 121
    making always visible, 125
    making invisible, 125–126
    minimizing, 122–123
    moving, 121–122
    removing buttons from, 124–125
    running as icon, 13
    sizing, 119–121
    starting applications with, 8–9, 13
OLE. *See* object linking and embedding
Options dialog box, Microsoft Mail, 177

P

Paste command, 43–44
Paste Special dialog box, 62
    embedding objects with, 88
pasting data to one or more applications, 51–53
permanent folders, Microsoft Mail, 178
Picture format, for linked objects, 59
pixel, 162
plus sign (+), 2

pointing-hand pointer, 26
PowerPoint presentations
    creating a Word document from, 156–159
    creating from a Word outline, 147–154
    creating Word tables in, 139–140
    editing Word tables in, 141–143
Present It, Word
    creating a PowerPoint presentation with, 147–154
    toolbar button, *152*
presentations. *See* PowerPoint presentations
private folders, Microsoft Mail, 178

R

Reference Information, 24
    Help topic, *27*
Report It, PowerPoint
    creating a Word document with, 147, 156–159
    toolbar button, *157*
Routing Slip dialog box, Microsoft Mail, 184, *185*
RTF (Rich Text Format), 58
Run dialog box, opening, 3

S

saving edited changes, 90–91
Scale dialog box, opening, 63
Search dialog box, *30, 31, 109*
    clearing all text boxes in, 107
    displaying definitions in, 31
    Go To button in, 30
    opening, 29, 106
    searching for files with, 106–107
Send Note form, Microsoft Mail, 173–177, *174, 177*
server application, 86. *See also* source application
Setup file, modifying, 192–193
shared folders, Microsoft Mail, 178
Sign In dialog box, Microsoft Mail, 169
source application, 57, 86
source file, 57, 76, *77*. *See also* linked data; links
Summary Info box, 106
Summary View Help topic, 28

T

Task List
    displaying, 14
    opening dialog box for, 95
toolbar. *See* Office toolbar; Microsoft toolbar
toolbar buttons. *See also specific button names*
    customizing, 11
    Cut, Copy, and Paste, *43*
Toolbar options, 11
ToolTips feature, activating, 11–12, *12*

U

Unformatted Text, for linked objects, 58
updating
    linked objects, 67
    links, 64–69

V

View options, displaying with View tab, 11

W

Windows Clipboard, 43
Windows Help History box, *29*
    displaying, 25
    Summary view, 29
Word
    creating a PowerPoint presentation from, 148–154
    creating a table for in PowerPoint, 139–140
    creating a document for from a PowerPoint presentation, 156–159
    editing converted PowerPoint text in, 160
    editing a table for, in PowerPoint, 141–143
    moving text from, to a PowerPoint slide, 44–46
work directory
    creating, 3–4
    hard-disk space required for, 3–4
worksheets. *See* Excel worksheets

The Quick and Easy Way to Learn.

Teaches DOS 6
The Quick and Easy Way to Learn 
ISBN: 1-56276-100-5
Price: $22.95

Teaches WordPerfect 6.0
The Quick and Easy Way to Learn
ISBN: 1-56276-105-6
Price: $22.95

Teaches Word 6.0 for Windows
The Quick and Easy Way to Learn
ISBN: 1-56276-139-0
Price: $22.95

We know that PC Learning Labs books are the fastest and easiest way to learn because years have been spent perfecting them. Beginners will find practice sessions that are easy to follow and reference information that is easy to find. Even the most computer-shy readers can gain confidence faster than they ever thought possible.

The time we spent designing this series translates into time saved for you. You can feel confident that the information is accurate and presented in a way that allows you to learn quickly and effectively.

Teaches Microsoft Access
ISBN: 1-56276-122-6
Price: $22.95

Teaches FoxPro 2.5 for Windows
ISBN: 1-56276-176-5
Price: $22.95

Teaches OS/2 2.1
ISBN: 1-56276-148-X
Price: $22.95

Teaches cc:Mail
ISBN: 1-56276-135-8
Price: $22.95

Teaches WordPerfect 6.0 for Windows
ISBN: 1-56276-020-3
Price: $22.95

Teaches Ami Pro 3.0
ISBN: 1-56276-134-X
Price: $22.95

Teaches Microsoft Project 3.0 for Windows
ISBN: 1-56276-124-2
Price: $22.95

Teaches Excel 4.0 for Windows
ISBN: 1-56276-074-2
Price: $22.95

Teaches 1-2-3 Release 2.3
ISBN: 1-56276-033-5
Price: $22.95

Teaches Windows 3.1
ISBN: 1-56276-051-3
Price: $22.95

Teaches PowerPoint for Windows
ISBN: 1-56276-154-4
Price: $22.95

Teaches Lotus Notes 3.0
ISBN: 1-56276-138-2
Price: $22.95

ZIFF-DAVIS ZD PRESS

Also available: Titles featuring new versions of Excel, 1-2-3, Access, Microsoft Project, Ami Pro, and new applications, pending software release. Call 1-800-688-0448 for title update information.

Available at all fine bookstores, or by calling 1-800-688-0448, ext. 103.

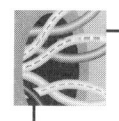

Imagination. Innovation. Insight.

The How It Works Series from Ziff-Davis Press

"... a magnificently seamless integration of text and graphics ..."
Larry Blasko, The Associated Press, reviewing *PC/Computing How Computers Work*

No other books bring computer technology to life like the *How It Works* series from Ziff-Davis Press. Lavish, full-color illustrations and lucid text from some of the world's top computer commentators make *How It Works* books an exciting way to explore the inner workings of PC technology.

PC/Computing How Computers Work
A worldwide blockbuster that hit the general trade bestseller lists! *PC/Computing* magazine executive editor Ron White dismantles the PC and reveals what really makes it tick.

ISBN: 094-7 Price: $22.95

How Networks Work
Two of the most respected names in connectivity showcase the PC network, illustrating and explaining how each component does its magic and how they all fit together.

ISBN: 129-3 Price: $24.95

How Macs Work
A fun and fascinating voyage to the heart of the Macintosh! Two noted *MacUser* contributors cover the spectrum of Macintosh operations from startup to shutdown.

ISBN: 146-3 Price: $24.95

How Software Works
This dazzlingly illustrated volume from Ron White peeks inside the PC to show in full-color how software breathes life into the PC. Covers Windows™ and all major software categories.

ISBN: 133-1 Price: $24.95

How to Use Your Computer
Conquer computerphobia and see how this intricate machine truly makes life easier. Dozens of full-color graphics showcase the components of the PC and explain how to interact with them.

ISBN: 155-2 Price: $22.95

All About Computers
This one-of-a-kind visual guide for kids features numerous full-color illustrations and photos on every page, combined with dozens of interactive projects that reinforce computer basics, making this an exciting way to learn all about the world of computers.

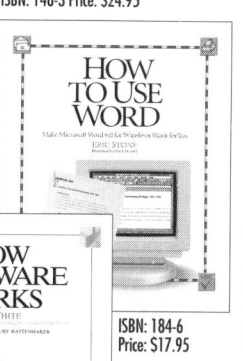

ISBN: 166-8 Price: $15.95

How To Use Word
Make Word 6.0 for Windows Work for You!
A uniquely visual approach puts the basics of Microsoft's latest Windows-based word processor right before your eyes. Colorful examples invite you to begin producing a variety of documents, quickly and easily. Truly innovative!

ISBN: 184-6 Price: $17.95

How To Use Excel
Make Excel 5.0 for Windows Work for You!
Covering the latest version of Excel, this visually impressive resource guides beginners to spreadsheet fluency through a full-color graphical approach that makes powerful techniques seem plain as day. Hands-on "Try It" sections give you a chance to sharpen newfound skills.

ISBN: 185-4 Price: $17.95

Available at all fine bookstores or by calling 1-800-688-0448, ext. 100.

ZIFF-DAVIS ZD PRESS

© 1994 Ziff-Davis Press

Capture all the power of Windows.™

ACT NOW, save 52%, and get FREE SOFTWARE!

Let *Windows Sources* show you how you can maximize the rewards of using Microsoft® Windows.™

Windows Sources is your monthly source of inside user tips and tricks...exclusive expert guidance...leading-edge technical information...benchmark test results — plus detailed data on how to choose and use the best Windows products.

Start your subscription now and get the next 12 issues (that's one full year) for only $16.94. You save 52% off the annual cover price.

What more, you'll receive exclusive **FREE** software — "**1001 Windows Hints & Tips.**" This all-new, deluxe collection of tips, tricks and solutions shows you how to work smarter, faster and better in Windows! FREE with your paid subscription.

CALL TOLL FREE TO SUBSCRIBE
1-800-365-3414

To qualify for these special savings, mention this code to the Customer Service Representative who answers your call: **4ZZ4**

Savings based on annual cover price of $35.40; basic one year subscription $27.94. Canada and foreign add $16.00. U.S. funds only. Canadian GST included. Please allow 30 days for shipment of first issue. FREE disk will be sent upon payment.

It's Software For Your Brain.

Get and keep your system up and running with *PC Magazine*. Every issue gives you in-depth product reviews... comprehensive evaluations...benchmark test results from PC Labs...news about emerging trends and new technologies...on-target buying tips...and a lot more.

Save 66% and get PC Magazine's 3-Disk Utilities Library — FREE!

Act now and get one year — that's 22 big, fact-packed issues — for just $29.97. You save 66% off the newsstand price.

Plus, your paid subscription gets you the "PC Magazine Utilities Library" — 3 disks loaded with 146 power-utilities for DOS and Windows.™

CALL TOLL FREE TO SUBSCRIBE
1-800-289-0429

To qualify for these special savings, mention this code to the Customer Service Represen-tative who answers your call: **4ZZ4**

Savings based on annual cover price of $86.90; basic one year subscription $49.97. Canada and foreign add $36.00. U.S. funds only. Canadian GST inculded. Please allow 30 days for shipment of first issue. FREE disks will be sent upon payment.

Ziff-Davis Press Survey of Readers

Please help us in our effort to produce the best books on personal computing. For your assistance, we would be pleased to send you a FREE catalog featuring the complete line of Ziff-Davis Press books.

1. How did you first learn about this book?

Recommended by a friend	-1 (5)
Recommended by store personnel	-2
Saw in Ziff-Davis Press catalog	-3
Received advertisement in the mail	-4
Saw the book on bookshelf at store	-5
Read book review in: _____	-6
Saw an advertisement in: _____	-7
Other (Please specify): _____	-8

2. Which THREE of the following factors most influenced your decision to purchase this book? (Please check up to THREE.)

Front or back cover information on book	-1 (6)
Logo of magazine affiliated with book	-2
Special approach to the content	-3
Completeness of content	-4
Author's reputation	-5
Publisher's reputation	-6
Book cover design or layout	-7
Index or table of contents of book	-8
Price of book	-9
Special effects, graphics, illustrations	-0
Other (Please specify): _____	-x

3. How many computer books have you purchased in the last six months? _____ (7-10)

4. On a scale of 1 to 5, where 5 is excellent, 4 is above average, 3 is average, 2 is below average, and 1 is poor, please rate each of the following aspects of this book below. (Please circle your answer.)

Depth/completeness of coverage	5	4	3	2	1	(11)
Organization of material	5	4	3	2	1	(12)
Ease of finding topic	5	4	3	2	1	(13)
Special features/time saving tips	5	4	3	2	1	(14)
Appropriate level of writing	5	4	3	2	1	(15)
Usefulness of table of contents	5	4	3	2	1	(16)
Usefulness of index	5	4	3	2	1	(17)
Usefulness of accompanying disk	5	4	3	2	1	(18)
Usefulness of illustrations/graphics	5	4	3	2	1	(19)
Cover design and attractiveness	5	4	3	2	1	(20)
Overall design and layout of book	5	4	3	2	1	(21)
Overall satisfaction with book	5	4	3	2	1	(22)

5. Which of the following computer publications do you read regularly; that is, 3 out of 4 issues?

Byte	-1 (23)
Computer Shopper	-2
Home Office Computing	-3
Dr. Dobb's Journal	-4
LAN Magazine	-5
MacWEEK	-6
MacUser	-7
PC Computing	-8
PC Magazine	-9
PC WEEK	-0
Windows Sources	-x
Other (Please specify): _____	-y

Please turn page.

6. What is your level of experience with personal computers? With the subject of this book?

	With PCs	With subject of book
Beginner...........	☐ -1 (24)	☐ -1 (25)
Intermediate.......	☐ -2	☐ -2
Advanced..........	☐ -3	☐ -3

7. Which of the following best describes your job title?

- Officer (CEO/President/VP/owner)........ ☐ -1 (26)
- Director/head...................... ☐ -2
- Manager/supervisor................. ☐ -3
- Administration/staff................ ☐ -4
- Teacher/educator/trainer............ ☐ -5
- Lawyer/doctor/medical professional... ☐ -6
- Engineer/technician................. ☐ -7
- Consultant......................... ☐ -8
- Not employed/student/retired........ ☐ -9
- Other (Please specify): _____ ☐ -0

8. What is your age?

- Under 20.......................... ☐ -1 (27)
- 21-29............................. ☐ -2
- 30-39............................. ☐ -3
- 40-49............................. ☐ -4
- 50-59............................. ☐ -5
- 60 or over........................ ☐ -6

9. Are you:

- Male.............................. ☐ -1 (28)
- Female............................ ☐ -2

Thank you for your assistance with this important information! Please write your address below to receive our free catalog.

Name: _____

Address: _____

City/State/Zip: _____

2729-10-01

Fold here to mail.

BUSINESS REPLY MAIL
FIRST CLASS MAIL   PERMIT NO. 1612   OAKLAND, CA

POSTAGE WILL BE PAID BY ADDRESSEE

Ziff-Davis Press
5903 Christie Avenue
Emeryville, CA 94608-1925
Attn: Marketing

NO POSTAGE
NECESSARY
IF MAILED IN
THE UNITED
STATES

■ TO RECEIVE 5¼-INCH DISK(S)

The Ziff-Davis Press software contained on the 3½-inch disk included with this book is also available in 5¼-inch format. If you would like to receive the software in the 5¼-inch format, please return the 3½-inch disk with your name and address to:

Disk Exchange
Ziff-Davis Press
5903 Christie Avenue
Emeryville, CA 94608

■ **END-USER LICENSE AGREEMENT**

READ THIS AGREEMENT CAREFULLY BEFORE BUYING THIS BOOK. BY BUYING THE BOOK AND USING THE PROGRAM LISTINGS, DISKS, AND PROGRAMS REFERRED TO BELOW, YOU ACCEPT THE TERMS OF THIS AGREEMENT.

The program listings included in this book and the programs included on the diskette(s) contained in the package on the opposite page ("Disks") are proprietary products of Ziff-Davis Press and/or third party suppliers ("Suppliers"). The program listings and programs are hereinafter collectively referred to as the "Programs." Ziff-Davis Press and the Suppliers retain ownership of the Disks and copyright to the Programs, as their respective interests may appear. The Programs and the copy of the Disks provided are licensed (not sold) to you under the conditions set forth herein.

License. You may use the Disks on any compatible computer, provided that the Disks are used on only one computer and by one user at a time.

Restrictions. You may not commercially distribute the Disks or the Programs or otherwise reproduce, publish, or distribute or otherwise use the Disks or the Programs in any manner that may infringe any copyright or other proprietary right of Ziff-Davis Press, the Suppliers, or any other party or assign, sublicense, or otherwise transfer the Disks or this agreement to any other party unless such party agrees to accept the terms and conditions of this agreement. This license and your right to use the Disks and the Programs automatically terminates if you fail to comply with any provision of this agreement.

U.S. GOVERNMENT RESTRICTED RIGHTS. The disks and the programs are provided with **RESTRICTED RIGHTS**. Use, duplication, or disclosure by the Government is subject to restrictions as set forth in subparagraph (c)(1)(ii) of the Rights in Technical Data and Computer Software Clause at DFARS (48 CFR 252.277-7013). The Proprietor of the compilation of the Programs and the Disks is Ziff-Davis Press, 5903 Christie Avenue, Emeryville, CA 94608.

Limited Warranty. Ziff-Davis Press warrants the physical Disks to be free of defects in materials and workmanship under normal use for a period of 30 days from the purchase date. If Ziff-Davis Press receives written notification within the warranty period of defects in materials or workmanship in the physical Disks, and such notification is determined by Ziff-Davis Press to be correct, Ziff-Davis Press will, at its option, replace the defective Disks or refund a prorata portion of the purchase price of the book. **THESE ARE YOUR SOLE REMEDIES FOR ANY BREACH OF WARRANTY.**

EXCEPT AS SPECIFICALLY PROVIDED ABOVE, THE DISKS AND THE PROGRAMS ARE PROVIDED "AS IS" WITHOUT ANY WARRANTY OF ANY KIND. NEITHER ZIFF-DAVIS PRESS NOR THE SUPPLIERS MAKE ANY WARRANTY OF ANY KIND AS TO THE ACCURACY OR COMPLETENESS OF THE DISKS OR THE PROGRAMS OR THE RESULTS TO BE OBTAINED FROM USING THE DISKS OR THE PROGRAMS AND NEITHER ZIFF-DAVIS PRESS NOR THE SUPPLIERS SHALL BE RESPONSIBLE FOR ANY CLAIMS ATTRIBUTABLE TO ERRORS, OMISSIONS, OR OTHER INACCURACIES IN THE DISKS OR THE PROGRAMS. THE ENTIRE RISK AS TO THE RESULTS AND PERFORMANCE OF THE DISKS AND THE PROGRAMS IS ASSUMED BY THE USER. FURTHER, NEITHER ZIFF-DAVIS PRESS NOR THE SUPPLIERS MAKE ANY REPRESENTATIONS OR WARRANTIES, EITHER EXPRESS OR IMPLIED, WITH RESPECT TO THE DISKS OR THE PROGRAMS, INCLUDING BUT NOT LIMITED TO, THE QUALITY, PERFORMANCE, MERCHANTABILITY, OR FITNESS FOR A PARTICULAR PURPOSE OF THE DISKS OR THE PROGRAMS. IN NO EVENT SHALL ZIFF-DAVIS PRESS OR THE SUPPLIERS BE LIABLE FOR DIRECT, INDIRECT, SPECIAL, INCIDENTAL, OR CONSEQUENTIAL DAMAGES ARISING OUT THE USE OF OR INABILITY TO USE THE DISKS OR THE PROGRAMS OR FOR ANY LOSS OR DAMAGE OF ANY NATURE CAUSED TO ANY PERSON OR PROPERTY AS A RESULT OF THE USE OF THE DISKS OR THE PROGRAMS, EVEN IF ZIFF-DAVIS PRESS OR THE SUPPLIERS HAVE BEEN SPECIFICALLY ADVISED OF THE POSSIBILITY OF SUCH DAMAGES. NEITHER ZIFF-DAVIS PRESS NOR THE SUPPLIERS ARE RESPONSIBLE FOR ANY COSTS INCLUDING, BUT NOT LIMITED TO, THOSE INCURRED AS A RESULT OF LOST PROFITS OR REVENUE, LOSS OF USE OF THE DISKS OR THE PROGRAMS, LOSS OF DATA, THE COSTS OF RECOVERING SOFTWARE OR DATA, OR THIRD-PARTY CLAIMS. IN NO EVENT WILL ZIFF-DAVIS PRESS' OR THE SUPPLIERS' LIABILITY FOR ANY DAMAGES TO YOU OR ANY OTHER PARTY EVER EXCEED THE PRICE OF THIS BOOK. NO SALES PERSON OR OTHER REPRESENTATIVE OF ANY PARTY INVOLVED IN THE DISTRIBUTION OF THE DISKS IS AUTHORIZED TO MAKE ANY MODIFICATIONS OR ADDITIONS TO THIS LIMITED WARRANTY.

Some states do not allow the exclusion or limitation of implied warranties or limitation of liability for incidental or consequential damages, so the above limitation or exclusion may not apply to you.

General. Ziff-Davis Press and the Suppliers retain all rights not expressly granted. Nothing in this license constitutes a waiver of the rights of Ziff-Davis Press or the Suppliers under the U.S. Copyright Act or any other Federal or State Law, international treaty, or foreign law.